HIGH-TECH CYCLING

Edmund R. Burke, PhD

University of Colorado at Colorado Springs

Editor

Human Kinetics

Library of Congress Cataloging-in-Publication Data

Burke, Ed, 1949-
  High-tech cycling / Edmund R. Burke.
    p. cm.
  Includes bibliographical references and index.
  ISBN 0-87322-535-X (pbk.)
  1. Cycling--Physiological aspects. I. Title.
  RC1220.C8B873 1996   95-81020
  612'.044--dc20   CIP

ISBN: 0-87322-535-X

Copyright © 1996 by Edmund R. Burke

Developmental Editor: Marni Basic; **Assistant Editors:** Ed Giles, Ann Greenseth, Kirby Mittelmeier, and Susan Moore; **Editorial Assistant:** Alecia Mapes Walk; **Copyeditor:** Joyce Sexton; **Proofreader:** Kathy Bennett; **Indexer:** Joan K. Griffitts; **Typesetter:** Kathy Boudreau-Fuoss; **Layout Artist:** Denise Lowry; **Text Designer:** Robert Reuther; **Photo Editor:** Boyd LaFoon; **Cover Designer:** Jack Davis; **Photographer (cover):** John Kelly; **Illustrators:** Keith Blomberg, Craig Ronto, Denise Lowry, Jennifer Delmotte, and Tom Janowski; **Printer:** United Graphics

Human Kinetics books are available at special discounts for bulk purchase. Special editions or book excerpts can also be created to specification. For details, contact the Special Sales Manager at Human Kinetics.

Printed in the United States of America   10 9 8 7 6 5 4 3

Human Kinetics
Web site: http://www.humankinetics.com/

United States: Human Kinetics, P.O. Box 5076, Champaign, IL 61825-5076
1-800-747-4457
e-mail: humank@hkusa.com

Canada: Human Kinetics, 475 Devonshire Road, Unit 100, Windsor, ON N8Y 2L5
1-800-465-7301 (in Canada only)
e-mail: humank@hkcanada.com

Europe: Human Kinetics, P.O. Box IW14, Leeds LS16 6TR, United Kingdom
(44) 1132 781708
e-mail: humank@hkeurope.com

Australia: Human Kinetics, 57A Price Avenue, Lower Mitcham, South Australia 5062
(088) 277 1555
e-mail: humank@hkaustralia.com

New Zealand: Human Kinetics, P.O. Box 105-231, Auckland 1
(09) 523 3462
e-mail: humank@hknewz.com

Contents

Preface   **vii**

Acknowledgments   **ix**

Credits   **xi**

Chapter 1   Selecting Cycling Equipment   **1**

Chester R. Kyle, PhD

Learn how the design of bicycle components can benefit cycling performance.

Chapter 2   Bicycle Suspension Systems   **45**

John Olsen, MSME

Examine the goals and components of suspension systems in this overview of bike physics, engineering, and performance.

Chapter 3   Body Size and Cycling Performance   **65**

David P. Swain, PhD

Explore how body size influences various aspects of cycling performance and how this can be described through the concept of "scaling."

Chapter 4   Body Positioning for Cycling   **79**

Edmund R. Burke, PhD, and Andrew L. Pruitt, EdD

Learn how you can minimize injuries and increase your efficiency, power, performance, and comfort through proper bicycle fit.

Chapter 5　Optimal Pedaling Cadence　101

J. Richard Coast, PhD

Explore the factors that contribute to optimal cadence in this overview of the concept of optimization.

Chapter 6　Cycling Optimization Analysis　117

Steve A. Kautz, PhD, and Maury L. Hull, PhD

Find out how the technique of analytical optimization has been used in an attempt to determine the optimal equipment adjustment for cycling.

Chapter 7　Cycling Biomechanics　145

Jeffrey P. Broker, PhD, and Robert J. Gregor, PhD

Read about the latest advances in cycling biomechanics, including instrumented pedals, new research into pedal loading, and the characteristics of the cycling "engine."

Chapter 8　Energy Expenditure During Cycling　167

James Hagberg, PhD, and Steve McCole, MS

Learn how air resistance—the major force that cyclists must overcome—is affected by riding speed, body position, drafting, and aerodynamic equipment.

Chapter 9　Nutrition for Cycling　185

W. Michael Sherman, PhD

Discover how various manipulations of dietary carbohydrate intake have the potential to improve endurance cycling performance.

Chapter 10 Resistive Exercises for Off-Road Cycling **207**

Ronald P. Pfeiffer, EdD, ATC, and Shane R. Johnson, MS

See how analysis of the joint and muscle actions of off-road cycling has helped provide a year-round strength training protocol for competitive off-road riding.

Chapter 11 Preventing Overuse Knee Injuries **251**

Maury L. Hull, PhD, and Patricia Ruby, MS

Survey the latest scientific research aimed at developing preventive technologies for common overuse knee injuries.

Index **281**
About the Contributors **289**
About the Editor **293**

Preface

During the last decade there has been a remarkable expansion of the application of scientific principles to the sport of cycling. More and more cyclists, from elite competitors to fitness enthusiasts, are applying these principles to their own programs. Indeed, many cyclists now realize the importance of acquiring basic scientific information that can be put to good use.

The need for this book became clear after the completion of *Science of Cycling* in 1986 and the *Medical and Scientific Aspects of Cycling* in 1988, when I continued to see scientific information being produced that needed to be disseminated to all of us in order to perform at our best. This book picks up where the others left off. In it you'll find the most recent research in the many facets of cycling science and medicine.

High-Tech Cycling has been possible only because the contributors made time to write their chapters while balancing research and teaching responsibilities. My request of them was to provide scientifically accurate, comprehensive, and readable reviews of the information available on their topics. I also asked them to suggest how to use this information in training and competition and how it might be used to stimulate further research. The authors have met these objectives, and as a result this book is a valuable resource for those who compete, coach, perform research, or engage in the clinical practice of sports medicine. Serious recreational riders with an appetite for accurate and up-to-date information about their sport will also want this book in their collections.

In planning *High-Tech Cycling*, I sought a balance between the physiological, biomechanical, nutritional, and scientific training aspects of cycling. In addition, I have included topics specific to mountain biking, the fastest growing segment of the sport.

The volume begins with criteria for equipment selection in road cycling. Chester Kyle presents information he has collected from his research during the last few years. Next, in chapter 2, John Olsen instructs us on the basics of mountain bike suspensions for comfortable and efficient cycling. He includes a series of very instructive figures for both experts and novices in the sport.

Although we all recognize the effects of body weight on cycling, we rarely consider the crucial role of body size on cycling performance. In chapter 3, David Swain discusses the important roles of body size and weight in cycling performance. Next, Andrew Pruitt and I focus on the importance of proper positioning on the bicycle for preventing injuries and improving cycling performance. Cycling is a marriage between the human body, which is somewhat adaptable, and a machine that is somewhat adjustable.

The following three chapters investigate the important topics of optimization and biomechanics of cycling. We often think of pedaling cadence for the serious cyclist as needing to be above 90 rpm; but what about individual preferences? What is the most efficient cadence for climbing and time trialing? In chapter 5, J. Richard Coast deals with these important questions. In chapter 6, Steve Kautz and Maury Hull do an excellent job of introducing us to cycling optimization, a tool for improving cycling performance. Next, Jeffrey Broker and Robert Gregor give us a comprehensive review of the biomechanics of cycling and current and future research directions in this field, sharing with us data they have collected on some of the world's elite cyclists.

The next two chapters discuss the important topics of energy cost of cycling and ways to optimally refuel the body for endurance cycling. In chapter 8, James Hagberg and Steve McCole report on the energy cost of cycling on the road with various positions on the bicycle and the effect of drafting on energy consumption. These are critical for a complete understanding of the interactive effect between aerodynamics and the rider's physiology. Fluid replacement and the timing of food intake are crucial to performance during competition or long-distance tours on a bicycle. In chapter 9, W. Michael Sherman focuses on the importance of fluid replacement and carbohydrate intake during cycling. He shares with us his many years of research into these areas of sport nutrition.

Chapter 10, by Ronald Pfeiffer and Shane Johnson, introduces us to a movement-oriented resistance training program for the competitive off-road cyclist. This work is based on studying the biomechanics of the cycling movements and working toward designing specific resistance training exercises for increasing overall body strength for improved performance. Finally, in chapter 11, Maury Hull and Patricia Ruby address the problems of knee injuries in cycling, the most common chronic injury in the sport. They give us insight into how pedal design and cycling mechanics may help reduce the incidence of knee injuries.

The following pages present the most current cycling research and offer a framework of knowledge and training principles from which all readers can benefit. The chapters will, I hope, increase your cycling knowledge and performance.

Edmund R. Burke

Acknowledgments

I am indebted to many people for the information presented in this book, most importantly the scientific researchers that have contributed to this book. In addition, I would like to thank all of the coaches and athletes of the U.S. Cycling Team who have helped me better understand our sport, and Marni Basic who helped put this book together for me.

And finally, I owe a lot to my wife, Kathleen. She unselfishly works behind the scenes, allowing me to devote an excessive amount of effort to my work.

Credits

Figure 1.2 from *Bicycling Science* (2nd ed.) (p. 51), by F.R. Whitt and D.G. Wilson, 1982, Cambridge, MA: MIT Press. Copyright 1982 by MIT Press. Reprinted with permission.

Figure 1.5 and Table 1.3 from "New aero wheel tests," by C.R. Kyle, 1991, *Cycling Science*, **3**(1), pp. 27-30. Adapted with permission.

Figure 1.6 from "New aero wheel tests," by C.R. Kyle, 1991, *Cycling Science*, **3**(1), pp. 27-30. Reprinted with permission.

Figure 1.10 from "Frictional resistance in bicycle wheel bearings," by K. Danh, L. Mai, J. Poland, and C. Jenkins, 1991, *Cycling Science*, **3**(3-4), pp. 28-32. Adapted with permission.

Figure 4.5, 4.8, 4.11, 4.12a, and 4.13b from *Serious Cycling* (pp. 175-183), by E.R. Burke, 1995, Champaign, IL: Human Kinetics. Copyright 1995 by Edmund R. Burke. Reprinted with permission.

Figure 6.8 from "The design of variable ratio chain drives for bicycles and ergometers—application to a maximum power bicycle drive," by N.R. Miller and D. Ross, 1980, *Journal of Mechanical Design*, **102**, pp. 711-717. Copyright 1980 by the American Society of Mechanical Engineers. Reprinted with permission.

Figure 6.9 from "Physiological response to cycling with both circular and non-circular chainrings," by M.L. Hull, M. Williams, K. Williams, and S.A. Kautz, 1992, *Medicine and Science in Sports and Exercise*, **24**, pp. 1114-1122. Copyright 1992 by Williams & Wilkins. Adapted with permission.

Figures 8.3 and 8.5, and Table 8.3 from "Energy expenditure during bicycling," by S.D. McCole, K. Claney, J-C. Conte, R. Anderson, and J.M. Hagberg, 1990, *Journal of Applied Physiology*, **68**, pp. 750-751. Copyright 1990 by the American Physiological Society. Reprinted with permission.

Figure 8.4 from "The effect of drafting and aerodynamic equipment on energy expenditure during cycling," by J.M. Hagberg and S.D. McCole, 1990, *Cycling Science*, **2**(3), p. 20. Copyright 1990 by *Cycling Science Publications*. Reprinted with permission.

Figure 8.6 photo courtesy of Photosport International®.

From "Wind tunnel tests of aero bicycles," by C.R. Kyle, 1991, *Cycling Science*, **3**(3-4), pp. 57-61. Reprinted with permission.

Table 1.8 from "Wind tunnel tests of aero bicycles," by C.R. Kyle, 1991, *Cycling Science*, **3**(3-4), pp. 57-61. Reprinted with permission.

Table 6.1 reprinted from the *Journal of Biomechanics*, **22**, H. Gonzalez and M.L. Hull, "Multivariable optimization of cycling biomechanics," pp. 1151-1161. Copyright 1989, with kind permission from Elsevier Science Ltd, The Boulevard, Langford Lane, Kidlington OX5 1GB, UK.

Table 10.1 from "Strength Training for Cycling," by H. Newton. In *Science of Cycling* (p. 24) by E.R. Burke (Ed.), 1986, Champaign, IL: Human Kinetics. Copyright 1986 by Edmund R. Burke. Adapted with permission.

1

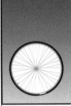

Selecting Cycling Equipment

Chester R. Kyle, PhD

Appropriate cycling equipment can save time, save energy, or improve convenience; it can add to comfort, maneuverability, or safety. Every year at bike shows, hundreds of new equipment items make their appearance, promoted by major corporations, smaller companies, and private individuals, all with the hope of finding a winning ticket into the market.

The majority of new products quickly disappear. There are three principal reasons for product failure: Capital for marketing and production is insufficient, the market is crowded with similar products that are usually better and cheaper, or the products simply have little beneficial effect on cycling performance. I hope the information in this chapter will help cyclists to avoid products in this last category.

Since all-terrain bicycles are discussed elsewhere, this chapter will concentrate on bicycles that are normally ridden on paved surfaces. These include conventional recreational or commuting road bicycles as well as competition road and track bikes and hybrid bikes that can be ridden either on or off the pavement. However, before we talk about cycling equipment, let's briefly discuss the principal ingredient that makes a bicycle go fast—human power. Power or energy consumption affects all of the topics in this chapter, so a summary will be useful.

Human Power

Naturally, the speed at which you can propel a bicycle depends upon what kind of equipment and technique you use. But more than anything else it depends upon how much power you can apply to the pedals. Almost any healthy adult can produce about 0.1 horsepower (75-100 W) continuously—even someone past 70 years old. This will move you along at about 10 to 15 mph (16-24 kph), depending upon what kind of bicycle and what kind of riding position you use (Kyle, 1973; Kyle & Edelman, 1975).

In 1975 at a Sportshochschule in Cologne, Germany, professional cyclist Eddy Merckx produced over 0.6 horsepower for 1 hr (455 W) on a cycling ergometer. In 1972, Merckx had set a world record of 30.7 miles (49.431 km) in 1 hr at Mexico City using a classical track bike without aerodynamic components (Okajima, 1990; Peronnet, Bouissou, Perrault, & Ricci, 1991). His record has since been broken several times by cyclists on modern aero bikes. In an hour ride, modern equipment can make a small difference in speed (about 2 mph, 2-3 kph); however, principally the speed depends upon athletic ability.

The capability of most cyclists lies somewhere between the performance of an average healthy adult and a champion professional athlete. The power you can produce is a direct function of how much muscle mass you have. This of course depends upon your weight and percent body fat (well-conditioned cyclists normally have from 7 to 18% body fat for men and slightly more for women). Figure 1.1 shows the amount of power you can produce versus your body weight and the speed you can maintain on the level with no wind. The curves were drawn for cyclists of average build using lightweight racing bicycles and riding in a low racing position with hands on the drops (Sjogaard, Nielsen, Mikkelsen, Saltin, & Burke, 1982; Swain, Coast, Clifford, Milliken, & Gundersen, 1987). For example, if you can maintain 20 mph and you weigh 170 lb (77 kg), you are producing about 160 W or 0.21 horsepower. In riding positions other than a low racing position, you would have to produce more power to go the same speed.

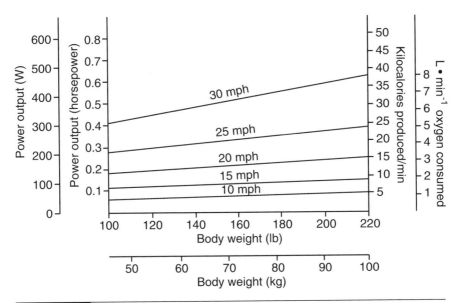

Figure 1.1 Power, speed, calories, and oxygen consumption versus body weight. Data from Swain et al. (1987) and Sjoggaard et al. (1982).

If you are taller than average for your weight you will have a higher wind resistance and must also produce more power, whereas those who are more compact and muscular need less power. The body surface area and frontal area and thus the wind resistance all increase as the height squared, so thin tall bicycle racers are a rare commodity.

However, your potential for endurance or speed depends more upon what type of muscles you have and the condition of your cardiovascular system than upon your body type. Fast-twitch muscle fibers, which make up the bulk of a cycling sprinter's muscle mass, are great for short bursts of speed but do not process oxygen as efficiently as do slow-twitch muscle fibers, which make up the bulk of an endurance athlete's muscle mass. This is why a superbly muscled athlete who can power a bicycle 40 mph (65 kph) or more in a 200-m sprint can easily be beaten over longer distances by a cyclist with much less physical strength. It happens all the time.

It is also well known that those of lighter body weight have an advantage when climbing hills. You can easily observe this in a pack when the gaps expand and contract as the slope changes. Downhill, the heavier riders have the advantage and can sometimes catch up if they haven't lost too much distance uphill. The optimum weight for elite male endurance racing cyclists seems to be between 140 and 160 lb (64-73 kg). Good sprinters, on the other hand, are massive, often weighing over 200 lb (91 kg).

For intervals of a few seconds, the body can produce perhaps five times the amount of power that it can produce continuously over intervals of several minutes (Whitt & Wilson, 1982). Short-term anaerobic exercise rapidly uses energy already stored in the muscles and does not involve the slower metabolism of oxygen. Once steady state is reached, the amount of long-term aerobic power you can produce depends upon the amount of oxygen you can absorb in the blood and convert to energy. You can improve your capacity to absorb oxygen approximately 20 to 30% by training (Sjogaard, Nielsen, Mikkelsen, Saltin, & Burke, 1982). Figure 1.2 shows the variation of power with the duration of exercise for typical cyclists (Whitt & Wilson, 1982).

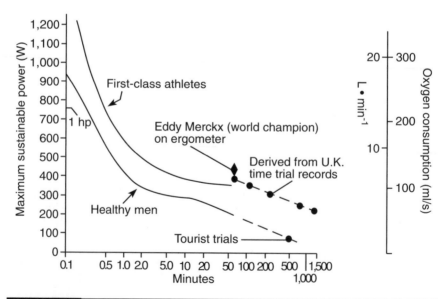

Figure 1.2 Power versus duration of exercise for various athletes. Reprinted from Whitt and Wilson (1982).

For those who wish to use cycling as a tool for weight reduction, Figure 1.1 shows the number of calories burned per minute versus speed and body weight and the oxygen absorption capacity of the cyclist. At 20 mph (32 kph), a person weighing 150 lb (68 kg) will use about 790 calories per hour and absorb about 2.8 L of oxygen per minute into the blood. Figure 1.3 shows the number of calories burned per mile on a level course. The energy consumed per mile is fairly constant until about 12 mph (19 kph), when wind resistance causes it to increase rapidly.

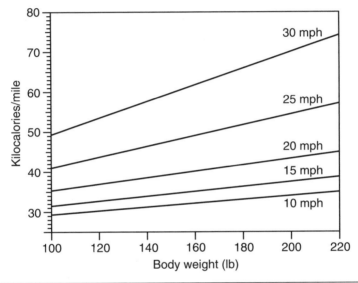

Figure 1.3   Calories per mile versus speed and body weight.

For a fixed distance you burn more energy by traveling fast. If you prefer to ride more slowly, you can compensate by traveling longer distances. Cycling takes about one third the energy per kilometer of walking or running, so you must travel longer distances on the bike to burn the same number of calories (Margaria, Cerretelli, Aghemo, & Sassi, 1963; Pugh, 1971). Because you travel faster, however, the time consumed per calorie burned is about the same.

How Bicycle Equipment Affects Speed

When a bicycle moves in a straight line, the resistance forces retarding motion are balanced by the thrust component developed by the rear wheel. Resistance forces are of five types:

1. Aerodynamic forces caused by wind and the bicycle's motion through the air
2. Gravity forces when the road is not level
3. Inertial forces experienced when the bicycle is accelerating or decelerating
4. Tire rolling resistance forces
5. Bearing friction

Efficient bicycle equipment can decrease all these forces.

On a level road with no wind, at speeds below 8 mph (13 kph), tire and bearing rolling resistance are the dominant retarding forces. However, the wind resistance increases as the square of bicycle speed while the rolling resistance increases only slightly with speed, so above 8 mph, the air resistance overshadows rolling resistance. In fact, at speeds above 25 mph (40 kph), wind resistance is responsible for over 90% of the total retarding force on a traditional road racing bicycle (Kyle, 1988a).

A simple equation will serve for analysis of the relative importance of the resistance forces and the benefits of equipment modification:

$$m(dv/dt) = T - [WSin(ArctanG) + WCrr_1Cos(ArctanG) + NCrr_2V + {}^1/_2C_dA_\rho(V + V_w)^2],$$

$$(1.1)$$

where m is the equivalent mass of the bicycle and rider, dv/dt is the acceleration rate, T is the propulsive thrust at the tire contact patch, W is the weight, Crr_1 is the rolling resistance coefficient, G is the fractional slope (the rise divided by the horizontal distance), N is the number of wheels (the equation also covers tricycles), Crr_2 is a factor defining the variation of rolling resistance with velocity, V is the cycle velocity, C_d is the aerodynamic drag coefficient, A is the frontal area, ρ is the air density (a value of 1.2 kg/m³ = .00233 slugs/ft³ was used in all calculations), and V_w is the velocity of a headwind or tailwind with the sign being positive for a headwind.

The first term in Equation 1.1 gives the inertial force due to acceleration. The second term gives the rider-generated net thrust after the losses through the chain, the gears, and the rear wheel. The third term gives the force component of gravity in ascending or descending. The sign of G is positive uphill and negative downhill. The fourth term gives the static rolling resistance of the tires and bearings. The sixth term gives the aerodynamic drag of the bicycle and rider.

The fifth term in Equation 1.1 combines the velocity-dependent drag due to wheel bearing and windage losses (rotational air drag) and also the velocity-dependent losses in the tires. Wheel bearing friction is a function of velocity and of total weight on the bearing. The friction of roller bearings is extremely small compared to other losses. The drag of tires increases with velocity because of dynamic friction in the tread and sidewalls. However, with high-pressure tires of 100 psi or more, dynamic friction is very small at the moderate speeds of a bicycle (10-40 mph, 16-70 kph). The rotational air drag of the wheel is also a function of velocity. A spinning wheel encounters air friction even on a stationary bicycle trainer.

For simplicity, it will be assumed that the coefficient Crr_2 includes only the windage losses of the wheels and that it is a function only of the number of wheels N and of the speed V. In a test using the General Motors tire test drum in 1987, a value of 0.0502 N · s/m (.00344 lb · s/ft) for Crr_2 was measured for a Moulton 17-in. bicycle tire with the spokes covered by smooth plastic wheel disks (Peronnet, Bouissou, Perrault, & Ricci, 1991). Since this factor has not been measured for other wheel sizes, a conservative value of 0.0502 N · s/m for Crr_2 will be used for all of the calculations.

Multiplying Equation 1.1 by the speed gives

$$mV(dv/dt) = P - WV[Sin(ArctanG) + Crr_1Cos(Arctan\ G)] + NCrr_2V_2 + {}^1\!/_2C_dA_\rho V(V + V_w)^2,$$

$$(1.2)$$

where P is the net mechanical power produced by the rider. If there is no acceleration, then the power shown in Equation 1.2 is the mechanical power necessary to overcome the drag forces. Depending upon the problem, Equations 1.1 and 1.2 can either be solved directly or be integrated numerically (Kyle & Burke, 1984). Now let's take a closer look at the factors that slow one down while cycling.

Aerodynamic Drag

Aerodynamic forces can be decreased by choosing shapes that move through the air efficiently. This is the process of streamlining, which all living creatures that move rapidly through air or water use to conserve energy. The drag coefficient C_d gives a relative measure of the aerodynamic drag: The higher C_d the higher the drag. See Figure 1.4 for the drag coefficients of typical shapes (Hoerner, 1965).

A standard road bicycle with the rider in racing position has a drag coefficient of between 0.8 and 0.9, while the total frontal area is usually between 3.4 and 4 ft^2 (0.32-0.37 m^2). Unfortunately, a traditional bicycle is made up of round tubes and cables and other unstreamlined shapes

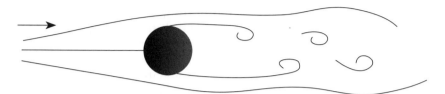

Air separates from a circular cylinder and leaves a turbulent wake with a low-pressure region in the rear of the cylinder. The pressure difference between the front and back creates a high drag. C_d =1.2.

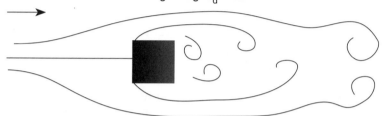

Shapes with sharp edges are much worse than cylinders. All edges should be rounded to avoid unnecessary drag. By putting a radius about 0.2 times the height on the corners of this box-shaped cylinder, the drag can be lowered from C_d = 2.0 to C_d = 1.3.

Air flows smoothly around a streamlined airfoil without turbulence. A wing shape takes less than 1/10 the energy to move through the air than a cylinder and less than 1/20 that of a box shape. The longer the airfoil is with respect to the thickness (chord-to-thickness ratio), the lower the drag. C_d = 0.1 or less.

When the rear of an airfoil is cut off, the drag increases because of the higher base drag due to turbulence at the rear. C_d = 0.3.

A two-to-one ellipse (width-to-height ratio) has a drag lower than that of a cylinder, but not as low as that of a cut-off airfoil section. C_d =0.6.

Figure 1.4 Aero drag of various shapes (Hoerner, 1965).

that have a relatively high aerodynamic drag. Streamlining the components on a bicycle can give a major reduction in air resistance. A round tube perpendicular to the wind, with a drag coefficient C_d of 1.2, takes more than 10 times the energy to move through the air than an airfoil, which can have a C_d less than 0.1. Objects with sharp edges, such as many cranks, pedals, and sprockets, are even worse than a cylinder. A sharp-edged box with a C_d of 2.0 takes more than 20 times the energy to move through the air than an airfoil. Drilling holes in components may be good for saving weight, but it is bad for aerodynamic drag. The speed loss due to air turbulence far outweighs the benefits due to weight savings. Rounding sharp edges can decrease drag from 15 to 50% (Hoerner, 1965). Unfortunately, rounding the sharp edges on a bicycle can escalate the production costs, so this detail is often neglected.

Apart from streamlining by changing the profile, there are other ways to lower the aerodynamic drag of bicycle components. One way is to decrease the frontal area. Bicycles with small-diameter tubes have a lower drag than bicycles with wide tubes. A bicycle pump parallel to the wind (like an arrow) has a lower drag than the same pump placed perpendicular to the wind (like a flagpole). A bicycle rider, by assuming a racing crouch, both streamlines the body and lowers the frontal area. Components placed in the wind shadow of others create a lower profile and a lower drag. A water bottle behind the saddle has a lower drag than the same bottle on the down tube.

Another way to decrease drag is to smooth the surfaces of components. Rough surfaces create turbulence. Smooth bicycle tubes have a lower drag than rough ones (Brownlie, Gartshore, Chapman, & Banister, 1991). There are two kinds of aerodynamic drag—surface friction drag and pressure drag. Friction drag is caused by viscous shear in the thin layer of air moving parallel to a surface. Surface roughness traps more air mass and increases the friction. Wind tunnel studies show that smooth, polished surfaces are almost always better within the speed range of a bicycle (Brownlie, Gartshore, Chapman, & Banister, 1991).

Pressure drag is caused by the difference in pressure on the surface between the leading and trailing sections of a moving object. When airflow separates from the trailing edges (see Figure 1.4), a low-pressure cavity develops, while on the leading edge, the pressure is higher than average. Differential pressure, acting over the entire surface, results in a drag force. At bicycle speeds, pressure drag is many times higher than friction drag. Streamlining is the most effective means of lowering the pressure drag.

Figure 1.5 and Figure 1.6 show the effect of lower aerodynamic drag upon a 40-km (24.9 mile) time trial (Kyle, 1991d). For example, if the measured drag on a bicycle in a wind tunnel is lowered by 50 g (0.11 lb) at 30 mph (48 kph), a cyclist who normally travels 20 mph (32 kph) can save 26 s in a 40-km time trial.

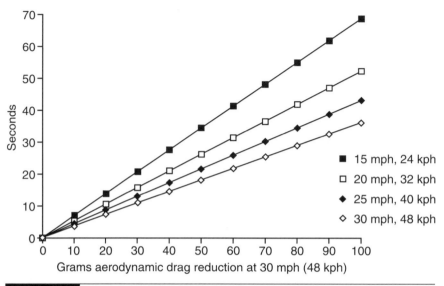

Figure 1.5 Time savings in a 40-km time trial versus aerodynamic drag reduction, small scale. Adapted from Kyle (1991d).

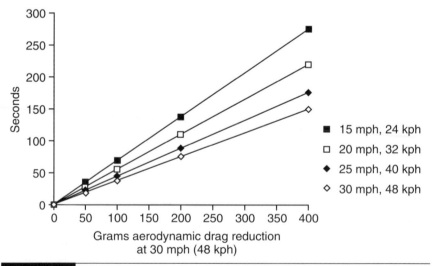

Figure 1.6 Time savings in a 40-km time trial versus aerodynamic drag reduction, expanded scale. Reprinted from Kyle (1991d).

Gravity Forces and Weight

Gravity forces have two important effects on bicycle speed. First, when a cyclist is climbing a hill, gravity will slow the rate of ascent, while during descent, gravity will speed up the bicycle. Unfortunately, the high downhill speeds never compensate for the slower climbing rate and a cyclist's average speed in hills will be less. Lowering the weight of a bicycle will increase the climbing rate, and the net time to cover a hilly course will improve. See Figure 1.7 for the effect of weight upon bicycle speed in hills.

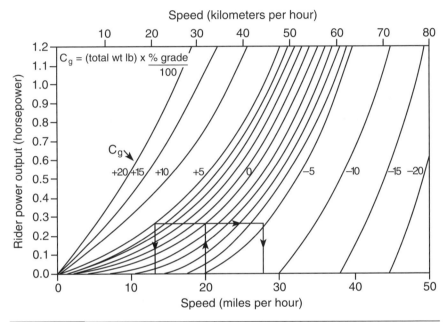

Figure 1.7 The effect of weight upon bicycle speed on hills. The bicycle used was a Le Jeune; rider in racing position. For a 200-lb cyclist riding on a 2.5% grade, C_g = 200 × (2.5/100) = 5. Level speed = 20 mph; downhill speed = 27.8 mph; uphill speed = 13.2 mph.

The second effect of gravity is more subtle. Higher weight deforms the tires and raises the bearing loads; this results in a higher rolling resistance. So even on level ground at a constant speed, a heavier bicycle is slower. However, the effect of weight on bicycle speed is small compared to that of aerodynamics. Figure 1.8 gives the time lost over a 40-km distance by the addition of weight to a bicycle, assuming a level course. Lowering the aerodynamic drag only 10 g (about the weight of two coins—a nickel and a quarter) equals the effect of removing one whole kilogram from a bicycle (2.2 lb). Ten grams of air resistance is the equivalent of a 4.5-in. pencil (12 cm) held perpendicular to a 30-mph wind (48 kph). Exposed cables can easily cause more than 10 g of drag. Cables should be run inside the handlebars and frame when possible.

Historically, cycle designers have put an enormous amount of effort and money into building lighter bicycles. There is no doubt that the

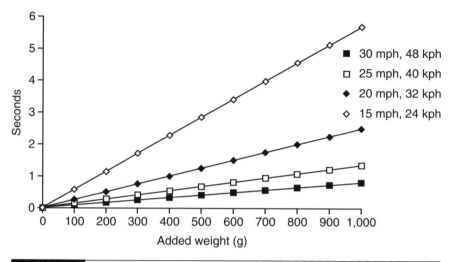

Figure 1.8 Time lost in 40 km versus added weight.

effort has paid off. Today's elegant road bicycles can weigh less than 20 pounds (9 kg). However during the past 10 years the relatively brief effort spent on improving bicycle aerodynamics has produced more record results than has any other equipment development during this century.

Inertial Forces

When a rider applies a force higher than equilibrium to the pedals, the bicycle will accelerate until the retarding force balances the new thrust force. Newton's second law of motion states, F = ma (net thrust force F, mass m, acceleration a), so the only way to boost the acceleration rate is to increase the applied force or to decrease the mass.

As with gravity, lighter bicycles are quicker than heavier ones. With acceleration, the effect of weight is relatively small but very important in racing. Acceleration is roughly proportional to the square root of the ratio of the masses. If a racing cyclist and bicycle weigh 80 kg and can accelerate from a stop to cover 100 m in 10 s, then if the bicycle is 1 kg heavier, the cyclist will lose about 0.06 s in 100 m; this would be a gap of about 0.8 m against an equal opponent on the lighter bicycle. Most roads are up and down, and there are always stops, so acceleration and deceleration is a constant process. Lighter equipment will get you there faster.

Rolling Resistance

Even though tire friction is small compared to wind drag, better tire designs have been responsible for significant improvement in cycle racing performance (Kyle, 1988b; Kyle & Burke, 1984). A good racing tire can weigh as little as 130 g and hold a pressure as high as 15 atmospheres (220 psi). The tires with the lowest rolling resistance have extremely thin walls, thin smooth tread, and thin tubes.

As a tire rolls, it flattens where it touches the ground, deforming the tread and the casing and scrubbing against the pavement. Internal and external friction and inelastic deformation of the tread cause energy losses that are exhibited as resistance to rolling. The rolling resistance is usually expressed in terms of a coefficient Crr, which is the friction force F divided by the wheel load W. The rolling drag decreases as a function of the following principal variables:

Pavement Roughness. In rolling, the tire deforms to fit small irregularities in the surface. Smoother pavement causes less tire distortion. The rolling resistance can easily double on rough pavement. See Table 1.1 for the effect of pavement type on rolling resistance.

Casing and Tread Construction. In general, thinner and more flexible, resilient casings and tread have lower rolling resistance. Natural rubber (latex) is better than manufactured butyl. Pinching tires between your fingers and feeling the ease with which they deform and rebound gives a good indication of their rolling resistance. See Table 1.1 for the rolling resistance of typical bicycle tires (Kyle, 1988a). The best wall materials are made from thin threads of silk, nylon, or Kevlar, since they have a high strength-to-weight ratio and are extremely flexible, thus minimizing both weight and hysteresis losses.

The tread pattern also influences rolling resistance. Tire tread concentrates the pressure at the contact patch where the tread squirms and deforms as it moves through the contact patch. Tread is meant to improve traction, not to lower rolling resistance. Fine tread patterns are better than coarse ones, but slick tires are best for low rolling resistance. Hybrid tread that has a broad smooth band in the center with tread lugs on both sides is a good compromise to give superior traction in corners or on soft surfaces and low rolling resistance on smooth pavement.

Tube Construction. Thin, lightweight natural rubber tubes (latex) have the lowest rolling resistance. The tube flexes with every wheel revolution; this influences rolling resistance about 1/2 to 1/10 as much as the tire does. Unfortunately, latex tubes lose air rapidly, so a mixture of latex and butyl gives both good rolling resistance and good air retention properties. Butylized latex tubes are commercially available. See Table 1.1 for tests on several tubes and liners.

Thick polyurethane tire liners, intended for flat protection, can nearly double the rolling resistance of a tire. Puncture sealants, latex liners, or puncture-resistant belts on tires cause less drag than thick polyurethane liners. However, probably the best solution for most riding conditions

Table 1.1 The Rolling Resistance of Bicycle Tires

Tire type		Pressure atm	Surface[1]		
			Linoleum	Concrete	Smooth asphalt
Tubular tires					
Continental Olympic	27 in. × 19 mm	6.8	0.19	0.17	0.22
Continental Olympic	24 in. × 19 mm	6.8	0.26	0.23	0.27
Clement Colle Main	27 in. × 19 mm	6.8	0.16		
Clement Colle Main	24 in. × 19 mm	6.8	0.21		
Clement Colle Main	20 in. × 19 mm	6.8	0.29		
Wired-on "clincher" tires					
Specialized Turbo S	700 × 19 C	6.8	0.26		0.29
Specialized Turbo S, Kevlar 700 × 19 C (with a latex tube)		6.8	0.23	0.27	
Same tire with a butyl tube		6.8	0.28		
Same tire with a butylized latex tube		6.8	0.25		
Same tire with a thin polyurethane tube		6.8	0.29		
Same tire with a polyurethane liner		6.8	0.54		
Same tire with a thick latex liner		6.8	0.32		
(The last two tests used latex tubes.)					

Tire	Size	Weight	Coefficient	
Touring tire	700 × 25 C	6.8	0.31	0.35
Same tire		8.2	0.28	
Knobby tread tire	27 in. × 2-1/4 in.	3.1	1.30	
Knobby tread tire	20 in. × 2-1/4 in.	3.1	1.70	
Avocet Fastgrip	20 in. × 1-3/4 in.	5.4	0.40	
Same tire		6.8	0.37	
Same tire		8.2	0.32	
Same tire worn tread		6.8	0.30	
Avocet Fastgrip	26 in. × 1-3/4 in.	6.8	Glass = 0.30; Smooth asphalt = 0.35; Rough macadam = 0.54	
Moulton	17 in. × 1-1/4 in.	5.4	0.34	
Same tire		6.8	0.30	0.39
Same tire		8.2	0.27	

[1]The rolling resistance coefficient in percentage. To get the resistance to motion, multiply the weight on the tire by the coefficient divided by 100. The tests were performed from 1984 to 1988 at California State University, Long Beach, for the U.S. cycling team, Specialized, General Motors, and Tom Petrie of Velimpex Marketing, El Cerrito, CA.

is to use tires with slightly more tread thickness. This will prevent most flats and will provide relatively low rolling resistance (see the 700 × 25 C touring tire in Table 1.1)

Tire Pressure.   With equal loads, higher tire pressures decrease the tire deformation. High tire pressure also helps prevent pinch flats, but the vibration dampening of the tire deteriorates. See Figure 1.9 (Kyle, 1988c) and Table 1.1 for the effect of tire pressure on rolling resistance. In racing, competitors will carry as high a pressure as is practical in order to decrease rolling resistance. Typical pressures are from 8 to 10 atmospheres (120 psi-150 psi) in road races and from 10 to 15 atmospheres (150 psi-220 psi) in track races.

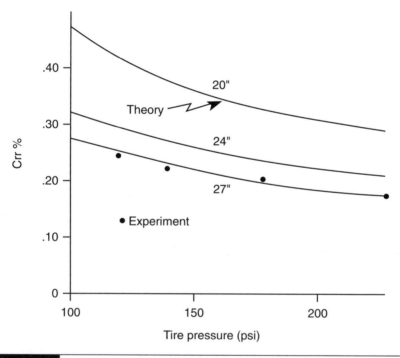

Figure 1.9   Rolling resistance coefficient versus tire pressure and wheel size. From Kyle (1988c).

Load on the Wheel.   Rolling resistance is directly proportional to the wheel load. Lighter loads lessen the tire deformation. Depending on the design of the tires and the road surface, the retarding force caused by tire friction can vary from about 0.22 to 0.5% of the weight on the tires (Kyle & Burke, 1984). The weight of the tire has three effects. Lighter tires have thinner casings and tread and therefore less internal friction. A lighter tire also decreases the wheel load, although this is a comparatively minor effect. In addition, because tire weight is concentrated at the rim, extra weight in the tire magnifies the inertial effects during acceleration. The equivalent inertial mass of a tire is double the inertial mass of a nonrotating weight, so light tires are doubly effective for quick starts.

Tire Cross-Sectional Diameter. Larger tire cross sections deform less under equal loads, given the same tire construction and tire diameter. However, narrow tire profiles are still extremely efficient, and they have a lower air resistance than wider tires.

Wheel Diameter. Larger wheels have less tire deformation for equal loads. They also roll over surface irregularities with less applied torque. As the wheel size decreases, with identical tire construction the tire must deform progressively more to support an equal weight; so tires with smaller wheels have an unavoidable higher rolling resistance even on perfectly smooth pavement (see Figure 1.9). On rough pavement they are at a double disadvantage: To overcome irregularities in the pavement requires a greater propulsive force for a small wheel than for a large wheel, and the friction losses are correspondingly greater (consider a roller skate trying to go over a rock half the size of the wheel). See Table 1.1 for the effect of wheel size and pavement roughness on rolling resistance.

Speed. Lower speeds decrease bearing friction, wind resistance, and dynamic tire distortion. All of these are usually included in some way with rolling resistance measurements. With high-pressure bicycle tires, dynamic distortion is very small, but bearing friction and wind resistance are always present.

Tire Temperature. Rubber viscosity decreases with higher temperatures, cutting internal friction. Also, air expands with heat, and this causes higher tire pressure.

Drive Torque. Tire deformation decreases with lower drive torques. The rear bicycle tire wears much faster than the front for two reasons. About 60% of the weight is on the rear tire, and the thrust force causes increased scrubbing on the pavement. For these reasons rear tires last about half as long as front tires.

Steering Angle. When the bike turns, tire friction goes up because the tire scrubs the pavement and centrifugal force increases the weight on the wheel. Steering a straight line will get you there faster (Kyle, 1991b).

Of the factors identified, pavement roughness, tire materials and construction, tire pressure, and wheel load are the major contributors to rolling resistance.

Bearing Friction

Bicycle wheel bearings are of two basic types, the cup and cone type and the cartridge type. As supplied by bicycle manufacturers, bearings are lubricated with grease. Ball bearings have a very low friction, and cause about 1/20th to 1/50th as much drag as high-pressure racing tires. Friction in bearings is so low that it can be measured only with a very accurate laboratory apparatus. Cartridge bearings usually contain seals that add to the bearing friction.

In 1991, Danh and his fellow researchers at Oregon State University measured the friction of bicycle wheel bearings of several types (Danh, Mai, Poland, & Jenkins). They found enormous differences between lubricants and between bearing types (see Figure 1.10). Their conclusions were:

- Cup and cone bearings, properly adjusted and lubricated with 20w oil, have the lowest friction. The friction of a cartridge bearing having no seal and lubricated with 20w oil is about seven times higher than that of cup and cone bearings. For racing, therefore, standard cup and cone bearings are superior.

- Bearings with grease have a friction about six to seven times higher than the same bearing with light 20w oil. For racing, therefore, the bearings should be cleaned and lubricated with light oil. The losses resulting from use of grease are the equivalent of climbing a 15-m hill during a 40-km time trial.

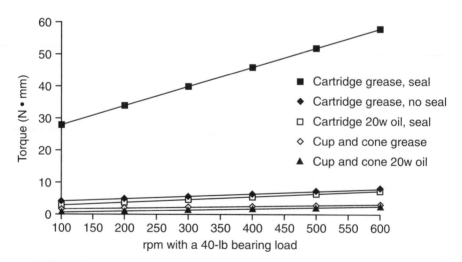

Figure 1.10 Effects of lubricant and seals on cartridge and cup and cone bearing friction. Adapted from Danh, Mai, Poland, and Jenkins (1991).

- Cartridge bearing seals can cause up to 10 times the friction of a free-running bearing without a seal. For racing, therefore, cartridge bearings should be of the shielded type, not sealed (the shield doesn't rub). For racing, the inner shield should be removed and the bearing lubricated with light oil.
- The friction of the bicycle wheel bearings does not seem to be affected much by the load; however, Danh and coworkers found that the friction increased linearly with the speed. Friction approximately doubled from 50 to 600 rpm.

The conclusions are generally correct with one qualification; Danh used new cartridge bearings, which give very high friction measurements. Worn bearings and seals that have been run in have a much lower friction than new bearings. Using a different test procedure, Kyle (1988a) reached basically the same conclusions as Danh. According to Danh's data, cone bearings could produce a 7-m lead in a 40-km time trial against an equal opponent using cartridge bearings with the seals removed and lubricated with light oil (Danh, Mai, Poland, & Jenkins, 1991).

To estimate the combined energy losses in the chain, sprockets, and bearings, a bicycle ergometer driven by an accurate dynamometer can be used (Kyle & Caiozzo, 1986b). Drivetrain losses are from 2 to 4% of the energy input. This extremely high efficiency is typical for a well-oiled sprocket and roller chain transmission. To minimize the transmission energy losses, a bicycle chain and gears should be clean and well lubricated.

A factor not commonly considered by inventors seeking to improve bicycle transmissions is the extremely high energy efficiency of a chain-sprocket drive—above 96%. For example, hydraulic transmissions are often proposed as a solution to bicycle gearing, but they are less than 75% efficient; this means that more than 25% of a rider's energy would be wasted. This is clearly impractical. It pays to beware of new infinitely variable transmissions or other drive schemes until the inventor measures the energy losses in the transmission. Anything with higher losses than a chain-sprocket transmission will not sell because the rider must overcome the added losses with muscle power.

Bicycle Components

The design and shape of various bicycle components also have a significant effect on aerodynamics.

Wheels

Numerous types of bicycle wheels are currently manufactured: round-spoked wheels with flat rims, bladed-spoked wheels with aero rims, composite disk wheels, Kevlar membrane aero wheels, composite three-spoked aero wheels, and an endless variety of combinations of spoke types and patterns, shapes, sizes, and weights. Several factors influence the performance of a bicycle wheel, including stiffness, weight, aerodynamic drag, strength and durability, and the efficiency of the braking surface. The fact is, however, that almost any type of wheel can be built to meet all of the important performance criteria except two, aerodynamic drag and weight. In other words, almost any type of wheel can have adequate strength, durability, stiffness (which influences the ride quality), and a good braking surface; however, all wheel types can't have low aerodynamic drag and low weight.

Table 1.2 shows the time advantage for elite cyclists when small aerodynamic drag reductions are achieved by the use of better equipment. Table 1.3 shows the air drag and weight of racing bicycle wheels tested at the University of California at Irvine low-speed wind tunnel. The measurements listed in Table 1.3 are for front wheels only. The rear wheel would provide about 60% of the advantage listed because the rear wheel is drafting in the slipstream of other components.

From the wind tunnel wheel tests, the following conclusions about the aerodynamics of wheels can be drawn (Kyle, 1991d):

The Effect of Wheel Size. Aerodynamically, there doesn't seem to be too much difference between the best wheels in 24-in., 26-in., and 27-in. diameter. Even though the 24- and 26-in. wheels have a smaller frontal

Table 1.2 The Racing Advantage of Aerodynamics

Drag decrease (grams)	Ft per mile advantage	Time decrease per mile(s)	1,000-m time trial	4,000-m pursuit
10	5	0.11	0.07 s	0.28 s
20	10	0.22	0.12 s	0.62 s
40	20	0.45	0.23 s	1.12 s
80	41	0.93	0.47 s	2.22 s
120	61	1.39	0.70 s	3.39 s
160	91	2.06	0.94 s	4.53 s
200	111	2.51	1.17 s	5.62 s

Adapted from Kyle (1990).

area, they must spin faster to achieve the same rim speed, so the corresponding drag is about the same. However, smaller wheels have many other advantages. They are lighter and stronger, and the bicycle frame can also be made lighter and stiffer with a consequent advantage in acceleration, cornering, and hill climbing. The center of aerodynamic lift of a disk wheel is ahead of the axle by about one fourth of the wheel radius, so a steering torque is generated by crosswinds. Small front disk wheels have more stability in unsteady crosswinds, so you can ride them in more severe wind conditions.

In a pace line, small-wheeled bikes can draft closer, and therefore the bikes in the pace line have a lower average wind resistance. Figure 1.11 shows the wind resistance of drafting riders in a pace line. Using 24-in. wheels, each drafting rider can have 5% lower wind resistance compared to riders in the same pace line with 27-in. wheels, so the pace line can travel faster. A reasonable estimate is 2 s faster in a 4,000-m team pursuit.

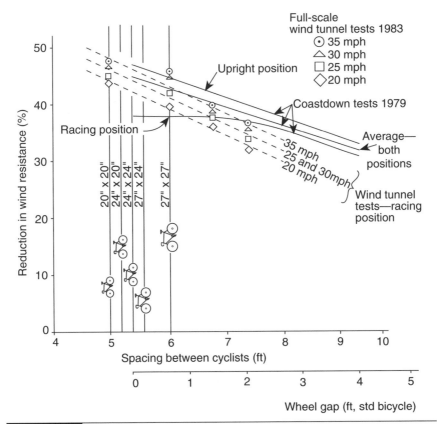

Figure 1.11 The wind resistance of drafting riders in a pace line.

Table 1.3 Bicycle Wheel Tests (U.C.–Irvine Wind Tunnel)

Wheels	Wheel weight (grams)	Drag in grams at 30 mph	
		Static tests (avg[1])	Rotating (avg[1])
24-in. wheels (18-mm tires)			
Flat carbon disk	950	74	97
Kevlar lens disk	480	76	100
12 spokes, deep aero rim	790	86	109
18 bladed spokes, aero rim	490	–	136
28 round spokes, flat rim[2]	610	–	182
26-in. wheels (18-mm tires)			
Kevlar lens disk	590	78	95
Flat carbon disk	900	73	101
HED CX 18 aero spokes	850	109	139
18 bladed spokes, aero rim	530	–	145
32 round spokes, flat rim[2]	700	–	208
27-in. wheels (18-mm tires)			
27-in. composite spoked wheels (3 and 4 spokes)			
Aerosports 3-spoke prototype	720	90	106
Trispoke (3 spoke)	720	87	112
Specialized (3 spoke)	1330	89	114

Zip (forward, 3 spoke)	850	102	129
Corima (4 spoke)	1590	100	131
Zipp (backward, 3 spoke)	850	108	146
27-in. disk wheels			
Gipiemme lens disk	1110	72	101
Flat carbon disk	1040	76	105
Zipp 950 carbon flat disk	950	77	112
HED flat carbon disk	1050	77	114
Kevlar lens disk	710	99	118
27-in. steel spoked wheels			
18 Aero spokes, aero rim	680	122	149
24 Aero spokes, aero rim	770	–	147
28 Aero spokes, aero rim	820	–	173
28 Oval spokes, aero rim	780	–	175
18 Round spokes, aero rim	700	–	206
36 Round spokes, std rim	960	–	258

[1]Tests performed for the U.S. Cycling Federation, Specialized, and Aerosports, at the U.C.-Irvine wind tunnel, 1987, 1989, and 1991. The basic accuracy of the wind tunnel balance is ±5 g, so many of the listed differences are not significant.

[2]22-mm tire.

Adapted from Kyle (1991d).

As we noted earlier, the only obvious disadvantage to small wheels is their higher rolling resistance. Considering the combined aerodynamic drag and rolling resistance, racing bikes can be built with a mix of wheel sizes and be very competitive. Table 1.4 compares several wheel combinations at 30 mph on a level course with a pair of standard 27-in. wheels as the baseline (Kyle, 1991d).

Table 1.4	The Net Drag of Various Bicycle Wheel Combinations
Wheel combinations	**Difference in drag (grams)**
27 × 27	0
27 × 26	−1
27 × 24	+9
26 × 26	+3
26 × 24	+13
24 × 24	+29

Data from Kyle (1991d).

So the difference among the various wheel size combinations used by time trial bikes is not very large, only about 29 g at 30 mph. This translates into a time difference of about 10 to 15 s in 40 km. Considering that small-wheeled bikes can be made much lighter, I suspect that all of the bikes listed would be about equal on a level course with no wind. On a rolling course where climbing is necessary, the lighter bikes with smaller wheels should be superior. And in a road race where there is constant acceleration and deceleration, the small-wheeled 24 × 24 should be best. Already, time trial bikes of 27 × 26, 27 × 24, 26 × 26, and 24 × 24 have won international races.

The Effect of Wheel Type. A comparison of the wheels in Table 1.2 shows that composite aerodynamic wheels have a uniformly lower drag than the best bladed-, oval-, or round-spoked wheels by 35 to 50 g per wheel.

When we compare composite three-spoked wheels to lens-shaped or flat disk wheels, the three types are about the same. There is another major difference, however, between disk wheels and three-spoked aero wheels. When there is a buffeting crosswind, a front disk wheel often causes steering instability that makes it impossible to ride a straight line. Rear disk wheels cause few problems—they can be ridden in nearly any wind condition. Three-spoked composite front wheels have much more stability in crosswinds, making them ideal for racing under almost any conditions. In fact, the aero drag of both three-spoked composites and disk wheels decreases in a mild crosswind, because the wheel actually develops lift (the sail effect). In contrast, the drag of conventionally spoked wheels increases in a crosswind (Kyle, 1990). Thus the advantage of aero wheels over steel spoked wheels improves with side winds.

The Effect of Tire Width. The width of tires should be about equal to the width of the rim for minimum aerodynamic drag. Air should flow smoothly around the tire and rim. If the tire is wider, it causes flow separation and turbulence, raising the drag. The wider the tire, the higher the aerodynamic drag. Some racers put a smooth bead of silicon caulking between the tire and rim to improve the flow. Since tire width makes little difference in rolling resistance, there is no advantage to using wide tires in time trialing or road racing. On rough pavement or in gravel or dirt, wide mountain bike tires handle much better than narrow road tires.

Bicycle Frames

Modern bicycle frames come in a bewildering variety of sizes, shapes, and materials. Frames of different styles have sloping top tubes, monocoque composite frame members, various wheel sizes, different seat tube angles, and so on. Because of this variety, it has become difficult to classify frame size by traditional methods. In fact, the frame size (58 cm, 60 cm, etc.) has little meaning for many custom bicycles. What is important is that the bars, the saddle, and the relative position of the cranks should be adjustable enough to fit the preferred riding position of the cyclist. For rider comfort, the triangle composed of the body contact points—crank, saddle, and handlebars—should remain unchanged no matter what frame style the rider is using. From a side view, the riding position should be identical from one bicycle to the next. A variety of bicycle sizes and geometries can feel comfortable and provide stable riding.

Stability is an obvious necessity for any bicycle. A rider must be able to ride a straight line and corner cleanly with near-effortless control. Unfortunately, there is really no useful way of defining bicycle stability except subjectively through rider feel. There are few absolutes in bicycle geometry. Dimensions and angles can vary a great deal and still be suitable. For most bicycles the steering head angle is between 65° and 75° as measured from the horizontal. The trail is the most critical geometric parameter. This is the distance between a projection of the steering axis where it hits the pavement and the center of the tire contact patch. The trail normally varies from 1.5 to 2.5 in. Within these ranges, bicycles feel stable and are very ridable. A head angle of 73° and a trail of 1.75 in. are typical of a racing bicycle, and 65° and 2.5 in. are typical of mountain bikes. Steeper head angles and less trail make a bicycle quicker in steering but less stable at racing speeds. More trail and lower head angles make the bicycle sluggish in steering, but very stable and easy to handle over bumps and rough pavement. Preferred bicycle geometry (frame size, rake, trail, etc.) is a matter of personal preference. Cyclists can ride anything from a child's sidewalk bike to a unicycle.

On the other hand, rider position and aerodynamics is not a matter of personal preference but is subject to the laws of physics. With aero bars that place the rider in a low crouch and the torso close to horizontal, the position of the steering axis is important. If the rider is too far forward over the steering axis, the added forward mass can make the bicycle difficult to steer. Lengthening the top tube, and thus the wheelbase, makes steering more sluggish but easier to manage. At 30 mph, the combined air resistance of a bicycle and a rider (6 ft, 165 lb) varies from about 5.5 lb to over 10 lb, depending upon the riding position and the bicycle. The aerodynamic drag of the bicycle is only 25 to 35% of the total, with the cyclist's body being the remainder. Consequently, body position is the biggest single factor in achieving low aerodynamic drag. Figure 1.12 shows the effect of riding position upon the power required to pedal a standard racing bicycle (Kyle, 1991c). The hill descent position (hands together, elbows in, low crouch) is the most efficient aerodynamically. This is only slightly better than the position achieved with the use of new elbow-rest aero handlebars. With aero bars, wind tunnel studies show that the drag of a rider is lowest if the back is flat (not

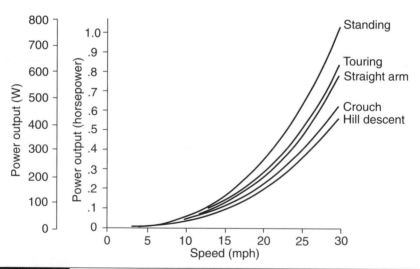

Figure 1.12 Power versus speed for various riding positions. The bicycle used was a Raleigh track bike; the rider was 6 ft 2 in., 180 lb. Results of coastdown tests conducted by Chester Kyle at California State University–Long Beach, 1983-1984.

arched), the elbows are held in so that the front arm profile is narrower than the body, and the angle of the arms is from 0° to 30° as measured from the horizontal (Kyle, 1989).

In the wind tunnel at the California Institute of Technology in 1986, we also tested some unusual riding positions (Kyle, 1991e, see Table 8). In 1986, elbow-rest handlebars were not commercially developed and we built a special cable steering system that allowed riders to place their arms behind the seat in a typical speed skater's position. We used an aerodynamic chest support to stabilize the riders and keep them in a tuck position while they were steering from behind the seat. Holding the arms horizontal and behind lowered the drag nearly 0.7 lb at 30 mph, which is enough for a 1-min advantage in 40 km. The more recent development of elbow-rest handlebar systems halted any further consideration of the strange rear steering arrangement.

For long races, the elbow-rest aero bars allow a rider to maintain an efficient aerodynamic posture for long periods without fatigue; however, for short races another arm position may be superior. By placing the hands on horizontal handlebars about chest width apart, doubling up the arms, and resting the chest on the bars, Graeme Obree of Great Britain succeeded in breaking the world hour record in July, 1993, riding 51.596 km at sea level in Hamar, Norway. According to reports, his unique riding position is very uncomfortable but has a lower drag than the position held with conventional aero bars. One week later, on July 23, 1993, Chris Boardman of Great Britain broke Obree's record at 52.270 km in Bordeaux, France. Boardman used the standard elbow-rest aero bar riding position.

The body type of a cyclist makes an enormous difference in aerodynamic drag. For the same weight and height, riders can have a wide variety of limb lengths, chest and neck size, and so on, and consequently a widely varying aerodynamic drag. Table 1.5 shows the physical

Table 1.5	Physical Characteristics of Six Cyclists						
Name	Gender	Age (yr)	Height (m	ft/in.)	Weight (Kg	lb)	Body type
M.R.	Female	34	1.619	(5'4")	47.7	(105)	Slender
K.K.	Female	19	1.625	(5'4")	54.5	(120)	Stocky
K.S.	Male	25	1.753	(5'9")	59.9	(132)	Slender
R.R.	Male	23	1.797	(5'11")	69.0	(152)	Medium
C.C.	Male	22	1.829	(6'0")	65.8	(145)	Slender
D.M.	Male	26	1.854	(6'1")	79.2	(160)	Slender

Reprinted from Kyle (1991b).

Table 1.6 Wind Tunnel Test Results Showing Bicycle Drag at Varying Yaw Angles

Drag force (Fx) and side force (Fy), pounds

Bike	0°		10°		20°		30°	
	Fx	Fy	Fx	Fy	Fx	Fy	Fx	Fy
M.R., triathlon bike	5.171	0.07	5.360	5.967	5.537	13.392	5.715	21.509
K.K., triathlon bike	5.925	0.29	6.021	4.648	6.062	11.82	6.696	20.66
K.S., triathlon bike	5.219	0.14	5.460	5.522	5.446	12.968	5.779	22.486
R.R., triathlon bike	5.619	0.66	5.764	5.612	5.656	13.386	5.674	23.258
Average, triathlon bike	5.484	0.29	5.651	5.437	5.675	12.892	5.966	21.978
C.C., track bike	8.006	0.21	8.398	4.062	9.098	7.990	—	—
C.C., aero bike	7.597	0.30	7.484	4.752	8.216	8.346	—	—
D.M., road bike	10.575	1.913	11.437	1.643	12.026	5.580	13.709	13.118

Note. All speeds and forces are given with respect to the bike axis. Wind speed 30 mph. **Triathlon bike:** Vitus aluminum frame, special flat 100k bars, a 27-in. × 19-mm front wheel with aero rim and 18 bladed spokes, a 27-in. × 19-mm Hed lens rear disk, single-disk front sprocket. The riders wore Giro aero helmets with Lycra covers and Lycra skin suits. All were in aero position with back flat and elbows pulled in resting on bars with the hands together in front. Wind tunnel tests were performed in January, 1990, at Texas A&M by Chet Kyle, Mike Melton, and Gary Hooker at the Hed Triathlon Camp. **Track bike:** Conventional Raleigh with drop bars and two 27-in. × 22-mm standard rim 36-round-spoke wheels. **Aero bike:** Prototype with helicopter aero strut tubing, bull horn bars with aero tubing, two 20-in., 18-round-spoke wheels with aero rims, 60-mm narrow front hubs, 110-mm rear hubs, a single-disk front sprocket with aero cranks. The riders on the track and aero bikes sat upright, head up, with elbows straight and hands on the bull horns; rider was bare-headed and wore a loose Lycra USA suit and high wool socks. Track bike and aero bike, wind tunnel tests performed in June, 1983, by Chet Kyle and Jack Lambie at Texas A&M for USOC. **Road bike:** Conventional round tube frame with drop bars, 27-in., 36-spoke wheels, and a carrier rack in the rear. Rider rode in a full crouch with hands on drops, wearing a loose cotton T-shirt, a wool ski cap, and loose cotton touring shorts. Wind tunnel tests were performed at Calspan in New York, October, 1980, by D.M. for Alex Moulton Bicycles. *Note.* The road bike test was actually performed at 20 mph, to get comparative drag figures at 30 mph; the measured drag was multiplied by 2.25 [(30/20)^2].

characteristics of six cyclists, and Table 1.6 shows the aerodynamic drag of these same subjects on a triathlon bike in identical riding positions. One of the shortest and lightest of the subjects had a stocky build and surprisingly had the highest aerodynamic drag. A slender torso is an advantage in cycling as far as aerodynamic drag is concerned (Kyle, 1991e). Many cyclists have a slender torso and arms but well-developed leg muscles—a body type ideal for cycling.

The data in Table 1.6 also include the drag of bicycles at wind yaw angles up to 30° (the equivalent of a crosswind). The yaw angle data demonstrate that bicycles with disk wheels or aero tubing perform far better in crosswinds than round-tube bicycles with conventional wheels. In fact, the prototype aero bicycle shown in Table 1.6 actually had a lower drag at 10° yaw angle than at 0°. The triathlon bike with disk wheels also performed very well.

Table 1.7 shows the air drag of various bicycle types in wind tunnel tests (Kyle, 1989, 1991b, 1991e). At 30 mph, aero funny bikes have almost 1 lb less drag than standard road bicycles, giving them an enormous advantage in time trials. The two Dupont bicycles listed had prototype monocoque frames similar to that of the Lotus/Mike Burrows funny bike used by Chris Boardman in winning the 1992 Olympic 4,000-m individual pursuit. The Dupont bikes were built by Don Guichard and Chester Kyle for the 1988 U.S. Olympic cycling team, but were declared illegal by the UCI (Union Cycliste Internationale) before the Olympics. The UCI reversed the ruling in 1991, making composite monocoque bicycles legal. Because it is possible to mold composites into optimum aerodynamic shapes, they make ideal, if expensive, materials for building racing bicycles. However, in the wind tunnel tests so far, metal tube aero bikes such as the Hooker Elite have performed as well as or better than composite bicycles. In the period from 1990 to 1993, the Hooker bike won dozens of national and international medals.

Shifting Systems

Index shifters with fingertip controls have several advantages over conventional systems in which the shifters are on the down tube. Fingertip shifters allow faster and more frequent shifts, giving the proper gear when it is required, not later. If the shifter is on the down tube, the rider must release the handlebar and reach down. This sometimes causes steering problems and often interrupts the pedaling effort. Reaching down also increases aerodynamic drag because of the position of the rider's arm. It shouldn't be necessary to move the arm to shift gears. With fingertip shifters, it isn't. Index shifters also permit changing gears under load, which permits a steadier pace.

Electronic rather than manual shifting is still in the development stage, but it could be an improvement that would save time and weight

Table 1.7 The Aerodynamic Drag of Bicycles at 30 mph

Bicycle	Wheels	Drag (pounds)	
		Bike bare	Bike with rider
Road bikes			
Gleb Derujinski, aero composite[1,2]	27" × 28 aero spokes front, 32 spokes rear	1.90	6.89
Trimble prototype, aero composite[1,2]	2 27" × 36 round spokes	2.46	7.07
Kestrel prototype, aero composite[1]	Same	2.52	7.27
GIOS (standard round steel tubes)[1]	Same	2.64	7.37
Trek (aluminum round tubes)[1]	Same	2.71	7.36
Cannondale (aluminum round tubes)[1]	Same	2.72	7.25
Time trial bikes			
Kyle prototype (steel aero tubes)[1]	27" rear flat disk, 24" front lens disk	1.45	6.48
Hooker Elite[3]	27" flat disk rear, 24" × 18 aero spoke front	1.38	6.66
1986 Huffy aero composite[1,2]	27" rear lens disk, 24" front lens disk	1.89	6.71
Kyle prototype[3]	27" flat disk rear, 24" flat disk front	1.33	6.72
Huffy Triton[3]	Same wheels as Hooker Elite	2.23	6.80
KHS[3]	Same wheels	2.29	6.94
Time Machine[3]	Same wheels	2.93	7.03
Rigideol aero (steel aero tubes)[3]	2 27" lens disks	2.02	7.06
Team pursuit bike			
Huffy aero composite[1]	2 24" lens disks	1.54	6.33

(continued)

Table 1.7 (continued)

Bicycle	Wheels	Bike bare	Bike with rider
Individual pursuit bikes			
Gleb Derujinski aero composite[1,2]	27″ rear lens disk, 24″ front lens disk	1.44	6.30
Dupont aero composite #1, S frame[1,2]	Same	1.20	6.41
1986 Huffy aero composite[1,2]	Same	1.57	6.42
Dupont aero composite #2, V frame[1,2]	Same	1.21	6.56
Brent Trimble composite monocoque[1,2]	Same	1.44	6.56
Tesch aero (aluminum aero tubes)[1]	Same	1.56	6.84
Schwinn track (steel round tubes)[1]	2 27 × 32 bladed-spoke wheels, aero rims	2.41	6.98

[1]These tests were performed at California Institute of Technology, November 4-10, 1986. The same rider was used in all tests and was in the same crouched racing position. The rider was 6 ft 2 in. tall and 170 lb, and wore Lycra tights with a long-sleeved wool jersey and a U.S. team aero helmet. The road bikes used standard drop bars except the Gleb, which used composite bars with an aero cross section and standard drop handgrips. Road and time trial bikes included water bottles. [2]These composite aero bikes were illegal for UCI-sanctioned races prior to 1991, when the rules were changed to permit monocoque bikes with no restrictions on tubing dimensions. [3]These tests were performed at Texas A&M, January 9-10, 1990. The same rider was used in all tests with elbow rest bars and with the torso horizontal. The rider was 6 ft 1 in. tall and 170 lb, and wore a Lycra skin suit and a Giro aero helmet. The Kyle prototype is the same bike as the first time trial bike listed except that it has special aero elbow rest handlebars designed by David Spangler of Hooker Industries. The bars are nearly identical to those on the Hooker Elite. Reprinted from Kyle (1989, 1991b, 1991e).

and make shifting more accurate. The miniaturization and automation of 35-mm cameras is an example of the process that could lead to better electronic shifting systems.

Drinking Systems

In rides of 1 to 2 hr, liquid supplements are not necessary for maximum performance (Coggan, 1990; Coyle, 1989; Noakes, 1990). But it has been shown by Edward Coyle of the University of Texas that the onset of exhaustion in exercise over 2 to 3 hr can be extended from 30 to 60 min by the intake of a carbohydrate supplement during exercise. To do this a cyclist must drink frequently and ingest about 50 g of carbohydrate per hour (Coyle, 1989).

Drinking from bottles carried on the down tube or seat tube works well, but there are problems. When riding in a pack, riders often find it hard to take one hand off the bars and drink. When they do, they must relax their pedaling intensity, reach down for the bottle, tilt the head back, squeeze the bottle, drink, and put the bottle back in the cage. These actions will temporarily slow riders down every time they drink. This is so because the aerodynamic drag will increase when the arm and head are out of position and because the rider must relax his or her pedaling while drinking.

There are several systems that allow cyclists to drink without changing position or slowing down. Probably the simplest is placing a bottle with a plastic straw on the handlebars. But because the bottle and straw are exposed to the wind, this solution creates a higher air resistance than with the bottle on the down tube. Another device places water on the back in a flat soft bag worn either outside or under the jersey (the CamelBak); the rider drinks though a tube attached to the helmet strap. This works well, doesn't raise the aero drag significantly, and permits the cyclist to concentrate on riding. However, many cyclists don't like the extra weight on the back or the feel of the bag if it is worn inside the jersey. Several other systems use pressurized bottles either behind the seat or on the down tube. The rider drinks through a standing tube clipped to the bars by biting a squeeze valve in the mouthpiece. Despite some minor problems, the new drinking systems are probably superior for most racing or recreational applications.

Clothing

Bicycle clothing has many functions; among these are providing safety, protection, or comfort, keeping the wearer cool or warm, lowering the aerodynamic drag, and even adding color or decoration to the rider. Except for the last item, all these can help improve performance.

Suits. During wind tunnel tests on bicycles at Cal Tech in 1986 (Kyle, 1991e), we conducted some experiments with clothing (see Table 1.8). At the time the tests were run, efficient aerodynamic clothing was not as common as it is today; however, the results still contain valuable information. Briefly, the use of slick, tight-fitting, smooth clothing without wrinkles can reduce the air drag dramatically. A rubberized Lycra suit was the best, but plain Lycra spandex was nearly as effective. Rougher materials such as wool or polypropylene used in jerseys or tights could slow a rider down over 1 min in 40 km. A skin suit with separate tights seemed to be about as good as a one-piece suit with tights and sleeves. The tests merely verified that a well-fitting skin suit is a requirement for any serious time trialer.

There may be some materials that have a lower aerodynamic drag than those now used in bicycle clothing. In 1990, Len Brownlie of the University of British Columbia tested various fabrics on a cycling mannequin in a full-scale wind tunnel (Brownlie, Gartshore, Chapman, & Banister, 1991). He found that a material called Cosmopion with a

Table 1.8 The Air Drag of Bicycle Clothing at 30 mph and the Effect of Arm Position

30 mph air drag tests	**Drag (pounds)**
Clothing	
1986 USA rubberized Lycra skin suit, long sleeves	5.78
Full Lycra skin suit with long sleeves and tights	5.80
1986 USA Lycra skin suit, long sleeves	5.83
Wool jersey with long sleeves	6.31
Polypropylene warm-up suit	6.46
Arm position	
Both arms back in speed skater's position	5.58
One arm back, one arm forward, hand on bars	6.10
Both arms in standard racing position, hands on bars	6.31

Note. All tests are at 0° yaw angle. The rider for both tests was 6 ft 2 in., 170 lb. For the clothing tests, the rider was on the Kyle aero road bike, in a crouched racing position, wearing a USA team aero helmet. For the tests of arm position, the rider was on the Kyle aero road bike, wearing a wool jersey, Lycra tights, and a USA team aero helmet. Tests were performed at Texas A&M, January 9-10, 1990.

Reprinted from Kyle (1991e).

slight surface roughness had a significantly lower drag than Lycra. Kyle noticed a similar phenomenon in wind tunnel clothing tests in 1986 (Kyle, 1986; Kyle & Caiozzo, 1986a). At bicycle racing speeds, cylindrical or oval shapes such as the legs, arms, or body undergo a transition in which the flow in the wake changes from laminar to turbulent. When this happens, the size of the wake decreases and the pressure on the trailing surface rises, lowering the drag abruptly to between one half and one third of what it was. If the flow transition can be prematurely induced at a lower speed by a slightly rough surface, then a significant drag reduction can occur (Brownlie, Gartshore, Chapman, & Banister, 1991; Hoerner, 1965; Kyle, 1986; Kyle & Caiozzo, 1986a). In field tests, Brownlie found that his wind tunnel data were correct; the Cosmopion suit was the fastest of the several suits he tested. Unfortunately, Cosmopion (made in Japan) is no longer produced, but some other similar material would definitely be worth developing.

As a point of interest, skin hair raises the air drag of the human body, so for minimum air resistance serious racers should shave the limbs exposed to the air and cover the head (Kyle, 1986).

Reflective and Evaporative Cooling.   Larry Berglund of the John B. Pierce Foundation Laboratory of Yale University has shown that in direct sunlight, light-reflective clothing can lower sweat loss and improve cooling in exercising cyclists (1987). At high noon, the uncovered human body can absorb about 100 W of radiative energy from the sun, and this energy must be dissipated by convective cooling, radiation, or evaporative cooling. Berglund found that aluminized fabric was best for cycle clothing, followed by white and light-colored fabric. The aluminum-impregnated fabric was superior to bare skin in the ability to dissipate heat. The right fabric, in other words, can cut down on water losses in endurance events (Berglund, 1987).

Helmets.   As with clothing, helmets can lower the aerodynamic drag of the rider while providing head protection and adequate cooling. Aero helmets that have no ventilation holes and have a teardrop shape produce the lowest drag. Examples include the helmets that were used by the U.S. Olympic cycling team from 1984 to 1992, the helmet used by Greg LeMond to win the Tour de France in 1988, and the helmets used in almost all world record time trial attempts. Helmet tests on a mannequin in the wind tunnel have uncovered some interesting facts (Kyle, 1990; Kyle & Burke, 1984):

- Aero helmets have a lower drag than no helmet at all. The drag of even short human hair is higher. An aero helmet smooths the flow over the head and lowers the drag by about 100 g at 30 mph.
- Unstreamlined, blunt, blocky helmets, commonly used in racing today, may weigh little and have good cooling, but their air

resistance is from 110 to 180 g higher than that of a good aero model. Standard helmets will lose more than 1 s per mile to an aero helmet. Therefore, aero helmets should be used in all important time trials up to 1 hr, where cooling is not usually a problem. Helmets with smooth, rounded edges and a polished surface are superior to those with a rough finish and sharp edges or ridges.

- For each helmet there is an optimum head position at which the drag will be minimal. If the head is tipped higher or lower than this, the drag will increase. Usually the best position for aero helmets is one in which the head is held such that the bottom of the helmet is parallel to the upper back and there is a gap between the back and the helmet. Some recent aero helmets, such as the one used by Graeme Obree, have a streamlined tail that is specially contoured to fit the rider's back; the helmet curves over the ears and under the chin. These potentially have a lower drag than older aero models.

Shoes and Pedals. Today's bicycle shoes are made for service and comfort, not for speed. An ideal shoe would have a very low weight and a smooth contour so that the airflow around the foot would be streamlined. In contrast, almost all cycling shoes have straps that disturb the airflow, a rough cloth and leather exterior surface with seams, ridges, and holes, plus a thick sole for rigidity that adds to the weight. Although aerospace materials and design concepts are used elsewhere on the bicycle, they have yet to be applied effectively to commercial cycling shoes.

In 1984, Peter Cavanagh of Pennsylvania State University built a pair of prototype streamlined cycling shoes with an integral pedal (the pedal was part of the shoe and only the axle protruded from the side of the shoe). Cavanagh's shoe/pedal lowered the air drag of the feet over 200 g at 30 mph (Kyle, 1986). The streamlined shoes would have provided over a 1-min advantage in a 40-km time trial. Unfortunately, the shoes were declared illegal by the UCI because most of their contour was not utilitarian but was for the sole purpose of lowering the air resistance. Even if fully streamlined shoes are not legal, much can still be done within the regulations to improve racing cycling shoes. A shoe with perfectly smooth and rounded contours and an integral pedal is not only legal but practical; however, producing it would require an expensive design and development effort by shoe manufacturers. The general concept used for a molded rear-entry ski boot would work very well.

In purchasing shoes and pedals for racing, there are several points to consider. The shoes should have a smooth upper surface if possible. The pedals should have a small frontal area and be as smoothly contoured as is practical. The pedal should allow lateral motion of the foot. The shoe cleat and pedal should be as small and light as possible. The

Shimano SPD mountain bike pedal system, except for its higher-than-average weight, is as suitable as any for road use.

Directions for Future Research

Future research in cycling should demand a more cycling-specific approach. There needs to be a greater focus toward cycling-specific experimental design, equipment, subject selection, and protocols to answer questions particular to the competitive and recreational aspects of cycling. The following are some areas that need to be studied.

Alternative Drive Mechanisms

Oval sprockets, linear lever drives, infinitely variable transmissions, variable-length cranks, and cam drives—for the past hundred years, inventors have sought a better way to propel a bicycle. They are still seeking an alternative drive system to replace the traditional sprocket and chain transmission. This is a daunting challenge. In order to be competitive, an alternative drive mechanism must be at least as good as the traditional system. This means that it must meet certain criteria, some of which are (Kyle, 1991a):

- **Weight**. The drive system must be relatively light.
- **Cost**. The cost should compare to that of a chain drive.
- **Gear changes**. There should be a wide range of gear ratios.
- **Noise**. The transmission should be relatively silent.
- **Maintenance**. The drive should require little maintenance or adjustment. Repair costs should be low. Maintenance or adjustments should be simple enough that the owner can easily perform them. With any successful drive, it should be easy to remove the rear wheel and change a tire.
- **Reliability**. The transmission should be rugged and almost failure free.
- **Mechanical efficiency**. The internal mechanical efficiency of the drive system should be greater than 95%. In other words, only 2 to 5% of the energy input should be wasted in internal friction. This automatically eliminates small hydraulic transmissions that are only about 60 to 75% efficient.
- **Biomechanical efficiency**. The caloric efficiency of human power production should not be impaired by the pedaling motion. Even today, inventors often claim that their new drive mechanism will

allow a rider to immediately increase power production from 15 to 25%. Given the high mechanical efficiency of a chain-sprocket drive and the high metabolic efficiency of the circular crank motion, this is an absurdly false claim. If it were true, the new mechanism would instantly be adopted by all bicycle racers, and this has not happened yet.

- **Operation**. The drive system should shift easily and rapidly and function smoothly with simple, easily accessible rider controls. It should be possible to push the bike backward without the rear wheel locking. The cyclist should be able to climb, accelerate, or pedal on the level with equal facility as with a standard gear-sprocket transmission.

- **Retrofit**. Any transmission that is to be commercially successful should be easily installed on a standard bicycle.

- **Kinetic energy conservation**. Any energy fed into the system to accelerate the legs or the mechanical parts should be recovered sometime during the pedaling cycle. For example, muscular energy should not be required to retard leg movement at the end of a power stroke. A circular crank motion satisfies this requirement.

It may be possible to overlook one or two of these criteria and still succeed, depending upon the application; but if any of the critical requirements (such as efficiency or reliability) are ignored, the transmission is doomed to failure in the marketplace. Instead of the emergence of a revolutionary new system that replaces the chain drive, the past century has seen a continual improvement of the chain drive that has made it even harder to displace. Better derailleurs, chains, and gears plus index shifters have made sprocket-chain drives more efficient than ever.

One recent alternative drive system, the Shimano Biopace, met most of the mentioned criteria and achieved a short-term commercial success, probably because of an intense advertising campaign and not because it was an improvement. The Biopace used oval drive sprockets that sped up the pedal travel by 7 to 17% in the power region. Unfortunately there has been no evidence that the system was in any way superior to a standard drive; in fact, in climbing hills the Biopace tended to bog down due to the slower pedal travel over the top and bottom of the crank cycle. Although it was an acceptable alternative transmission, the Biopace is little used at present, since it demonstrated no real advantage over the standard drive.

In theory it should be possible to improve the combined metabolic and mechanical efficiency of a bicycle drive system by 1 or 2%, but so far this has proved impossible or impractical. This will not stop inventors from trying; new drive systems still appear every year at bicycle shows.

We can hope that a breakthrough will occur before another hundred years have passed.

Instruments

At present, small bicycle computers are available that display such performance variables as speed, average speed, cadence, distance, time, altitude, and heart rate. They are inexpensive, accurate, and easy to use and are a valuable aid in training. Like all electronic devices, they will be subject to continual improvement (Sargeant, 1990). What new functions should we expect in cycling computers in the next few years? The future of microelectronics is clear. Everything will get smaller. As this happens, the power of small computer chips will slowly improve, allowing higher-performance designs for the same cost and size (Sargeant, 1990).

Let's list the functions that might be measured by a sophisticated bike computer: that is, those that could be useful for training, research, or analysis, to the coaches, trainers, athletes, and scientists who need to precisely define cycling performance. Some of the functions are already common in bike computers, but most are not. All of them are possible with today's technology. As electronic devices improve, more and more of the functions will be standard options on tomorrow's bike computers:

- ❏ Speed, average speed, maximum speed
- ❏ Cadence, average cadence, maximum cadence
- ❏ Trip distance, split distance, total distance
- ❏ Trip time, split time, clock time
- ❏ Power, average power, maximum power
- ❏ Hill slope in percent, average slope, maximum slope
- ❏ Elevation, trip gain or loss in elevation, maximum elevation
- ❏ Wind velocity and direction relative to the bike
- ❏ Air temperature
- ❏ Compass direction
- ❏ Heart rate, average heart rate, maximum heart rate
- ❏ Breathing rate, average breathing rate, maximum breathing rate
- ❏ Body core temperature

From this list, you can see that to display more than a few of the functions would be impractical and would make a bike computer as complex as an aircraft instrument panel. And such a complicated bike computer would be nearly impossible for the average person to operate without continual reference to an instruction manual. Any more than two buttons on a cycle computer becomes confusing. However, if all of the functions could be stored in memory, the handlebar display could be simplified to include perhaps speed, time, distance, power, and heart rate, and the additional stored information could be fed to a computer for later analysis.

Probably the most valuable instrument that has yet to be marketed successfully is a power meter. If cyclists could read average power, updated every few seconds, they could maintain a constant power without regard to wind conditions, weather, or terrain. They could systematically plan workouts and be certain of an absolute gauge of their performance. To compute power one must accurately measure force and velocity. Velocity is easy, but force is not. As a rider pedals, the thrust force and therefore the power varies unevenly from zero to maximum during each pedal cycle, meaning that the power must be integrated and averaged over several pedal cycles. Balboa Instruments of Newport Beach, California, has built a power meter called the Power Pacer that will do this, but it is only available for research. Others such as Look have built and marketed power meters, but these have not performed successfully.

A Comparison of Road and All-Terrain Bicycle Technology

Only a decade ago in the United States, most commuting and touring road bicycles were carbon copies of road racing bicycles. As such they were not well suited for general use, and the public freely registered their complaints. Road bikes required too much maintenance. The saddles were too narrow and too hard and were uncomfortable to ride. The high-pressure tires had too many flats. The tires gave a rough ride and were hard to steer over uneven pavement or in sand or gravel. The racing drop handlebars were uncomfortable and caused sore necks, hands, and shoulders if the cyclist rode on the drops. The brakes were hard to keep in adjustment and didn't give good stopping power on steep slopes. The wheels were too flimsy and kept slipping out of true. Potholes would bend the rims and cause pinch flats. There weren't enough gears to easily climb hills. All of these complaints were valid. It takes a fair amount of skill and knowledge to keep a racing bike adjusted, and the bikes just aren't designed for comfort or convenience—they are designed for speed. It takes training to become comfortable on a road bike.

Then came mountain bikes and their cousins, the hybrid city bikes. This new breed of machines used an upright riding position, comfortable grips, better saddles, and wide rugged tires, plus a strong frame and wheels. In fact they cured almost all of the complaints about road bikes. The sales of road cycles soon plummeted, and mountain and hybrid bikes captured about two thirds of the bicycle market in the United States. Mountain bikes were no doubt more fun, they could be ridden off road, and they were very comfortable on pavement. They could be ridden off curbs or over railroad tracks without fear, and cracks in the pavement were no problem. Suspensions were available that absorbed the ride shocks.

In spite of their loss in popularity, road bikes won't disappear just yet; they are still a necessary but specialized breed. However, cyclists who want a general purpose bicycle can put smooth tires with side lugs on a mountain bike and ride almost anywhere with safety, comfort, efficiency, and convenience. They won't go as fast as they could on a road bike, but that is a small price to pay considering the advantages. The mountain bike has become the equivalent in the United States of the European utility bike.

Technology transfer between road and mountain bicycles is a lively and continuous process that has already improved both types. There are mountain bikes with aero bars and slick tires, and road bikes with suspensions and 24 speeds. This technology transfer is a healthy trend that will continue to benefit all cyclists.

References

Berglund, L. (1987). *Evaporative weight loss as a measure of absorbed radiation in the human*. Paper presented at the 8th Conference of Biometeorology and Aerobiology, American Meteorological Society, Boston, MA.

Brownlie, L.W., Gartshore, I., Chapman, A., & Banister, E.W. (1991). The aerodynamics of cycling apparel. *Cycling Science*, **3**(3-4), 44-50.

Coggan, A.R. (1990). Carbohydrate feeding during prolonged cycling to improve performance. *Cycling Science*, **2**(1), 9-13.

Coyle, E.F. (1989). Carbohydrate and cycling performance. *Cycling Science*, **1**(1), 18-21.

Danh, K., Mai, L., Poland, J., & Jenkins, C. (1991). Frictional resistance in bicycle wheel bearings. *Cycling Science*, **3**(3-4), 28-32.

Hoerner, S.F. (1965). *Fluid dynamic drag*. Hoerner Fluid Dynamics, 7528 Straunton Place N.W., Albuquerque NM 87120.

Kyle, C.R. (1973). *Factors affecting the speed of a bicycle*. (Rep. No. 1). Long Beach, CA: California State University, Mechanical Engineering.

Kyle, C.R. (1986). Athletic clothing. *Scientific American*, **254**, 104-110.

Kyle, C.R. (1988a, June). How friction slows a bike. *Bicycling*, pp. 180-185.

Kyle, C.R. (1988b). The mechanics and aerodynamics of cycling. In E.R. Burke, & M.M. Newsom (Eds.), *Medical and scientific aspects of cycling* (pp. 235-251). Champaign, IL: Human Kinetics.

Kyle, C.R. (1988c). Sunraycer, wheels, tires and brakes. *Lecture 3-3, G.M. Sunraycer Case History.* Warrendale, PA: Society of Automotive Engineers.

Kyle, C.R. (1989). The aerodynamics of handlebars and helmets. *Cycling Science,* **1**(1), 22-25.

Kyle, C.R. (1990). Wind tunnel tests of bicycle wheels and helmets. *Cycling Science,* **2**(1), 27-30.

Kyle, C.R. (1991a). Alternative bicycle transmissions. *Cycling Science,* **3**(3-4), 33-38.

Kyle, C.R. (1991b). The effect of crosswinds upon time trials. *Cycling Science,* **3**(3-4), 51-56.

Kyle, C.R. (1991c). Ergogenics for bicycling. In D. Lamb, & M. Williams (Eds.), *Perspectives in exercise science and sports medicine* (pp. 373-412). Indianapolis: Brown & Benchmark.

Kyle, C.R. (1991d). New aero wheel tests. *Cycling Science,* **3**(1), 27-30.

Kyle, C.R. (1991e). Wind tunnel tests of aero bicycles. *Cycling Science,* **3**(3-4), 57-61.

Kyle, C.R., & Burke, E.R. (1984). Improving the racing bicycle. *Mechanical Engineering,* **109**(6), 35-45.

Kyle, C.R., & Caiozzo, V.J. (1986a). The effect of athletic clothing aerodynamics upon running speed. *Medicine and Science in Sports and Exercise,* **18**(5), 509-515.

Kyle, C.R., & Caiozzo, V.J. (1986b). Experiments in human ergometry as applied to human powered vehicles. *International Journal of Sports Biomechanics,* **2**, 6-19.

Kyle, C.R., & Edelman, W.E. (1975). Man powered vehicle design criteria. In H.K. Sachs (Ed.), *Proceedings of the Third International Conference on Vehicle System Dynamics* (pp. 20-30). Amsterdam: Swets & Zeitlinger.

Margaria, R., Cerretelli, P., Aghemo, P., & Sassi, G. (1963). Energy cost of running. *Journal of Applied Physiology,* **18**, 367-370.

Noakes, T. (1990). The dehydration myth and carbohydrate replacement during prolonged exercise. *Cycling Science,* **2**(2), 23-28.

Peronnet, F., Bouissou, P., Perrault, H., & Ricci, J. (1991). The one hour cycling record at sea level and at altitude. *Cycling Science,* **3**(1), 6-20.

Pugh, L.G.C.E. (1971). The influence of wind resistance in running and walking and the mechanical efficiency of work against horizontal or vertical forces. *Journal of Physiology,* **213**, 255-276.

Okajima, S. (1990). Development of Shimano Pedaling Dynamics (SPD). *Cycling Science,* **2**(3), 7.

Sargeant, B. (1990). An overview of cycling instrumentation. *Cycling Science*, **2**(3), 13-18.

Sjogaard, G., Nielsen, B., Mikkelsen, F., Saltin, B., & Burke, E. (1982). *Physiology in bicycling*. Ithaca, NY: Mouvement.

Swain, D., Coast, J.R., Clifford, P.S., Milliken, M.C., & Gundersen, J.S. (1987). Influence of body size on oxygen consumption during bicycling. *Journal of Applied Physiology*, **62**(2), 668-672.

Whitt, F.R., & Wilson, D.G. (1982). *Bicycling science*. Cambridge, MA: MIT Press.

Bicycle Suspension Systems

John Olsen, MSME

Bicycle suspension is certainly one of the hottest current subjects in bicycling. What follows is an overview of some of the physics, engineering, and performance issues involved in suspension, not necessarily to allow you to proceed to design suspension systems with no further research, but to get potential designers and intelligent users thinking about concepts in suspension design arrived at over a century of work in other vehicular fields. Any subtopic in suspension design would require this whole book to cover in detail. This chapter is not intended to provide academic rigor, but rather to introduce and explain suspension concepts that may be new to many in the bicycle community.

Suspension Without Suspension

To understand how suspensions work, it may be best to start with an unsuspended bike. Once you understand how such a bike responds to bumps and road roughness, it is easier to understand the function of suspension systems. First of all, there is no such thing as an unsuspended bike; all bikes offer some ride-improving features. For most "unsuspended" bikes, much of that shock absorption comes from the flex of the tires and from enveloping, another feature of the pneumatic tire.

Tires contact the ground over a span of several inches, depending on tire pressure and wheel diameter. A stone, say 1/8th of an inch in diameter, would impress the tread that rested on it, but it would have very little effect on the overall tire-ground contact area; the stone would simply be swallowed up by the tire, and the axle would lift much less than 1/8 in. as a result. This is called *enveloping*, and all tires do it. Enveloping is an averaging effect: The roughness of the ground under the contact patch is averaged out by the tire, greatly reducing the effect of small, peaky bumpettes. The larger the tire diameter, and the softer the tire pressure, the greater the enveloping effect. Tire enveloping works like a low-pass filter, screening out higher-frequency input.

Larger obstacles, like an expansion joint between uneven concrete slabs, are at least partially eaten by the flex of the tire's sidewall—again, depending on the wheel diameter, tire pressure, and tire construction. Tires running at low pressures swallow bumps better than do those at higher pressures, and larger tires can swallow bigger bumps without pinch flats.

Bumps large enough to survive the passage through the tire also have to find their way through the flexible rim and spokes, up the flexible fork blades and steerer tube, and out the flexible handlebars before they can do their nefarious work on the rider's hands. If the bump strikes the rear wheel, then the path that the bump's energy must traverse includes the tire, rim, spokes, rear frame triangle, seat post, and saddle. Let us not forget the beneficial effect of relaxed, flexible arms—a loose set of arms provides marvelous shock and vibration protection to the upper body, saving the rider valuable energy. The rider's body is not, nor can it be modeled as, a rigid component.

On an efficient road bike, all of the mechanical components are relatively stiff, even the tire. Yet a sensitive and experienced cyclist can tell the difference in ride from one tire type to the next, from one spoke lacing pattern to the next, from one fork bend and blade material to the next, and even from one frame material to the next. All of these apparently stiff parts do their share in taking some of the tingle out of our rides; as evidence for this, I offer the observation that many experienced riders believe they can discern the differences in feel between an aluminum and steel frame set.

The "Why" of Mountain Bike Suspension

What happens when you take the bicycle, designed for nothing worse than Belgian pavé, and subject it to the rigors of the woods, deserts, and mountains—sans paving? Suspension advocates would say that you get pinched tubes, bent rims, wrist injuries, crashes, broken frames, and general mayhem. Mountain bikes have, until recently, been unsuspended—not rigid, but unsuspended. Many riders felt, and a decreasing few still feel, that the big, soft tires that equip serious mountain bikes offer all of the isolation you really need, and that any attempt at suspension is just so much extra weight. Unfortunately, the wonderful challenge of mountain biking comes from the fact that we are riding surfaces that are not as flat and smooth as possible: There are bumps out there—big ones, small ones, sharp ones, dull ones. These bumps are so often big that they overwhelm the flexibility of the tire and the rest of the bicycle. The rider becomes the suspension system, and this extra job exacts costs in oxygen consumption, reduced concentration, reduced control, and fatigue.

Of course, a rider can increase the fraction of obstacles that the tires can swallow by lowering tire pressures, but that can go only so far before pinch flats result. You can opt for forks and bars of greater flexibility, but these are minor, incremental improvements that may have other costs, like reduced fatigue life, loss of handling precision, or brake chatter. In the end, most open-minded riders would probably agree that mountain bikes really would be better with perfect suspension, suspension that worked well enough to offset the inevitable increase in weight, cost, and complexity—a suspension that is a net improvement, not a net loss!

Perfect Suspension

These are the basic goals of any suspension system:

1. To isolate the rider from the roughness of the road, reducing fatigue and discomfort, while leaving the rider with enough feel for optimum control. This goal requires the isolation of relatively small, medium-, and high-frequency bumps.
2. To absorb the energy and shock that come from hitting obstacles and bumps, and dissipate this effect before it does too much damage to the equilibrium of the rider. This function requires the absorption of higher-amplitude, low-frequency bumps.
3. To keep the wheels on the ground over rough terrain, where they can provide useful functions like driving, braking, and steering.
4. To avoid adding to the bicycle (because of the presence of the suspension system) undesirable characteristics such as "pogoing" (the bicycle suspension's working while the rider is just pedaling hard).

This last goal sounds easy enough, but in reality suspension systems that do well with goals 1, 2, and 3 are difficult to implement without violating objective 4. This is particularly true, to date, for rear suspensions. The challenge in any suspension design is to accomplish all four goals simultaneously.

The Components of Suspension

Springs

We've already seen that the deflection of tires and components provides some of the benefits claimed for suspension systems. If some deflection is good, let's add more. To do so, we have to design controlled vertical flexibility into our frame—somewhere. A bump hitting a wheel has to be able to harmlessly compress something in the system, somewhere before the violence gets to the rider. This "suspension travel" can be located in the front fork, in the down tube, in the seat support structure, in the stem, or in the rear triangle; or it can be in more than one location. All of these options have strengths and weaknesses, proponents and opponents. As of yet, no single suspension compliance location has shown a dominating superiority in performance, despite strident claims to the contrary. Other factors are more important.

For simplicity, let's assume for now that the suspension travel will occur in a telescopic front fork. If we simply provide a sliding joint in our fork, the fork will collapse, so we need to add a device that will provide some kind of restoring force to hold our bicycle's front end up.

This device is a spring, and springs come in a variety of types. You can choose a steel or titanium or carbon fiber coil spring, a spring that works by twisting a strong solid material. Gas springs trap air, or some other gas, in a cylinder that compresses the pressurized gas as the suspension travels. Elastomer springs compress, stretch, shear, or otherwise work "rubber." Liquid springs compress a pressurized liquid. All springs provide more *restoring force* (if you push on them, they push back) the more they are compressed. These spring types differ in several respects, including complexity, linearity, and energy storage efficiency. Some spring types (steel leaf springs, for example) store very little energy for their weight, while other springs (certain types of elastomer springs, or liquid springs) weigh very little for the amount of energy they store. Some springs, like steel coil springs, are inherently linear; that is, they provide force in strict proportion to the amount that they are compressed. If a linear spring gives you 100 lb when it is compressed 1 in., it will give you 200 lb when it is compressed 2 in. The spring rate (stiffness) for a linear spring is the force you get at a certain amount of spring compression, divided by the amount of compression, in units of pounds per inch. Linear springs can be described by a single spring-rate number.

Other springs, like piston-in-cylinder gas springs, some elastomer springs, and taper-wire coil springs, provide an inherently rising rate—the spring rate is higher at full compression than it is at the start of compression: Such springs get stiffer as they are compressed. This is generally good; suspensions using such springs can be soft for small bumps, but they can be stiff enough at the end of travel to avoid bottoming on the big bumps. Such nonlinear, rising-rate springs provide a smoothly increasing range of spring rates. Note that you can make a linear spring provide a nonlinear force at the rear wheel by employing it with a nonlinear mechanism. Such mechanisms are often employed in motorcycle suspension design, allowing a rising rate from basically linear steel coil springs.

Elastomer springs are usually not made of "rubber"; the material comes from a beaker, not the inside of a rubber tree. They are usually solid or foam blocks of some sophistication—sophistication in shape, in density, and in material. The right combinations of shape, material, and density can provide a rising-rate spring effect, helping avoid bottoming in much the same way as does a gas spring.

It is important to understand that springs (except elastomer springs) do not absorb energy, they merely store it, and give it back with little loss. Some people talk about springs as absorbers, but they are not. A pure spring, by itself, is a pogo stick. In order to avoid getting all of that stored energy back when you don't want it, the energy stored in the spring has to be converted from mechanical energy into some other kind of energy, usually heat. Springs do the work of holding you up, but they are unruly beasts with a mind of their own. It is necessary, or at least strongly desirable, to ally springs with some energy dissipation mechanism in order to keep them from returning all that energy with uncontrolled timing.

Travel

How much suspension deflection, called "travel," should a suspension system have? Imagine a rider attacking a rough course. The faster he or she goes, the harder the bumps will try to compress the suspension. Most suspension systems are designed so that it takes a force equaling two to three times the normal weight on the suspension system (2 or 3 gs) to fully compress the spring. If you have lots of travel available, the spring can be softer than is the case when it is limited in travel.

If there is a static load of 100 lb on a fork, then we might design the fork to bottom (to run out of travel) at a load of 300 lb. If we have 10 in. of travel, we need a total linear spring rate of only 30 lb per inch, while if we have only 2 in. of travel, we will need a linear spring rate of 150 lb per inch to bottom on the same bump as did the long travel spring. The softer, longer travel spring, all other factors being equal, will provide much better isolation from small, repetitive, or sharp bumps than will the short-travel spring. Thus, long travel lets us use soft springs to store a given amount of energy. If we are employing a nonlinear spring, then we can get tricky, starting soft but ending stiff, even with limited travel.

Preload

You may have noted that if you have a total spring rate of only 30 lb per inch, and if the fork is going to carry a static load of 100 lb, then the fork will collapse more than 3 in. when you sit on the bike! In fact, off-road motorcycles, blessed with copious travel (12 in. is not uncommon), do sag almost this much when supporting the weight of the rider. If you, a bicyclist with little travel, don't want some of your precious suspension travel used up in supporting the load even when you aren't moving (this load is called the "static load"), then you have a choice. You can opt for a very stiff spring, or you might employ *preload*.

Take a linear coil spring with a rate of 100 lb per inch, a spring that will be forced to be 10 in. long when trapped inside the structure of the fork. What if we make that spring 11 in. long when it is lying on your workbench? Then we will have to compress the spring 1 in. when we install it. Since it is already compressed when it is waiting for action in the uncompressed suspension, it will have a preload of 100 lb/in. $\times$ 1 in. = 100 lb, and it will be able to support the static load with no deflection. Thus, the suspension won't collapse at all when it takes its designed load, even though its spring rate is only 100 lb per inch.

If we preload the spring 2 in., what happens? The spring will push against the fully extended fork structure with a force of 200 lb, while the static load is applying only 100 lb. The fork won't compress at all until you hit a bump with enough vigor to generate an additional force of more than 100 lb. This means that the fork will be ineffective in dealing with small bumps, because the bicycle may not generate that much force as it rolls over them. The forces from these smaller bumps will go right into the rider, just as they did with the "unsuspended" bicycle, if they aren't eaten by the tire, fork, etc. The lesson is that big preload means poor protection from small bumps.

Remember that preloading a coil spring does nothing to change the spring's rate. If the spring is a linear spring, it will have the same spring rate no matter how much we compress, or preload it.

Gas springs and elastomeric springs can have preload, too. To change the preload in a gas spring (a RockShox, for instance), you merely increase the gas pressure. The preload is proportional to the initial gas pressure. However, the spring rate of a gas spring also increases as you add initial pressure. This usually works out well, since those who need more preload often need more stiffness as well. Both gas springs and elastomeric springs can be designed to have almost infinite spring rates at full compression, making them very difficult to completely bottom. Figure 2.1 illustrates the change in spring rate that comes with a change in the preload of a typical air spring.

Damping

What do we do with all of that energy that we left stored up in the spring? If we let it come bombing back out unimpeded, it might come out at a bad time and throw the rider flat on his or her back. It may bounce the tire off the ground, spoiling traction for climbing, turning, or braking. As you will see later, repetitive bumps may drive the undamped suspension into resonance, producing a huge response from a small input.

We need to convert some of that stored mechanical energy in the spring into heat. One way to do that is via friction. If our fork has some "stickiness" built into it (and all have some), then some of the stored energy will be lost to that friction and converted to heat. The downside to this simple remedy is that friction also locks the fork up for small bumps, which get transmitted right on through to the rider. A suspension system with both a lot of preload and a lot of friction is not able to deal with small bumps, and the bike is basically unsuspended over such bumps.

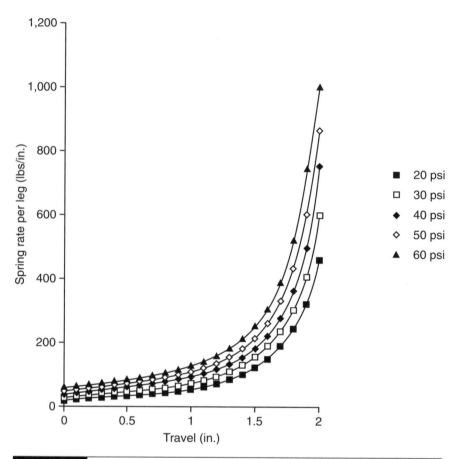

Figure 2.1 The change in spring rate that comes with a change in the preload of a typical air spring.

All suspension systems have friction, but conventional wisdom would have a suspension designer work very hard to minimize it. Pivots, instead of telescoping joints, and careful bearing and bushing design, help minimize friction. At least one clever suspension design (the front fork on the Monolith bicycle) employs designed-in friction to help the suspension resist moving in response to the bobbing of the rider's body. This bobbing creates friction-enhancing side loading on the suspension bushings, preventing easy movement. Yet the suspension breaks free relatively easily when a larger bump strikes the front wheel and creates a force vector pointing nearly straight up the axis of the fork. This design gives a feel like that of an unsuspended bike in routine maneuvering, but large bumps disappear nicely. I offer this bicycle as evidence that friction isn't *always* bad in suspension. Just usually.

We could also choose a spring material that has inherent energy loss built into it. Elastomeric springs have this property to varying degrees; when they are compressed and released, they heat up. This energy is stolen from the mechanical energy that they store when they are compressed. This type of energy loss has some advantages. It is simple, with no moving parts; it can deal with small bumps (unlike friction), given that the suspension unit isn't set up with too much preload; it is light in weight for the amount of energy it can absorb. Negatives include a large temperature sensitivity, fairly rapid breakdown with repeated loading, and problematic repeatability (matching spring rates can be challenging).

The energy loss scheme favored by the vast majority of motor vehicles is hydraulic damping. It is used on most cars, motorcycles, trucks, and airplanes because it can be very strong; hydraulic damping can provide lots of force to control strong springs. Most hydraulic dampers work like pumps: They pump special oil through a small hole (an orifice), and the oil resists this flow with a resistance that depends in a nonlinear way on the velocity with which the pump is moving, and thus, the amount of oil that needs to flow. This resistance can be very strong, and it can be customized to provide different amounts of force in different directions through use of various types of one-way valves and spring-loaded blowoff valves in the piston.

If the compression-damping orifice is forced to stay closed or highly restricted, the suspension unit can be locked out. The nearly incompressible hydraulic oil is trapped, rendering the suspension unit inoperative. If the rider can perform this lockout on the fly, he or she can choose to disable the suspension while climbing to keep the bike from bobbing up and down in response to the rider's torso motion during standing climbing, for instance. The big rubber dial atop the Cannondale Delta V front suspension is a good example of a suspension lockout. The necessity of a lockout provision is a matter of rider preference, and many riders who initially use lockout eventually stop using it, having gotten accustomed to the motion of the suspension in response to torso movements on climbs, for instance.

Damping can also help the spring prevent bottoming. Any compression damping provides a force that works with the spring to slow the plunge toward full travel. Compression damping can be tailored to get stronger as the suspension unit nears full travel; this is called hydraulic snubbing. Hydraulic snubbing could also be employed near full extension to prevent the clunking that happens when most current suspension systems "top out," or return to full extension.

Hydraulic damping also has a dark side. A suspension with substantial compression damping that strikes a sharp-edged bump will strongly resist the rapid motion of the wheel as it tries to climb the bump. The spring can accommodate this rapid movement; it is only a slight exaggeration to say that springs aren't sensitive to velocity, they just care about how much they are compressed. The compression damping, however, produces a force whose magnitude depends on how fast the wheel is rising, and thus how much oil the fork is trying to pump through that small, restrictive orifice. At some velocity, the orifice can't accommodate any more flow rate, and the column of oil lifts the bicycle, transmitting shock. Unless the valving that controls the damping is arranged to let a big hole open up under these circumstances, such a hydraulically damped suspension system can be harsh on sharp bumps. Such a big hole is called a "blowoff valve," and all good hydraulic dampers incorporate them in some form in the compression valving.

Hydraulic damping can also transmit little bumps, if the damping is too strong, since rapidly repeating bumps also want the wheel to move quickly, as will be shown in the next section.

Finally, if rebound damping is too strong compared to the stiffness of the spring, a suspension system can pump down. If strong rebound damping prevents the suspension from coming back to its normal ride height before the next bump comes along, and if there are a series of bumps at the right spacing, then the suspension can pump itself down until there is no suspension travel left. This can happen to a hydraulically damped telescopic fork with too little air pressure or too soft a coil spring.

Frequency Response

If you rest a mass on a spring in such a way that the mass can only move up and down with no friction, and if you give the mass a sharp whack with a hammer, you will notice that the mass moves up and down at a certain frequency. (Frequency is the number of cycles per second, a unit called hertz, abbreviated Hz.) The frequency that the mass naturally bobs at, called the "natural frequency," depends on the amount of mass and the spring rate of the spring. A larger mass means a lower natural frequency; a lower mass means a higher natural frequency. A stiffer spring means a higher natural frequency, whereas a softer spring lowers the natural frequency.

Figure 2.2 shows how a simple mass sitting on a spring behaves if the bottom of the spring is shaken up and down steadily at a constant frequency and amplitude. If you shake the bottom of the spring up and down very slowly, the mass moves almost the same distance as does the bottom of the spring. This is analogous to a suspended bike riding over long-wavelength whoop-de-dos at a slow speed. If you slowly increase the frequency at which the spring base is shaken (imagine the rider on the whoops speeding up slowly), eventually you reach a frequency at which the mass goes wild, smashing up and down a great deal further than the base of the spring is moving. This is called resonance, and it happens at the natural frequency. This is, of course, bad news for the rider on the whoop-de-dos, unless that rider's suspension has lots of damping. Notice in Figure 2.2 how much less the mass moves at resonance if there is damping present. Much of that mechanical energy is being converted into heat.

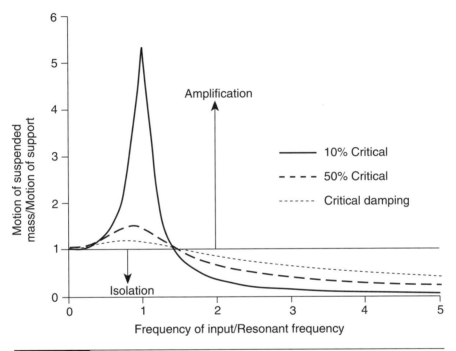

Figure 2.2   The frequency response of a mass resting on a spring with damping. *Note.* Critical damping is the amount of damping that just keeps the mass from oscillating when the spring is compressed and the mass released.

Note that you can avoid tremendous mass motion at the natural frequency by doing all of those things that, at other times, are bad to do with a suspension system: using lots of preload, limiting the travel, and introducing friction. At resonance, a suspension system with lots of preload may not even know that it is being shaken at its natural frequency, if the bumps are small enough that the spring doesn't see more than the preload force. At resonance, a suspension system with limited travel will simply slam into its travel stops, making lots of noise and fuss, but at least not achieving a low orbit. A lot of friction will also keep the mass on the planet—but controllable damping is better.

If you shake the base of the spring at a frequency higher than the natural frequency (our valiant rider has survived his resonance problem and accelerated through it), the behavior of the mass calms down. Soon, at a frequency roughly 1.4 times the natural frequency, the mass will be moving no more than the base of the spring once again, just as it did at very low frequencies. As you shake the base of the spring faster and faster, the mass moves less and less. When the spring is being shaken at a frequency much higher than the resonant frequency, the mass barely moves at all. The mass is now enjoying excellent isolation. High input frequencies are generated by riding at speed over small bumps and by striking sharp edges.

However, if the suspension has lots of damping, the very damping that helped so much at resonance hurts at high frequencies, passing force into the mass that reduces isolation. At high frequencies, the oil column transmits substantial force to the bike and rider, reducing the amount of isolation that the suspension can provide at these frequencies and increasing the suspension's harshness. Ideally, a suspension system would offer strong damping at low frequencies, and especially at resonance, for good control, and yet provide very little damping above the natural frequency, for good isolation.

What does all of this mean? If you want to design a suspension system for an environment consisting of numerous small, repetitive bumps (a chip-sealed road, say, or, perhaps, the Paris-Roubaix course), you would want a soft suspension system working with the mass of the rider to provide a low natural frequency relative to the spacing of the bumps, with little preload and very little damping. This would provide maximum isolation, maximum comfort, and minimum fatigue. This is the "Father's Oldsmobile" school of suspension design, typified by the Allsop Softride beam and stem.

If you weren't sure about the frequencies that you were going to encounter but feared that you would have a wide range of bump spacings to contend with, then it would be inevitable that you would be operating around resonance some of the time. It would be disastrous to have little damping in this circumstance, so you have to add damping. If you are also concerned about absorbing the energy from big bumps and impacts, and if you have limited travel to work with, then you would want a stiffly sprung system with lots of damping and preferably a rising spring rate. You wouldn't get much isolation over those small bumps, but you would survive the resonance-causing bumps and be far better off than without suspension when hitting the big stuff. This is the Aircraft Landing Gear school of suspension design, typified by the RockShox Mag 21 and other hydraulically damped suspension systems.

Or, you could compromise by employing an elastomeric spring with as much travel as you could get out of it (usually not much), with moderate damping, and with whatever preload other design factors called for. This is the Useful Compromise school of suspension design, typified by RockShox Quadra elastomer forks, or the Offroad ProFlex rear suspension, among many.

The Effect of Unsprung Weight—Why Less Is More

Remember our mass resting on a spring? What if another, smaller mass (we'll call it unsprung weight) is added to the bottom of the spring, and then another spring is added below the new mass? Instead of one mass on a spring, and one natural frequency, we would now have two masses free to vibrate, and two natural frequencies to worry about and to cause resonance.

This is a simple model of a bicycle with unsprung weight. The top mass represents the weight of the rider and whatever portion of the bicycle rests on the springs of the suspension system, and the stiffness of the top spring represents stiffness of the suspension spring(s). The new, bottom mass stands for the mass of the bicycle that lies below the suspension system, and the lowest spring is the stiffness of the tire(s). Impact one mass or the other, and both masses would vibrate, at different frequencies, at the same time. The motion of one mass would, through the interconnecting spring and damper, affect the motion of the other mass. In fact, if we could build such a simple bicycle with only two masses connected like this, there would be a certain speed over a given wavelength of bump at which the unsprung mass would resonate. At this speed, this resonance would make for a bumpy ride on the sprung mass—the tail would be wagging the dog. Now, if there is enough damping between the unsprung and sprung masses to control the resonance of the much heavier sprung mass, then the resonance of the relatively light unsprung mass will be very heavily damped, and very little resonance will occur.

It is always a suspension designer's goal to reduce unsprung weight as much as possible, but in bicycle suspension, other factors can dominate the equation. For instance, the Allsop suspension system (Figure 2.3e) suspends only the rider, leaving almost the whole bicycle to contribute to unsprung weight. However, the Allsop rides very smoothly in most, but not all, circumstances because its design concept allows it to employ a very soft spring with very little damping, thus allowing much better high-frequency isolation than can the typical high-pivot rear suspension system (a system that must deal with chain tension problems and limited travel with a stiff spring, lots of preload, and, hopefully, lots of damping). The Allsop system gets exciting in circumstances that drive the resonance of the rider on the beam, and this is not a function of unsprung weight. Thus, most of the hysteria in the media against the Allsop system's high unsprung weight is misplaced. The detractors are probably referring to a problem that is typical of a softly sprung, lightly damped suspension system: It resonates in response to big, low-frequency bumps, unless the rider is ready and stiffens his legs. So would a Specialized FSR or a Cannondale Super V or an Offroad Proflex if they were set up for good high-frequency isolation, with a soft spring rate, little preload, long travel, and little damping!

Figure 2.3   Types of rear suspension: (a) Low pivot, (b) High pivot, (c) Low-forward pivot, (d) Four-bar linkage, (e) Cantilevered beam suspended saddle (Allsop), (f) Telescopic seat post suspended saddle, (g) Unified rear triangle.

Rear Suspension

To all of the intricacies of front suspension design, rear suspension systems add an additional challenge: the pulsatile force transmitted by the chain to the rear wheel. The reaction of this drive force into the rear suspension, coupled with the inertial reaction of the bike and rider, causes a potential coupling of the tension in the chain and the force in the suspension spring that can result in several forms of disruptive and unpleasant behavior.

And yet, despite its design challenges, a successful rear suspension system can be extremely valuable. It can, like front suspension, help a rider maintain control on hard, fast, bumpy descents; but it can also, even more than front suspension, be an ally to speed up a bumpy climb. How? Every time an unsuspended bike's rider sees a 3-in. bump coming along, he or she must do a pull-up on the handlebars as the rear wheel approaches the bump, getting the heavy torso out of the way of the soon-to-be-rapidly-rising saddle. Failure to do so means pain, pinch flats, and perhaps an unplanned halt. A compliant rear suspension system can absorb much of that destructive energy, allowing the rider to remain seated and relaxed, concentrating on maintaining the best line up the hill and putting out a smooth flow of power.

Chain-Suspension Interaction

Imagine a motorcycle-like suspension system, with a swing arm pivoted right behind, and slightly below, the bottom bracket, and a spring/shock unit with little preload (the suspension sags when the rider is in position; see Figure 2.3a). Every time the rider pushes on the pedals, the chain compresses the suspension system by creating a torque that makes the suspension close, making the bike squat. Such a bike would inch-worm down the trail, squatting every time the chain pulled on the rear cogs, unless the suspension spring was so stiff or so heavily preloaded that the sum of the static weight and the pedaling forces couldn't compress it. Such a stiff suspension would move only in response to very big impacts, say, on a fast downhill, but it would do little to help on a climb.

Now imagine that you have the ability to raise the swing arm pivot relative to the frame and chain line. At some point, the net force vector from the rear tire's contact patch will point directly at the swing arm pivot. With the pivot in this position, the tension in the chain cannot create any torque to extend or compress the suspension, and the suspension and drivetrain will be decoupled. Near this "ideal" location, the suspension could be set up with minimal preload, allowing maximal suspension effectiveness without resulting in pogoing. Unfortunately, the location of this decoupled point varies from gear to gear, so that a totally decoupled bicycle design with derailleurs would require a moving pivot.

Move the pivot above this point, and chain tension will cause the suspension to move in the opposite sense, extending with tension rather than compressing. The bike would "anti-squat." If the static load on the suspension was enough to compress the spring some amount, then the chain tension pulses could pull the suspension unit to its maximum length with every pedal stroke. The suspension would top out on hard pedal strokes, possibly causing a clunking noise if no provision for topping out gently was designed into the unit. This, again, is inchworming, only in the opposite direction.

In a sense, the suspension extension that comes with any pivot location above the neutral point may be valuable: It jams the rear tire into the dirt just as the pedal stroke calls for the maximum traction, mimicking the action of skilled climbers. However, most riders find any noticeable inchworming alarming and unpleasant; most feel that it must waste energy. And it may, at least on smooth surfaces; we just don't know how much, or know how significant that loss is.

Inchworming in a high-pivot rear swing arm suspension can be totally avoided by running so much preload that the suspension can support its static load with no compression; that is, it is always topped out except when in the act of absorbing a big impact. In fact, most high-pivot bikes are designed to be set up this way, with lots of preload. However, as mentioned previously, substantial preload means efficient transmission of small bumps, and a suspension that is active only during big hits.

Where does the ideal pivot point lie? Papadopoulos (1993) has shown that the neutral point's location can be approximated by extending a "ground reaction line" at a 45° angle, up and forward from the rear tire's contact point, to the intersection with the top run of the chain. Extend another line forward from the rear axle through this intersection point (see Figure 2.4). If the swing arm pivot lies along this line, then, for the gear (and chain location), the tension in the chain will have very little effect on the rear suspension. A shift from one chainring to another causes more change in this ideal location than does a shift from one rear cog to another, so the pivot location would have to move when the chain changed chainrings in order to maintain neutrality. For the normal, fixed pivot location, the amount (and perhaps even the sense) of pogoing will vary from one chainring to the next.

The maximum torque and acceleration occur when the bike is in the small chainring, so it probably makes sense to optimize the pivot location for the lower range of gears. This means a relatively low pivot location, somewhere close behind the intersection of the top run of the

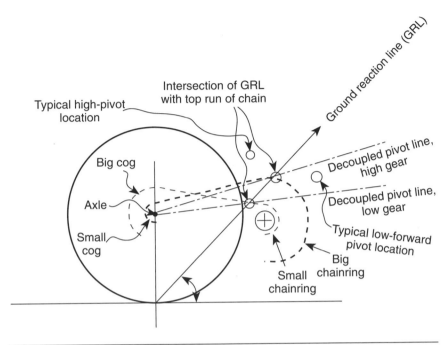

Figure 2.4 Finding a swing arm pivot point that will decouple chain forces from suspension (Papadopoulos, 1993).

chain and the small chainring. On most bikes, the front derailleur cage is in the way, so a short, simple, motorcycle-like swing arm is moderately challenging to implement. (The Raleigh M9000 is a good example of a well-implemented, simple swing arm system with a pivot in this location.) An increasing number of suspended bikes get around this issue by curving the swing arm up and over the front derailleur, coming down to a pivot ahead of the front derailleur and seat tube, just above the chainwheels. Most bikes with this configuration are close to neutral in the middle chainring and exhibit moderate pogoing in the small chainring.

Multilink suspension systems, as in the Fisher RS-1 and the Specialized FSR, are four-bar linkages, and they can be designed to put the "instant center" (the imaginary point in space about which the link holding the rear axle rotates, initially) in just the right place for a chosen chainring, even if the front derailleur is there.

It is interesting to note that the tendency toward smaller chainrings, led by Suntour with their 20-tooth Microdrive system, exacerbates the pogoing problem for most high- and low-forward-pivot rear suspension bicycles, whereas it reduces the squatting tendencies of low-pivot rear suspension bikes. Many riders experiencing excessive pogoing with any of the small chainring systems would experience an improvement by installing larger chainrings (the "old-fashioned" equipment). Conversely, low-pivot bikes (like the Manitou) would behave better with Microdrive.

Bump-Pedal Feedback

The second major chain-induced phenomenon that troubles in-frame rear suspension systems is bump-pedal feedback. When a bike with rear suspension strikes a bump with the rear wheel, and the bump is large enough to cause the suspension to deflect, some rear suspension geometries will tug on the chain, producing a very noticeable slowing or acceleration of the pedals. In extreme cases (for instance, a high-pivot bike with little preload), this behavior can be very annoying and distracting. Papadopoulos (1993) has shown that the rear swing arm pivot point that minimizes bump-pedal feedback is not the same point that minimizes pogoing. He points out that bump-pedal feedback is minimized by a fairly low swing arm pivot design that places the effective line of the swing arm tangent to a circle coaxial with, but somewhat smaller than, the smallest chainwheel. It is this author's experience that placing the pivot location close to that chosen by low pivot designs (see Figure 2.3a and c) would offer relatively little bump-pedal feedback.

Another, simpler, way around the chain-to-spring coupling problem is to avoid the issue altogether by suspending the rider above the frame, leaving the frame rigid. Whether by an Allsop Softride composite beam (Figure 2.3e), or by a sprung seat post (Figure 2.3f), the chain tension has no direct effect on the suspension system. Because they are totally decoupled, these suspension systems can be very soft, giving excellent isolation from small, high-frequency bumps, and sharp-edged steps, at the expense of increased unsprung weight.

Conclusion: Future Research

Front suspension systems have been around for half a decade or more, and such systems are accepted by all but the most conservative mountain bikers and road riders. The real design issues remain those centered on rear suspension design and the interaction between front and rear suspension.

A majority of the time spent riding mountain bikes involves relatively slow climbing and traversing level surfaces. In the author's experience, a full suspension bike with little or moderate coupling between chain tension and suspension forces, equipped with a moderately damped, relatively soft spring, can aid overall efficiency and speed in these conditions if the surfaces traversed are rough enough. This seems to be partially due to more uniform contact between the rear tire and the ground, to decreased fatigue because the rider can relax on the saddle even when hitting fairly large obstacles, and to the overall physiological benefits accruing from a smoother ride. These benefits decrease with very stiff suspension systems. If the riding surfaces are very smooth, an active full suspension bike will be measurably slower than an unsuspended bike, in this author's experience. Fast, high-intensity descents are aided by almost any well-damped suspension design; in fact, it is apparent that many of the early full suspension designs—in particular, high pivot designs—are intended to function primarily in this regime. Limited work has been done in the area of cycling efficiency versus suspension type, primarily Berry et al. (1993).

Suspension design is a rich area for research, as many questions remain unanswered. Can rear suspension help overall efficiency on a climb? What type of suspension optimizes climbing efficiency? Do all active suspension designs reduce efficiency on smooth surfaces? Can rear suspension increase grip on a steep, loose, or slippery climb? What is the best trade-off between climbing efficiency and augmentation of grip?

Design and tuning issues could also be investigated, including questions such as these: What is the optimum travel front and rear for full suspension bikes in different circumstances? What is the optimum damping scheme to maximize high-speed control, big-bump energy absorption, and high-frequency isolation?

As full suspension mountain bikes take more and more of the market and, by corollary, move down the price scale, these questions will be relevant to more and more of the cycling public. Industry (and academia) cannot currently answer all of these questions, and so a very interesting rapid evolution process is playing itself out before our eyes. In the few years that full suspension bikes have been available, rapid progress has already been made, and some designs have already evolved out of existence. High pivots, for example, were becoming rare by the 1994 Anaheim bike show while low pivot designs and unified rear triangle designs (Figure 2.3g) were conspicuous. Well-conceived research will help clarify and guide this process.

References

Berry, M., Woodward, M., Christopher, D., & Pittman, C. (1993). The effects of a mountain bike suspension system on metabolic energy expenditure. *Cycling Science*, **5**(1), 8-14.

Papadopoulos, J. (1993). Designing bicycle rear suspensions to reduce pedal interaction. Manuscript submitted for publication. [Personal communication]

3

Body Size and Cycling Performance

David P. Swain, PhD

In most sports, there is a clear advantage to individuals with a particular body size—such as towering height among basketball players. In basketball, the reason for the size advantage is readily apparent: The object of the game is 10 ft off the ground. In other sports, the basis for a size effect on performance is less obvious. Why are gymnasts smaller than football players?

Many body size effects in sports are associated with a phenomenon known as scaling: variation in physical attributes that can be predicted from just knowing the heights of two similarly shaped athletes. If a normally proportioned adult were five feet tall, how would this person compare to a six footer with the same proportions? The six footer is 20% taller (6/5 = 1.2), but is he 20% stronger? 20% heavier? The answer to both questions is no.

Area scales with the square of linear dimensions (i.e., area = length × length), and volume scales with the cube of linear dimensions (i.e., volume = length × length × length). So the six footer has 1.2 × 1.2 = 1.44, or 44% more area than the five footer, and has 1.2 × 1.2 × 1.2 = 1.728, or 73% more volume. What does this have to do with strength or weight? Physiologists know that the strength of a muscle is proportional to its cross-sectional area (cut across the belly of a biceps to see how large the exposed area is). Therefore, the six footer isn't 20% stronger than the five footer, but is 44% stronger. These relationships are illustrated in Figure 3.1.

If the muscles and bones and other organs are made of the same basic material in the two individuals, then their weights will be directly related to their volumes. So the six footer isn't 20% heavier than the five footer, but is 73% heavier (e.g., 200 lb vs. 116 lb).

A very important consideration in many sports is how strong the athlete is relative to his or her own body weight. The six footer has 44% more absolute strength than the five footer, but since the six footer weighs 73% more, the six footer is relatively weaker when doing movements in which body weight is the resistance, like pull-ups and push-ups. Why are gymnasts smaller than football players? Gymnastics requires high strength relative to body weight, while football requires high absolute strength.

Bicycling is a complex sport in which many variables affect performance. Body size appears to have a significant impact. Observers of the sport are quick to notice that the best hill climbers are generally small cyclists whereas the best time trialists are generally large cyclists, and that only the largest cyclists make superb sprinters. The scaling of surface area and of weight, as described in the example of the two athletes, are important determinants of these effects in the sport of bicycling. But in order to explain them, it is necessary to first examine the energy demands that a cyclist encounters.

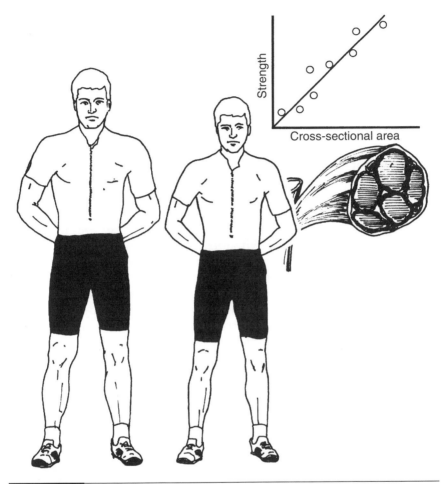

Figure 3.1 Illustration of a large and small cyclist. The inserts graphically depict the fact that strength is proportional to the cross-sectional area of a muscle rather than to height or weight.

The Energy Cost of Cycling

When a cyclist is out on the road, he or she must overcome three primary forces in order to move the bicycle forward. These are

1. the friction between the tires and the road surface, known as rolling resistance;
2. the "friction" that the cyclist's body and bicycle encounter as they push through the air, known as air resistance; and
3. the force of gravity when going uphill.

Of the three, rolling resistance makes the least contribution and will be ignored in the following discussion.

Air resistance is the primary force to be overcome in traveling on the flats, and it increases exponentially with speed, specifically, with the square of the cyclist's speed through the air. And the energy required to overcome that force increases with the cube of speed. Thus, traveling at 30 mph is not 50% harder than at 20 mph, but rather is almost three times harder (based on equations in DiPrampero, Cortili, Mognoni, and Saibene, 1979, after rolling resistance is factored in also; the energy cost of overcoming air resistance alone would increase $1.5 \times 1.5 \times 1.5 = 3.375$ times). This explains why many recreational cyclists can ride comfortably at 20 mph but cannot reach 30 mph except in brief sprints. Unless, of course, the recreational rider is drafting behind an elite cyclist. McCole and his colleagues demonstrated that the energy requirement of cycling can be reduced almost 30% by drafting behind another rider, and by nearly 40% when drafting at the back of a group (McCole, Claney, Conte, Anderson, & Hagberg, 1990).

When climbing, the cyclist must overcome the force of gravity in addition to air resistance. A cyclist already pushing at close to his or her physical limits must slow down in order to climb the hill. The steeper the hill is, the more the cyclist will slow down, and this causes an interesting shift in the forces the cyclist must overcome.

At these slower hill-climbing speeds, air resistance now comprises only a small part of the total force opposing the cyclist, and therefore, it no longer helps very much to draft. Individuals face steep hills virtually alone, even when they're surrounded by other cyclists. So, in a sense, hill climbing is a "race of truth," just as is the individual time trial.

On the downhill side, the force of gravity is added to any energy provided by the cyclist in the descent. However, if the hill is steep enough, freewheel descent speeds can exceed 50 mph. At such speeds, it is futile for the cyclist to attempt to pedal any faster, both because no one has gears high enough to match such speeds comfortably and because it would require an enormous amount of energy to accomplish even a marginal increase in speed. Remember that the energy needed to overcome air resistance increases with the cube of speed. An athlete with a maximal aerobic power ($\dot{V}O_2max$) of 75 ml · kg^{-1} · min^{-1} who is freewheeling at 50 mph could go only 53 mph by pedaling at full power (based on the equations of DiPrampero, Cortili, Mognoni, and Saibene, 1979). It would be better to rest during the descent, recovering from the uphill climb.

Variations in the body size of cyclists can have a significant impact on the energy cost of cycling. A number of scientific investigations have been performed to clarify this issue. However, it is important to recognize the limitations of laboratory research in studying an outdoor sport such as bicycling.

When subjects in a laboratory are asked to ride a stationary bicycle ergometer they do not face air resistance and they do not face hills. While it is possible to ride a bicycle on a treadmill and thus have a steady grade to climb, the wind resistance is still missing. A good example of the problem is the study of aerodynamic handlebars. Aero bars are well known to improve cycling performance and have been shown to reduce air resistance in wind tunnels. However, laboratory studies on the energy cost of cycling have revealed no advantage in the use of aero bars. Of course, none should be expected if the athlete is stationary on an ergometer.

Laboratory studies of the energy cost of cycling can contribute much to our knowledge of the sport; but only outdoor studies, which are difficult to perform, can answer some of the questions that need to be addressed.

Body Size Effects During Level Cycling

As noted earlier, the energy requirement of cycling on the flats is directly proportional to the frontal area that the cyclist and the bicycle expose to the airflow. Much can be done to reduce the drag associated with the bicycle through the use of aerodynamic components. The cyclist's drag also can be reduced through the use of an aero helmet, skin-tight clothing, aero bars, and a flat-backed tuck; but not much can be done about the inherent size and shape of each individual cyclist.

The surface area of different-sized cyclists scales with linear dimensions squared, while volume and weight scale with linear dimensions cubed, as discussed in the example with the gymnast and the football player. As a consequence, while larger athletes have a greater amount of absolute surface area, they have *less* surface area relative to their weight than do smaller athletes (just as football players have less muscle cross-sectional area relative to their weight than do gymnasts). This means that although the absolute energy cost of pushing themselves through the air is greater for larger cyclists, the energy cost *relative to their weight* is less for the large cyclists than for the small cyclists.

These theoretical considerations were demonstrated in an experiment performed on outdoor cycling (Swain, Coast, Clifford, Milliken, & Stray-Gundersen, 1987; see Figure 3.2). Large cyclists, weighing an average of 186 lb, needed 2.97 L of oxygen per minute to ride at 20 mph, whereas small cyclists, weighing an average of 131 lb, needed 2.66 L · min^{-1}, or about 10% less. The reason is that smaller cyclists expose less absolute frontal area to the wind. But the difference in frontal areas is much less than might be expected on the basis of only the weights of the athletes, and it was less than expected even on the purely theoretical

Figure 3.2 The setup used to measure the oxygen consumption of different-sized cyclists while riding on the flats. Exhaled air from the cyclist is collected in a sealed bag in the back of the pickup truck and then taken to a laboratory for analysis.

basis of scaling. Apparently, large cyclists are able to reduce their air resistance better than small cyclists when in a tucked position.

When expressed relative to the cyclists' body weight, the large cyclists had a much lower oxygen cost, requiring only 35.2 ml of oxygen per minute for each kilogram of body weight, compared to the 44.9 ml $\cdot$ kg^{-1} $\cdot$ min^{-1} that the small cyclists used. Thus large cyclists have a relative energy cost advantage in that they require 22% less oxygen per kilogram of body weight to ride on the flats.

If all cyclists had the same aerobic capacity in ml $\cdot$ kg^{-1} $\cdot$ min^{-1}, then larger cyclists would dominate in level cycling. The only way smaller cyclists could keep up would be to draft. However, on time trials, where drafting is not allowed, large cyclists would win every race.

This doesn't always happen because there is much variation in the $\dot{V}O_2$max of different athletes. Smaller athletes generally have greater aerobic power relative to body weight. Among competitive U.S. time trialists, a typical 175-lb cyclist might be expected to have a $\dot{V}O_2$max of 68 ml $\cdot$ kg^{-1} $\cdot$ min^{-1}, while a typical 140-lb cyclist would be at 70 ml $\cdot$ kg^{-1} $\cdot$ min^{-1} (Coyle et al., 1991; Swain, 1994).

There is also an advantage to smaller athletes as a consequence of scaling. Maximal oxygen consumption appears to be proportional to surface area, as it is probably limited by variables such as the surface area of capillaries in the muscles for the diffusion of oxygen and other surface and cross-sectional areas associated with oxygen transport. Since area scales with linear dimensions squared and the volume or tissue being served scales with linear dimensions cubed, large athletes have "too much" tissue volume relative to their oxygen supply in comparison to small athletes.

One might conclude that the advantage in relative $\dot{V}O_2$max that small cyclists enjoy would balance out the relative advantage that the large cyclists have in overcoming their air resistance, and that everyone would compete on equal terms. This doesn't happen, because the advantage to large cyclists in overcoming wind resistance is slightly greater, and therefore large cyclists tend to perform better in time trials.

In 1991, Coyle and his colleagues performed a comprehensive study of elite performance in the time trial (Coyle et al., 1991). A later analysis of the body weights of the cyclists in that study revealed a trend for faster times by the heavier athletes (Swain, 1994). On the basis of those findings, a typical 175-lb cyclist might expect to finish a 25-mile time trial 4 min faster than a typical 140-lb cyclist.

If small cyclists hope to be competitive in flat stage races, they must be intelligent users of drafting and look for the right moments for a breakaway—generally on hilly stretches if any are available. In time trials, small cyclists must do everything they can to maximize their aerodynamics. Greg LeMond, the premiere cyclist of the 1980s, was relatively small, weighing about 145 lb, and excelled on hills. However, he was also an excellent time trialist. This was mostly attributable to his extraordinary individual ability. But it was also attributable to his intelligent use of aerodynamics. This was most impressively displayed in his dramatic come-from-behind victory in the final time trial of the 1990 Tour de France, when his novel use of an aero helmet and aero bars had a significant role in the defeat of his larger rival, Laurent Fignon.

Body Size Effects During Uphill Cycling

Going uphill means going slow and, as discussed earlier, this means that resistance become less of a factor. In climbing, cyclists face the force of gravity on almost equal terms. That is to say, gravity is directly proportional to mass, so each cyclist must provide the same amount of energy relative to his or her own body weight plus the weight of the bicycle. This actually gives a slight advantage to the large cyclists, because their bicycles are a smaller percentage of their own weight than are the bicycles of small cyclists.

This advantage has been observed during uphill bicycling on a laboratory treadmill (see Figure 3.3): Large cyclists exhibited a trend for a slightly lower relative oxygen cost, in ml · kg^{-1} · min^{-1}, than small cyclists while climbing a 10% grade (Swain, 1994; Swain & Wilcox, 1993). However, this is a good case of the laboratory's not matching up with the outside world, because there is no advantage to the larger cyclists once the energy supply is factored in.

Figure 3.3 The laboratory setup used to measure the oxygen consumption of uphill cycling. The cyclist is riding at 7 mph up a 10% grade.

The energy available to each cyclist is not proportional to body weight. As we saw earlier, aerobic power is proportional to surface area and gives an impressive advantage to smaller athletes when expressed per kilogram of body weight. Therefore, if the energy required to go uphill is proportional to weight, but the available energy favors those with a low weight, small cyclists should excel at hill climbing despite their small disadvantage in relative bicycle weight.

This prediction refers only to long climbs that must be done under steady state, aerobic conditions, not to short hills that can be topped in a sprint. That situation will be dealt with in a later section.

The fact that small cyclists often specialize in hill climbing is nothing new to observers of the sport. Current specialists such as Claudio Chiapucci and Piotr Ugrumov bear this out. Recently, an analysis of the results of a major stage race added scientific backing to this observation. Cyclists who participated in the 1992 Tour du Pont were weighed, and their race times in different stages were compared (Stovall, Swain, Benedetti, Pruitt, & Burke, 1993). On the three hilliest stages, lighter cyclists performed significantly better than their heavier rivals. On the hilliest stage, a typical 140-lb cyclist finished the 98-mile course in 4 hr and 26 min, whereas a typical 175-lb cyclist finished 10 min back.

Large cyclists can improve their hill climbing by insuring that the body weight they carry up hills is mostly productive muscle tissue. Maintaining a very low body fat percentage, on the order of 5% for male cyclists, is essential for proficient climbing. Female cyclists must be aware of the deleterious side effects associated with low body fat—amenorrhea and osteoporosis—and consider both the personal health risks and competitive benefits of dropping too much below 15% fat.

Body Size Effects During Downhill Cycling

Everyone is familiar with the experiment in which Galileo dropped two balls of different weights from the leaning tower of Pisa, supposedly discovering that both hit the ground at the same time. Shouldn't, then, two different-sized cyclists descend a steep hill at the same speed? No. Today, physicists know that if Galileo had accurately measured the descent of the two balls, he would have found that the heavier one hit the ground first. Equal acceleration of different objects occurs only in a vacuum, not in the air surrounding the leaning tower of Pisa.

Objects are accelerated by gravity with a force that is proportional to their mass, whereas they are decelerated by a force, drag, that is proportional to their surface area and to the square of their speed. As a free-falling object's speed increases, the drag increases until it equals the gravitational force. At that point, the object continues to fall at a constant speed, known as terminal velocity. For example, terminal velocity for sky divers is approximately 120 mph.

Why would a heavier object fall more rapidly? If two objects are similarly shaped and made of the same material, like two balls or two cyclists, then scaling can be used to describe the relationships between their surface areas and weights. The lighter object has a greater ratio of surface area to weight, so the drag force will build during free fall to equal the gravitational force (i.e., the object's weight) at a lower velocity than for the heavier object. To put it another way, the greater *relative* air resistance slows the smaller object down more.

If these two objects are rolled down a slope, they will again accelerate until reaching a terminal velocity. But the terminal velocity on the slope will be less than that in free fall, because the effective force that gravity applies is reduced by the angle (specifically, it is equal to the force in free fall times the sine of the angle with the horizontal).

Using the equations worked out by DiPrampero and his colleagues, one can calculate that a typical 140-lb cyclist would make a freewheel descent of a 10% grade at about 42 mph, whereas a typical 175-lb cyclist would descend the same hill at 44 mph (DiPrampero, Cortili, Mognoni, & Saibene, 1979). Thus, large cyclists can gain back some of the time they lost going uphill. However, if the uphill and downhill sections of a course equal out, the large cyclist will lose far more time going uphill than he or she can gain back going downhill. The slow climbs take much longer, so differences in speed there will result in a bigger time gap.

Body Size Effects During Sprint Cycling

Sprinters are big, period. This is just as true in running as it is in cycling, and for the same reasons. Sprinting occurs at high speeds, so air resistance is the most important force to be overcome. As discussed earlier for cycling on the flats, the relative energy cost of overcoming air resistance favors larger athletes.

However, in the discussion of cycling on the flats we also saw that the energy supply, aerobic power scales in favor of the small athletes and partially compensates for the energy cost advantage to their larger competitors. This is not the case in sprinting, where the energy supply comes from stored adenosine triphosphate (ATP) rather than from aerobic metabolism.

Whereas aerobic metabolism is limited by surface areas, the storage of ATP within muscle fibers should be directly proportional to the volume or mass of the muscles. Thus, larger athletes have sufficient anaerobic power to fuel the demands of their larger muscles. With the aerobic disadvantage out of the picture, large athletes can fully exploit their air resistance advantage during sprints.

During racing, the large and powerful sprinters are a threat in criterium races and in flat road races. If there are no long hills to contend with, they will still be in the pack at the finish, ready to sprint for the win.

Putting It All Together— What's the "Best" Body Size?

From the previous discussion it should be clear that there is no single body size that is the best for cycling. Each athlete can excel at different aspects of this complex sport. Smaller cyclists generally are the best hill climbers, while larger athletes have an edge in time trials and a distinct advantage in sprinting. These differences are largely the result of surface area and body weight scaling and the ways in which this scaling affects factors like air resistance, aerobic capacity, and anaerobic capacity.

Although body size is an important determinant of cycling performance, the scientific studies that have been performed indicate that it accounts for only about 10 to 20% of the variation in race times. Many other variables also play significant roles in determining champion cyclists and can confound the scaling effects. Drafting is a feature of mass-start races that can be worked to its best advantage by team tactics. Genetic inheritance, conditioning level, body fat percentage, nutritional status, skill, and psychological preparedness are critical components of individual ability.

Miguel Indurain, four-time winner of the Tour de France, is the preeminent cyclist in the world today and a contender for Eddy Merckx's crown of best cyclist of all time. Larger than the average cyclist at 172 lb, Indurain totally dominates on time trials. But he is also one of the best hill climbers. How can he, like other great champions before him, excel at both events? Indurain was recently evaluated in an exercise physiology laboratory at the University of Navarra in Spain, and his $\dot{V}O_2$max was measured at 88 ml $\cdot$ kg^{-1} $\cdot$ min^{-1}. This is an awesome value of aerobic power, possibly the highest ever measured for a cyclist. Recall that among nationally competitive U.S. time trialists, a typical 175-lb cyclist has a $\dot{V}O_2$max of only 68 ml $\cdot$ kg^{-1} $\cdot$ min^{-1}, while smaller cyclists are generally in the 70s. Being blessed, through both genetics and hard training, with a nearly superhuman metabolism, Indurain is able to defeat rivals of any body size.

Miguel Indurain and Greg LeMond may represent the opposite limits of the size range needed for success in major stage races, given the current mix of time trials and mountain climbs in these competitions. There may be cyclists smaller than LeMond who are better hill climbers but who are not good enough at time trials to win the overall tour. Similarly, a cyclist larger than Indurain may be able to beat him in a flat time trial, but it is unlikely that such a person could be as effective in the hills. Such was the case in the 1994 Tour de France, when Chris

Boardman beat Indurain in the prologue, a very short time trial, but was unable to make much of a mark later in the race.

The 1994 Tour de France was a marvelous illustration of the search for the best body size. Tour organizers hoped to break Miguel Indurain's streak of consecutive victories, so they designed the Tour with more mountain climbing than usual and replaced one of the normally flat time trials with an uphill time trial. Thus, smaller cyclists were being given a chance to beat Indurain in the overall standings. Indurain once again dominated in the flat time trial, and small cyclists won in the mountains and the uphill time trial. But Indurain was able to stay close enough to the climbers on the mountain stages to emerge victorious over the entire Tour. Interestingly, the only large cyclist to win a mountain stage, Eros Poli, did so by going on a 100-mile solo breakaway on the flats. He took 20 min longer than the little guys to climb the mountain, but he had built up a 24-min lead before starting the ascent.

Suggestions for Future Research

While this chapter has explored the scientific findings concerning body size and cycling, much speculation has been included as well. More research is needed to provide a thorough understanding of the topic. For example, more studies should be done using outdoor cycling. No controlled studies of hill climbing or of descents have yet been performed on the road. Such studies would provide a more realistic measure of the energy cost associated with these activities and of the body size effects.

A great deal could be learned through the use of wind tunnel testing. Actual drag forces could be measured on many cyclists of different sizes and different body shapes to define these relationships more precisely. Scaling applies only to similarly shaped objects. Stocky versus lean cyclists have differences in air resistance that can not be predicted solely from their heights or weights. Cyclists with a stocky build should have a smaller ratio of surface area to body weight than their leaner competitors, and thus the stocky cyclists would be better at time trials and sprints. It would be too difficult to assess these factors with just a tape measure. Wind tunnel studies would provide definitive answers.

References

Coyle, E.F., Feltner, M.E., Kaytz, S.A., Hamilton, M.T., Montain, S.J., Baylor, A.M., Abraham, L.D., & Petrek, G.W. (1991). Physiological and biomechanical factors associated with elite endurance cycling performance. *Medicine and Science in Sports and Exercise, 23*, 93-107.

DiPrampero, P.E., Cortili, G., Mognoni, P., & Saibene, F. (1979). Equation of motion of a cyclist. *Journal of Applied Physiology, 47*, 201-206.

McCole, S.D., Claney, K., Conte, J.-C., Anderson, R., & Hagberg, J.M. (1990). Energy expenditure during bicycling. *Journal of Applied Physiology, 68*, 748-753.

Stovall, K.D., Swain, D.P., Benedetti, K., Pruitt, A.L., & Burke, E.R. (1993). Body mass and performance in the Tour du Pont. *Medicine and Science in Sports and Exercise, 25* (Suppl.), 169. (Abstract)

Swain, D.P. (1994). The influence of body mass in endurance bicycling. *Medicine and Science in Sports and Exercise, 26*, 58-63.

Swain, D.P., Coast, J.R., Clifford, P.S., Milliken, M.C., & Stray-Gundersen, J. (1987). Influence of body size on oxygen consumption during bicycling. *Journal of Applied Physiology, 62*, 668-672.

Swain, D.P., & Wilcox, J.P. (1992). Effect of cadence on the economy of uphill cycling. *Medicine and Science in Sports and Exercise, 24*, 1123-1127.

4

Body Positioning for Cycling

Edmund R. Burke, PhD • Andrew L. Pruitt, EdD

For the cyclist interested in performance, proper position on the bicycle is paramount. A properly fitted cyclist will be efficient, powerful, comfortable, and injury free on the bike. An efficient and powerful position is one that enables the cyclist to pedal the bicycle effectively, without a lot of wasted energy and improper pedaling mechanics. Being comfortable on the bicycle allows for the athlete's weight to be distributed between the saddle, pedals, and handlebars, so the skeletal system bears the weight instead of the muscles of the back and arms.

A good bike fit, then, is imperative not only for comfort but also for minimizing potential for injury. Improper positioning can often lead to overuse injuries and premature fatigue while riding. For the past 5 to 10 years, Andy Pruitt has been describing cycling as "a marriage between the human body, which is somewhat adaptable, and a machine that is somewhat adjustable." In fitting the bicycle to the cyclist, one needs to adjust the bicycle to the cyclist so that the cyclist has to adapt as little as possible (Burke, 1994).

Types of Bicycles

Choosing among the plethora of bicycle styles currently available can be confusing. In this chapter we will focus only on describing the proper positioning of a cyclist on a road racing bike, a mountain bike, and a time trial bicycle.

Road Racing Bicycle

The most important angle on a bicycle is that formed by the seat tube with the ground (Figure 4.1). As we will see later in this chapter, an important fitting dimension will require that your knee be over the pedal spindle (KOPS) of the forward foot when the crank arms are horizontal. The seat tube angle is usually designed to accomplish this. The most common angles for road racing frames are from 72° to 74°, which will allow for an average-sized cyclist to position his or her knee over the pedal spindle with only minor adjustments to fore and aft movement of the saddle.

Consequently, the seat tube angle is related to femur length. The longer the femur, the shallower (smaller) the angle; a shallower angle tends to move the cyclist back on the bicycle. If someone has a short femur, the seat tube angle would have to be steeper (larger) to position the knee far enough forward. In general, the smaller the bicycle the steeper the seat tube angle. More and more professional cyclists who are riding long road races with many climbs are also opting to use bicycles with a 72° seat tube angle. The steeper the seat tube, the harsher the ride, thus limiting your bicycle to shorter events.

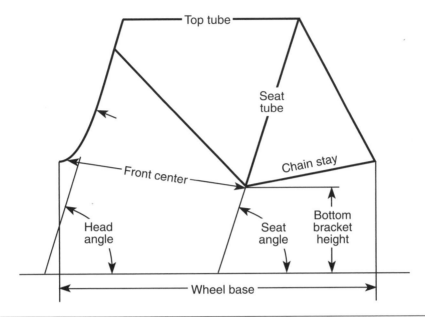

Figure 4.1   Basic bicycle geometry.

Head tube angle, meanwhile, is based on frame size, top tube length, seat tube angle, pedal clearance in relation to front wheel, and desired steering characteristics. It's commonly 73° to 75°. The steep head tube angle is usually combined with a relatively short fork rake, creating a reasonable amount of calculated steering trail for stability at high speed. This allows for the least amount of frame flex and minimum tendency to stray when the cyclist is riding on straight stretches or descending a steep mountain.

Chain stay length is about 16 in., which reduces frame flex and keeps the overall wheel base to somewhere between 38 to 40 in. A short wheel base increases steering responsiveness.

When you are selecting a frame, see that about 4 to 5 in. of seat post is showing once saddle height is established (we will consider saddle height in a later section). Select the smallest possible frame that affords a good mix of comfort and handling. As a rule, a smaller frame is lighter and stronger and handles better than a larger one. However, the frame should not be too small; this will cause the top tube to be short or will cause the seat post to be set past its maximum extension line.

Mountain Bike

As with road bikes, mountain bike sizes are usually determined by seat tube length, and some models have sloping top tubes that result in extremely short seat tubes. In these cases, smaller frame sizes fit larger cyclists. The clearance between crotch and top tube when the rider straddles the top tube in cycling shoes should be a minimum of about 3 in.— enough to allow quick, painless dismounts. A mathematical formula for selecting frame size is based on inseam length minus 14 in. For a cyclist with a 36-in. inseam, the formula would be 36 − 14 = 22-in. frame.

Whereas many road bike frames are measured from the center of the crank spindle to the center of the top tube, many mountain bike frame builders measure from the center of the crank spindle to the *top* of the top tube. If the bike has a sloping top tube, then measure to the top of where it would be if it were level with the horizon.

The seat tube angle on most mountain bikes is around 71° to 73°. With a few variants this has been the norm in the industry in the last few years. Entry level bikes usually have similar head tube angles to allow for slower and more predictable steering. Recently, head tube angle has become progressively steeper so the steering is more immediate and responsive.

Most racing cyclists will have the same position relative to saddle height and reach for both their mountain and road bicycles. This is so because many mountain bike cyclists also put in plenty of miles on their road bicycles and want to have the identical position on the two bikes to eliminate the chance of injury.

Lastly, there is a large variation (from 11-3/4 to 13 in.) in the bottom bracket height of most mountain bikes. A bike with an 11-in. bottom bracket height and one with a 12-in. bottom bracket height would have a difference in stand-over height of 1 in. If using a higher bottom bracket, some cyclists prefer to lower their saddle height slightly so as to not have too high a center of gravity. A lower position will allow for greater stability with minimal cost to efficiency. Cyclists should carefully review their position when saddle height is lowered, since this may cause riders to throw their knees out at the top of the pedal stroke and could put undue stress on the anterior and lateral aspect of the knee.

Time Trial Bike

Positioning on the time trial bicycle is one of the more exciting topics of discussion among cyclists because there is still so much experimenting and refining taking place with the seat tube angles and aero arm positioning. More and more we are seeing steeper seat tube angles, with these angles ranging from 75° to 90°. Chris Boardman's hour-record-setting bicycle had an effective seat angle of 80° and an effective head tube angle of 74°. Positioning for the time trial will be discussed in greater detail later in the chapter.

Proper Fit to the Bicycle

There are several things to consider when fitting a bicycle. Let's review the latest findings on what will provide comfort, prevent injury, and improve cycling performance.

Optimal Saddle Height

Optimal saddle height for cycling has been estimated on the basis of power output (Hamley & Thomas, 1967) and caloric expenditure (Hamley & Thomas, 1967; Nordeen & Cavanagh, 1975; Shennum & DeVries, 1975). These reports generally agree that oxygen consumption is minimized at approximately 100% of trochanter height (from greater trochanter [boney points at widest parts of the hips] of femur to the floor while standing barefoot), or 106 to 109% of pubic symphysis height (measured from the ground to the pubic symphysis [bony prominence, middle of pelvis in the crotch area] while standing barefoot). Experienced cyclists generally choose a saddle height close to optimum simply by adjusting the seat height for maximum performance (Gregor, Green, & Garhammer, 1982).

Muscle activity patterns (Desipres, 1974; Ericson, Nisell, Arborelius, & Ekholm, 1985; Gregor, Green, & Garhammer, 1982; Jorge & Hull, 1986), joint forces and moment patterns (Browning, Gregor, Broker, & Whiting, 1988; Ericson, 1986; Ericson, Bratt, Nisou, Nemeth, & Eicholm, 1986; Ericson, Ekblom, Svensson, & Nisell, 1985; Ericson, Nisell, Arborelius, & Ekholm, 1985), and pedaling effectiveness (Broker, Browning, Gregor, & Whiting, 1988) also have been reported to vary across seat heights. These relationships, however, have not been used to suggest optimal saddle heights.

Over the years, several formulas have been developed through use of the metabolic or empirical data mentioned to set saddle height for the cyclist on both the sport/tour and racing bicycle. Whenever fitting the bike to the cyclist, always recommend that the person wear the shoes he or she expects to wear the most when riding. This approach will allow for proper fit and comfort while riding.

Method 1. The simplest and usually the quickest method requires that the cyclist mount the bicycle on a wind-load resistance trainer and pedal comfortably while centered squarely in the saddle. The rider then unclips his or her feet, putting the heels on the top of the pedal, and pedals backward (Figure 4.2). The saddle height should be set at the point where the heels maintain contact with the pedals without the hips rocking from side to side as the cyclist reaches the bottom of the pedal

Figure 4.2   Estimating seat height from leg length.

stroke. This usually leads to a lower saddle height than that obtained with the other formulas we will review. When the cyclist is properly clipped into the pedals there should be a slight knee flexion when the pedal is at the bottom of the stroke.

Method 2.   One of the more common methods requires the subject to stand wearing cycling shoes with the feet about 2 in. apart on a hard floor and to hold a book or broomstick in a horizontal position while pulling it up firmly between the legs (Figure 4.3). Measure the distance (floor to

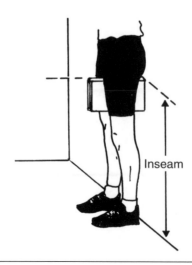

Inseam

Figure 4.3   Measuring inseam length to estimate saddle height.

crotch) and then multiply by 1.09 to get the distance from the center of pedal spindle (axle) to the top of the saddle (Figure 4.4) when the crank arm is parallel to the seat tube (Hamley & Thomas, 1967). This will give an upper limit to saddle height. Remember that the top of the saddle is the cupped part where one actually sits, not the front tip or the lip on the back of the saddle.

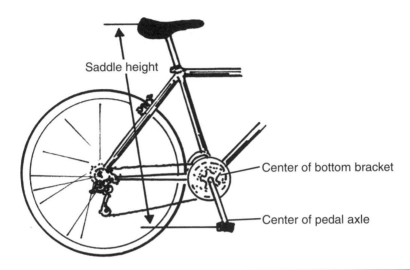

Figure 4.4   Saddle height is the distance between the top of the saddle and center of the pedal axle, measured when the pedal is down and the crank arm is in line with the seat tube. LeMond measures from the saddle to the center of the bottom bracket.

Method 3.   A third formula, recommended by Greg LeMond (1987), is to multiply the inseam measurement (floor to crotch as shown in Figure 4.3) by 0.883 to get the distance from the center of the bottom bracket to the top of the saddle (Figure 4.4). This works out to be about 1/4 in. to 1 in. lower than with the first method for most people. This formula was determined years ago by Cyrille Guimard, LeMond's former coach, using wind tunnel tests and power tests. LeMond also recommends that you subtract 3 mm from the final figure when using clipless pedals (Matheny, 1992).

Method 4.   Holmes, Pruitt, and Whalen (1994) recommend that the correct saddle height for an individual with no knee pain allow for 25° to 30° of flexion of the extended leg when the pedal is at bottom dead center (Figure 4.5). This angle is formed from the greater femoral trochanter to the lateral condyle to the lateral malleolus of the extended leg. This measurement should be made with a goniometer, which can be purchased at a medical supply store or can be made from a ruler and a protractor. Line the instrument up along the femur and the tibia, with the axis being at midpoint of the patella (knee). Flexion of 25° to 30° allows for adequate decompression of the knee to prevent anterior knee injuries and avoids the dead spot at the bottom of the pedal stroke. This position also decreases anterior knee stress by reducing patellar compression. Saddles that are too high can result in posterior knee pain, and saddles that are too low can produce anterior knee pain.

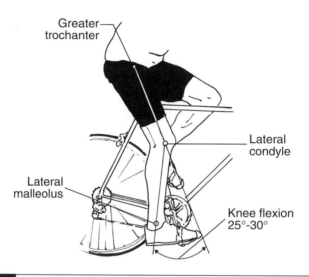

Figure 4.5 Saddle height is evaluated by measuring degrees of knee flexion at the bottom dead center of the pedal stroke. Reprinted from Burke (1995).

Remember that all these formulas are estimates. After the initial setup, the cyclist may need to slightly readjust the saddle height (and other measurements listed later in this chapter). Any initial changes and readjustments should be accomplished in small increments of approximately 1/4 in. every few riding sessions.

When you set up saddle height on a mountain bicycle (one that will be used primarily off road), the saddle height will be the same as on the individual's road bicycle or slightly lower. Because of the higher bottom bracket on mountain bikes, duplicating the same position as on a road bicycle from pedal spindle to top of the saddle may result in a center of gravity that is too high. A lower position will allow for greater stability and maneuverability, with minimal cost to efficiency (Burke, 1994).

Leg Length Discrepancies

Leg length inequalities that may be tolerable with walking can become problematic with cycling because of the cyclist's fixed position on the bike and because of the high number of repetitions completed each minute on the bicycle. Determine whether inequalities are functional or static, because corrections are specific for the type of discrepancy. Functional length differences that are due to foot mechanics (i.e., that occur at the ankle or foot) are corrected primarily with orthotics and bicycle fit adjustments. Static inequalities can be treated with spacers or saddle or foot position adjustments.

Static length discrepancies may be present in the femur or the tibia. A scanogram (Figure 4.6), which provides static segmental measurements and location of length differences, can reveal these discrepancies.

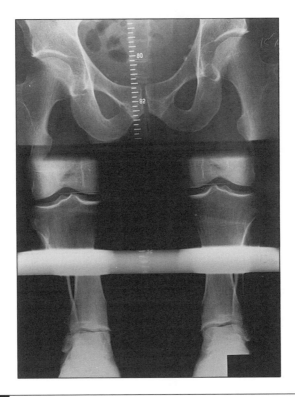

Figure 4.6 Scanogram of the static segmental measurements of a cyclist.

Functional length discrepancies can result from faulty foot mechanics. Radiographic evaluation with a standing anterior-posterior view of the pelvis can be used to detect functional length differences. In order for a radiographic evaluation to be accurate, the floor the cyclist is standing on must be perfectly level.

The saddle height for cyclists with leg length discrepancies should always be adjusted to the long leg. Length corrections are then made on the shoe or pedal of the short leg, or with the fore-aft positioning of the feet if the length discrepancy occurs at the femur.

Then there are tibial and femoral length discrepancies. Tibial length discrepancies can easily be treated by using spacers to equalize the lengths. These spacers can be placed between the shoe and the cleat, or in the shoe of an off-road cyclist. Femoral length discrepancies are more difficult to treat. One method, though anecdotal, is to use a combination of spacers and an adjustment in the foot position on the pedal to provide correction. For example, a 6-mm difference could be treated by placing a 3-mm shim between the shoe and the cleat and by moving the foot of the short leg back 1 mm on the pedal and the foot of the long leg forward on the pedal.

Corrections for length should always slightly undercompensate the total difference, since many cyclists slightly correct with "ankling" (exaggerated plantar or dorsiflexion of the foot). Length discrepancies of 4 mm or less do not need correction unless the cyclist is symptomatic.

Fore and Aft Saddle Position

The rule of thumb for saddle fore and aft placement specifies that your knees should be vertically positioned over the pedal spindles when the pedals are forward and horizontal with the ground. This rule is widely regarded as a good starting position for proper weight distribution on the bike. It also promotes good pedaling style. As we will see later, there are several reasons to alter the position. Nevertheless, it is a good place to begin.

With the cranks horizontal to the ground (3 and 9 o'clock position), place a straightedge (yardstick) on the front of the patella of the forward foot and extend it down to the end of the crank arm (Figure 4.7). Loosen the bolt (under the saddle) that holds the rails to the seat post and slide the saddle fore and aft until the straightedge is perpendicular to the ground. This is often referred to as the neutral knee position.

Some triathletes prefer to have the front of the knee up to 2 to 3 in. in front of this neutral position. The more forward position will probably require a frame with a significantly steeper seat tube angle than comes standard on most road bikes. Remember, though, that any time you move the saddle forward you are effectively lowering the saddle height, so you may have to adjust the saddle height again.

Some off-road specialists prefer to have the mountain bike seat set back from their road bike position. The front of the knee should fall about 1 cm behind the end of the crank arm as indicated by a straightedge. A cyclist who is climbing while seated on a mountain bike should sit as far back on the saddle as possible; this will allow for greater traction on the rear wheel.

Figure 4.7   In the neutral fore-aft position, with the pedal at 90°, a straight-edge is placed on the front of the knee and should fall to the end of the crank arm. Straightedge should be vertical.

You will see professional road cyclists using this same position (with the saddle pushed back all the way on the rails) because they sit relatively far behind the bottom bracket in order to push bigger gears while sitting down on long climbs. This position will be hard on a cyclist who has low back pain or hamstring problems.

Saddle Tilt

The saddle should be set either level or with a slightly elevated front end. To determine the proper saddle tilt, a carpenter's level may be placed along the longitudinal axis of the saddle to indicate that the saddle is level or slightly angled with the front end higher. Some women prefer that the front of the saddle be angled slightly downward to prevent pressure on the perineal area. Some men will opt to have their saddle tilted slightly upward, but this may lead to urologic and neuropathic problems.

Upper Body Position

Cyclists typically will adjust reach length according to what is comfortable, what is consistent with their level of back conditioning, and what can be maintained for desired distances. To find the proper stem length (extension), the cyclist should sit on the bicycle with the arms bent comfortably, the hands in the drops, and the head facing forward. The next step is to drop a plumb line from the tip of the rider's nose; it should bisect the handlebars in the center at the stem (Figure 4.8).

Figure 4.8   Hands are in the drops of the bars, back is about 45°, and elbows are bent. With the stem properly extended, a plumb line dropped from the nose while looking down at a 45° angle will fall about 1 inch behind the handlebar. Reprinted from Burke (1995).

Some determine stem length by assuming the position described and judging the stem length to be correct when the transverse part of the handlebar blocks out their view of the axle of the front wheel. Again, make sure that the cyclist is positioned on the drops and that the elbows are bent as for riding in a racing position. Greg LeMond recommends a position in which the elbow and knee are separated by about 1 to 2 in. (lengthwise), at their closest point, while the cyclist is riding in the drops of the handlebars with the arms bent at a 65° to 70° angle. Handlebar stems can be replaced to give proper extension.

The height of the bars should be at least 1 to 2 in. below the top of the saddle for a small cyclist, and as much as 4 in. for a tall cyclist. If the cyclist is complaining of hand numbness (cyclist's palsy) or pain in the neck, arms, or shoulders, he or she may want to raise the stem to take weight off the hands. In addition, cyclists should use well-padded cycling gloves to absorb road shock and vibrations and should attempt to keep their wrists in a neutral position.

The width of the bars on a road bicycle should be the same as the width of the shoulders; measure from the end of one acromion to the corresponding acromion across the front of the chest (Figure 4.9). Handlebar widths on a mountain bike generally range from 20 to 24 in. A wide bar is best for slow speed control, whereas a narrow bar allows for quicker turning and makes it easier to squeeze through wooded single-track trails. Most mountain bike specialists prefer handlebars that are around 20 to 21 in. wide. They do not need wider bars because of the addition of bar ends, which allow for extra leverage when climbing.

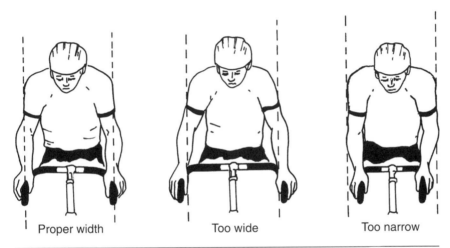

Proper width   Too wide   Too narrow

Figure 4.9   Handlebar width.

The position of the upper body is the least exact part of the bicycle fit because it tends to be a function of comfort, experience (years of riding), hamstring and back flexibility, back problems, and ability to rotate the hips. It may take time and patience to get a cyclist into an "ideal" position.

On a mountain bike the upper body position will in most cases be more extended. A more extended position on a mountain bike gives one enough room for lots of body English on climbs and descents and allows for no overlap of knees and elbows. As on the road bicycle, the top of the stem should be 1 to 2 in. below the imaginary horizontal line extending from the top of the saddle. Too high a position on the bike will raise the center of gravity and unevenly distribute the cyclist's weight between the front and rear wheels. A frame that is too small will force the cyclist to lean over too far because the handlebars are so far below the saddle. Too large a frame will also stretch someone out too far.

Handlebar Position

The bottom of the handlebar on a road bicycle should be level or angled down slightly toward the rear wheel hub. Place each brake lever so that the tip just touches a straightedge extended forward from under the handlebar. The best all-around riding position is with the hands placed around the top of the brake level hood; this provides for good steering, quick access to brake levers, and good grip for out-of-the-saddle climbing. This is the favorite position of most cyclists. If using a bicycle equipped with Shimano STI or Campagnolo Ergo brake levers, many cyclists mount the levers a little higher on the curve of the bars. This is because the levers add about 1 cm in reach to the cyclist's extension when riding with the hands around the top of the brake lever hoods. Mounting them higher shortens the effective reach of the cyclist.

Crank Arm Length

The consensus is that crank arm length should be matched to the cyclist's leg length. The standard crank arm length of 170 mm suits cyclists of average proportions between about 5'5" and 6'0". Shorter cyclists should consider crank arms of 165 or 167.5 mm. Cyclists under 5 ft tall should consider 160-mm crank arms. Cyclists around 6'0" to 6'2" might try 172.5-mm crank arms; 6'2" to 6'4", 175-mm crank arms; and taller individuals, 180- or 185-mm crank arms. Two cyclists may be of the same height with one having disproportionately longer legs. This cyclist may want to opt for slightly longer crank arms.

Crank arm length determines the size of the pedal circle, which relates to the vertical distance the rider's feet rise from the bottom of each pedal stroke to the top. This may affect comfort and does affect knee and hip flexion. For example, if a short rider uses long crank arms, the hips and knees may flex uncomfortably at the top of the pedal stroke even though the saddle is at the proper height. Crank arm length also influences the leverage and rpm rate that one produces while cycling. Long crank arms are good for pushing large gears and climbing at lower rpms, and shorter crank arms are good for low-gear, high-rpm pedaling. Most mountain bikes come with longer crank arms (172.5 mm–175 mm).

Most bicycles come with proportionally sized crank arms. If the cyclist needs a different arm length, a bicycle dealer can change crank arms. Remember, when crank arms are changed, saddle height may have to be readjusted.

Foot Position

Position the feet so that the widest part (ball of the foot, metatarsal head of the great toe) of the foot is directly over the pedal axle. To prevent knee pain, cleats should be adjusted so the angle of the foot on the pedal is neutral, as anatomically arrived at by the cyclist's own natural foot position on the pedal. The most efficient method of providing an accurate placement of the foot is to use a special instrument called the Rotational Adjustment Device (RAD). Most good bicycle shops have this device and can fit someone's cleats in about 20 min.

Under certain circumstances some cyclists have a preference for mounting their cleats on their cycling shoes so that the ball of the foot is ahead of or behind the pedal axle. When the ball of the foot is ahead of the axle, the effective lever arm from the ankle to the pedal axle is shortened. This requires less force to stabilize the foot on the pedal and puts less strain on the Achilles tendon and calf muscles. Some triathletes and time trial specialists use this position because it allows them to produce more force when using large gears. But it will limit one's ability to pedal at high cadences. A cyclist who is experiencing some soreness in the Achilles tendon or calf muscles should consider moving the ball of the foot forward a few millimeters on the pedal. Lastly, some cyclists with shoe sizes smaller than size nine may consider moving the ball of the foot slightly behind the pedal axle, and cyclists with a shoe size larger than size 11 may consider moving the ball of the foot slightly in front of the pedal axle.

Placing the ball of the foot behind the pedal axle effectively lengthens the lever arm from the ankle to the pedal axle and makes it harder to keep the foot as a rigid lever. Consequently, the calf muscles and Achilles tendon need to do more work to stabilize the foot on the pedal. Often, you see track cyclists using this position because it allows for higher rpms during fixed-gear events. But a cyclist may be flirting with potential injury, especially if using large gear ratios.

Most importantly, cleat position should reflect any anatomic variants that may be noted on an examination. For example, a cyclist with external tibial rotation should be placed in a slightly externally rotated or toed-out cleat position. This is especially critical for cyclists using fixed rather than floating cleat systems because there is no rotation to compensate for anatomic variants. Cyclists who have marked pronation, excessive toeing out, or varus alignments (bowleg) may benefit from adding spacers between the pedal and the crank arm (Figure 4.10). This can alleviate trauma to the medial malleolus for cyclists with excessive pronation and can improve hip-to-foot alignment for varus individuals.

Clip-On Handlebars

In recent years with the continued growth of the triathlon and time trial cycling, we have seen a new form of handlebar being used by athletes in these events. It was developed to reduce the aerodynamic drag of the

Figure 4.10 Spacers (washers) between the pedal and the crank arm.

cyclist, just as in downhill skiing. Using clip-on (aero) handlebars effectively requires mastering four elements of positioning: narrowing the arms, riding with a flat back, lowering the chin, and keeping the knees in while cycling.

Narrowing the arms. By narrowing the arms, the cyclist reduces the body's frontal area and allows for the wind to be directed around the body. The cyclist begins by gradually bringing in the armrest pads a few centimeters closer on the handlebars until it is possible to ride comfortably with the forearms almost touching for long periods of time (Figure 4.11). This may take several weeks or months. Once someone can ride like this comfortably and in a powerful position, he or she will have reduced aerodynamic drag greatly.

Riding with a flat back. The next task is to work on riding comfortably with a flat back (Figure 4.12). This is accomplished by rotating the pelvis forward on the saddle and working on lower back and hamstring flexibility. The saddle should be level and the stem length long enough to get the proper "stretch" of the back. This will eliminate the hump that you see in many cyclists' backs when viewing them from the side. Cyclists should not attempt this until they have been able to ride with the forearms positioned closely together for long periods of time.

Lowering the chin. Thirdly, the cyclist will need to lower the chin to fill in the gap between the arms and to help streamline the aerodynamic shape further (Figure 4.13). Riders need to remember not to drop the

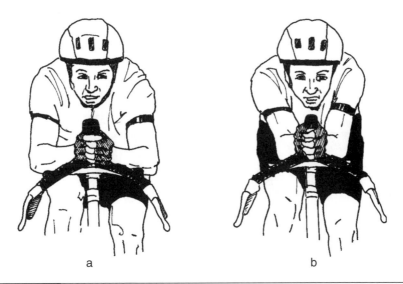

Figure 4.11 Reducing frontal area by bringing arms closer together. For example, a cyclist who rides with forearms wide (a) slowly moves the elbow in toward center (b). Reprinted from Burke (1995).

Figure 4.12 The key to a flat back is pelvic rotation. Figure (a) shows a cyclist who sits with the pelvis turned under, as though sitting on a chair, and cannot flatten out the back. With the pelvis rotated forward, the hump in the back can be eliminated (b). Reprinted from Burke (1995).

chin so low that they cannot safely look down the road. Lowering the chin will also lower the shoulders and make a more perfect aerodynamic object. It is important not to bury the head. Safety and comfort are key concerns while time trialing or while riding off the front of a group.

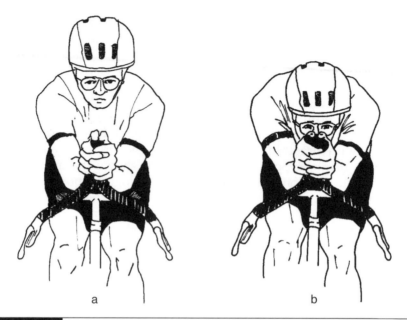

Figure 4.13 Lowering the chin (b) is not the same as lowering the head (a). Notice in (b), the cyclist has lowered the chin to fill in the hole between the upper arms. Reprinted from Burke (1995).

Keeping the knees in. Lastly, cyclists who have accomplished these three changes in upper body position need to be careful to keep the knees in while pedaling. If the other positional changes cause someone to throw out the knees while pedaling in order to avoid hitting the arms, he or she may have to raise the stem or shoulders slightly to allow the knees to stay in while pedaling. Keeping the knees in while pedaling is just as important in air drag reduction as keeping the forearms together, keeping a flat back, and lowering the chin. Research on pedaling rpm in the wind tunnel has shown no correlation between pedaling rate and reduction in air resistance (Kyle, 1989).

Adjusting the tilt of the bars helps one to accomplish these steps in positioning oneself comfortably on the bicycle. Most athletes keep the tilt of the bars upward somewhere between 15° and 30° to achieve optimum comfort, performance, and power.

Questions have arisen about the effect of this position on breathing and oxygen consumption. Research completed at the University of Utah (Johnson & Shultz, 1990) showed that using aerodynamic bars in this position had no measurable physiological cost upon cycling. In the laboratory under two different submaximal conditions, 15 highly trained subjects rode a bicycle ergometer fitted with either dropped road bars or the same bars fitted with clip-on-style bars. There was no evidence in the study to suggest that aero or clip-on bars interfered with breathing (ventilatory) mechanics. Not only was ventilation unaffected; there was no significant difference in oxygen consumption when the athletes worked at 80% of maximum during the 10-min steady state ride. Therefore, there is no foundation for concerns that the severely crouched position required with the use of an aerodynamic type handlebar will interfere with breathing. Recently, work by Origenes and others (Origenes, Blank, & Schoene, 1993) also has shown that riding in an aerodynamic position does not impair physiologic responses to high-intensity exercise.

As with any new piece of equipment, the more practice a cyclist has riding the bicycle with the aero bars before a long ride or race, the more familiar he will become with all aspects of riding technique and comfort. Not using aero bars or clip-ons is sure to put a cyclist at a disadvantage in certain events due to lack of optimum aerodynamic position on the bike.

Directions for Future Research

Positioning is undergoing continual changes with the advent of the "Obree" and "Boardman" positions on the bicycle. Because of the many questions raised by these radical positions, future research will see more interaction of the clinician, biomechanist, and cyclist in determining proper position on the bicycle. For example, while a particular position will dramatically reduce the aerodynamic drag on the cyclist or increase power output, or do both, it could lead to overuse injuries if practiced for many thousands of miles. The study of cycling biomechanics needs to be a more interdisciplinary science not only to lead to increases in performance, but also to reduce the incidence of injury.

Injury research is beginning to look into compensating for length differences through the use of a combination of elliptical chainrings and asymmetrical crank arms. These systems are in the developmental stages and to date have not been evaluated for their effect on pedaling mechanics in cyclists with leg length discrepancies. Work also needs to be continued on the effects of force application to the pedals, with "static" versus "floating" pedals; but along with this research, it is necessary to look at the effect of shoe design on the loading of the lower leg and on overuse injuries.

Lastly, future research on the effects of maintaining an aerodynamic position for extended periods of time needs to review the fatigue patterns in the lower and upper body musculature. This work is important to establish whether or not pathomechanical problems develop after several hours on the bicycle.

References

Broker, J., Browning, R., Gregor, R., & Whiting, R. (1988). Effects of seat height on force effectiveness in cycling. *Medicine and Science in Sports and Exercise*, **20**, 583.

Browning, R., Gregor, R., Broker, J., & Whiting, R. (1988). Effects of seat height changes on joint force and movement patterns in experienced cyclists. *Journal of Biomechanics*, **21**, 871.

Burke, E. (1994). Proper fit of the bicycle. In M.B. Mellion & E.R. Burke (Eds.), *Clinics in sports medicine: Vol. 13(1). Bicycle injuries: Prevention and management* (pp. 1-14). Philadelphia: Saunders.

Desipres, M. (1974). An electromyographic study of competitive road cycling conditions simulated on a treadmill. In R.C. Nelson & C. Morehouse (Eds.), *Biomechanics IV* (pp. 349-355). Baltimore: University Park Press.

Ericson, M. (1986). On the biomechanics of cycling. A case study of joint and muscle load during exercise on a bicycle ergometer. *Scandinavian Journal of Rehabilitative Medicine*, **16**, 1-43.

Ericson, M., Bratt, A., Nisou, R., Nemeth, G., & Eicholm, J. (1986). Load moments about the hip and knee joints during ergometer cycling. *Scandinavian Journal of Rehabilitative Medicine*, **18**, 165-172.

Ericson, M., Ekblom, J., Svensson, O., & Nisell, R. (1985). The forces on the ankle joint structures during ergometer cycling. *Foot and Ankle*, **6**, 135-142.

Ericson, M., Nisell, R., Arborelius, U., & Ekholm, J. (1985). Muscle activity during ergometer cycling. *Scandinavian Journal of Rehabilitative Medicine*, **17**, 53-61.

Gregor, R., Green, D., & Garhammer, J. (1982). An electromyographic analysis of selected muscle activity in elite competitive cyclists. In A. Morecki & K. Fidelus (Eds.), *Biomechanics VII* (pp. 537-541). Baltimore: University Park Press.

Hamley, E., & Thomas, V. (1967). Physiological and postural factors in the calibration of a bicycle ergometer. *Journal of Physiology*, **191**, 55-57.

Holmes, J., Pruitt, A., & Whalen, A. (1994). Lower extremity overuse in bicycling. In M.R. Mellion & E.R. Burke (Eds.), *Clinics in sports medicine: Vol. 13(1). Bicycle injuries: Prevention and management* (pp. 187-206). Philadelphia: Saunders.

Johnson, S., & Shultz, B. (1990). The physiologic effects of aerodynamic handlebars. *Cycling Science*, **2**(4), 9-12.

Jorge, M., & Hull, M. (1986). Analysis of EMG measurement during bicycle pedaling. *Journal of Biomechanics*, **19**, 683-694.

Kyle, C. (1989). The aerodynamics of handlebars & helmets. *Cycling Science*, **1**(1), 22-25.

LeMond, G., & Gordis, K. (1987). *Greg LeMond's complete book of bicycling* (pp. 118-145). New York: Perigee Books.

Matheny, F. (1992, December). Finding perfect saddle height. *Bicycling Magazine*, 46-50.

Nordeen, K., & Cavanagh, P. (1975). Simulation of lower limb kinematics during cycling. In P. Komi (Ed.), *Biomechanics V-B* (pp. 26-33). Baltimore: University Park Press.

Origenes, M., Blank, S., & Schoene, R. (1993). Exercise ventilatory response to upright and aero-posture cycling. *Medicine and Science in Sports and Exercise*, **25**(5), 608-612.

Shennum, P., & DeVries, H. (1975). The effect of saddle height on oxygen consumption during bicycle ergometer work. *Medicine and Science in Sports and Exercise*, **8**, 119-121.

5

Optimal Pedaling Cadence

J. Richard Coast, PhD

Most people who have an interest in cycling also have an idea of what constitutes an optimal pedaling rate. However, there are many different ideas about what the optimal cadence is, and for every cadence proposed as optimal, a different factor is suggested as the critical one to optimize. Many scientists who have studied cycling in the laboratory have used the measurement of oxygen consumption ($\dot{V}O_2$) or heart rate as the critical factor in determining optimal cadence and have found the lowest $\dot{V}O_2$ when pedal rate was held down to 50 to 70 rpm (Banister & Jackson, 1967; Gueli & Shephard, 1976). By using this variable to determine optimal cadence, these investigators are arguing that whole body metabolic rate is the critical factor in optimizing cadence. On the other hand, coaches and experienced cyclists will often tell new riders to "spin," or pedal at least 90 rpm, and sometimes faster. One reason is that pushing high gears at a low pedal rate makes the knees and muscles in the thighs hurt. When people use this reasoning, they are arguing that stress or torque on the muscles and joints is the critical factor in determining optimal cadence (Redfield & Hull, 1986a, 1986b). Others have shown, particularly in runners and walkers, that the leg segments act as pendulums and that the physical laws governing the action of pendulums are primary factors in determining the optimal frequency of motion (Holt, Hamill, & Andres, 1991). Might these laws also be active in cycling?

Bicycling does not place identical demands on all participants, or even on any single rider over time. The demands of the competitive or recreational event, and thus the inputs to determine optimal cadence, differ dramatically. In a single event, the power output can vary by almost tenfold. An example is the difference between cycling in the middle of a large group of riders at 40 kph versus sprinting at the end of a race at nearly 70 kph. Different demands are placed on a rider trying to maintain the highest possible speed throughout a race, such as a time trial or triathlon, than are placed on the rider in the middle of a group in a criterium race, which will include many cycles of braking into and sprinting out of corners. This difference in demands holds true even if the average speeds of the races are identical. Finally, different demands are placed on a rider in relation to the duration of the event. Road races in cycling may be as short as 10 km or as long as 250 km or more, taking anywhere from 12 min to 7 hr to complete.

In addition to the differences in events, there are differences between riders that may affect the choice of optimal cadence. Even for races longer than 10 to 15 min, in which the demand is mostly aerobic, there are critical factors in the rider that may determine cadence. These include the maximal aerobic capacity of the athlete. For example, if a person has a maximal $\dot{V}O_2$ of $4.5\ L \cdot min^{-1}$, an event that would demand $4.8\ L \cdot min^{-1}$ is impossible to continue for more than a few minutes. Even when the demand is less than the maximal capacity, there is a difference in the ability of riders to maintain high percentages of the maximal $\dot{V}O_2$. Therefore, the ability to produce energy may affect selection of a cadence. And since cycling is an activity that places demands on specific, rather small muscle groups, the activation, fatigue, or stress on these muscles and the joints they surround may play a role in cadence selection.

Might the answer to the question of optimal cadence actually be that the demands of the event and the limitations of the rider interact to determine the optimal cadence? This chapter will focus on the concept of optimization as it applies to cycling cadence. It will cover some of the past research on pedaling rate and methods of determining optimal cadence. It will also explore the reasons optimal cadences as determined in the laboratory are so vastly different from those generally used by cyclists on the road and will present some ideas about how to bring the two closer together. The last area to be considered is future research in pedal rate optimization, including possible strategies for road racing, track racing, and time trialing.

Optimization Research

Many methods have been used to tease out the factors that contribute to the optimization of cycling cadence. These range from whole body measurements such as oxygen uptake or heart rates to factors influenced more by the forces exerted by or on the muscles and joints. The preferences of cyclists have also been examined as clues to the perceptual cues and the importance of learning in the establishment of cadence. This section will describe some of the studies that have contributed to our understanding of cadence optimization.

Energy Production and Efficiency

Several groups of researchers in the early 20th century measured oxygen uptake or energy production during cycling in an attempt to determine the most efficient pedal rate. Work by Dickinson (1929) is among the most widely cited of this era. Dickinson had a subject pedal at cadences of approximately 10 to 120 rpm while she measured $\dot{V}O_2$. Her results showed that the subject was most efficient when pedaling at approximately 33 rpm. Drawbacks to this study include the differences in power output (7-112 W) with the different pedal rates (a variable known to affect efficiency), the use of only one subject, and the fit of the subject to the bicycle, which was described as "suitable for a bicyclist of larger build than the subject of these experiments" (Dickinson, 1929, p. 250). Another group, led by F.G. Benedict, also studied efficiency at different pedal rates by using either $\dot{V}O_2$ or energy expenditure measured in a calorimeter. They found that efficiency decreased with increased pedal rate. They did not use any cadences below 70 rpm, however, to establish whether or not there was a true minimum energy cost (Benedict & Cathcart, 1913). Their study was more applicable to the concerns of cyclists, though, because the subject used in the experiments was a professional cyclist.

Several other groups in the early 1900s improved on the work done by these researchers by either keeping the power output constant (Cathcart, Richardson, & Campbell, 1924) or using a greater number of subjects (Garry & Wishart, 1931). Regardless of the method however, the general results were similar—high pedal rates were uneconomical compared to low ones. Work from that time to the present has yielded results that corroborate these. Banister and Jackson (1967) showed that the $\dot{V}O_2$ during pedaling at 60 rpm was the same at a power output of 166 W as it was during pedaling at 120 rpm at 85 W, indicating that for the same amount of oxygen used, their subject could produce nearly twice as much power at the lower cadence. Eckermann and Millahn (1967) and Gueli and Shephard (1976) showed comparable results in both $\dot{V}O_2$ and heart rate. These studies are all in agreement that low pedal rates tend to be more economical than high ones.

More recent studies have yielded some evidence for higher optimal pedal rates in certain cases, though. Hagberg, Mullin, Giese, and Spitznagel (1981) had national-class cyclists ride their own bicycles on a treadmill at 20 mph and a 2.5 to 4.5% incline. The subjects rode at their preferred pedal rate and at pedal rates above and below the preferred frequency. Their $\dot{V}O_2$, blood lactate, and ventilation all exhibited U-shaped relationships with pedal rate, and the minimum (optimum) occurred at a pedal rate near the preferred cadence, which averaged 91 rpm. Further examination of the data indicates that the optimum cadence appears to be slightly lower than 91 rpm, closer to 80 rpm. Regardless of the actual cadence, however, this study was one of the first to provide evidence of a most economical cadence that was much higher than the typical 50 to 60 rpm. At least three variables could account for the difference between the results of this study and those of previous investigators. These are the power output used, which averaged approximately 300 W; the skill or training level of the cyclists, who were probably accustomed to the high cadences; and the use of a bicycle on a treadmill rather than a cycle ergometer, which may have different inertial characteristics.

Other Factors Affecting Efficiency and Cadence Optimization

The effect of power output on the measured optimal cadence has been studied by several researchers. Seabury, Adams, and Ramey (1977) found that if power output increased from 82 to 196 W, the metabolically optimum cadence increased from 42 to 58 rpm. Böning, Gönen, and Maassen (1984) showed that the pedal rate eliciting the lowest $\dot{V}O_2$ varied from about 40 rpm at 50 W to about 70 rpm at 200 W power output. Still, the highest optimal pedal rate reported was only about 70 rpm, much lower than that found in the study by Hagberg, Mullin, Giese, and Spitznagel (1981) and that used by competitive cyclists. Work from our laboratory (Coast & Welch, 1985) yielded higher pedal rates than these. Subjects rode at cadences ranging from 40 to 120 rpm at power outputs up to 330 W. At a power output of 100 W, the pedal rate yielding the lowest heart rate or $\dot{V}O_2$ was approximately 50 rpm. This increased to approximately 80 rpm when the power output was 300 W, agreeing with the data of Hagberg and colleagues (1981) as well as much of the data gathered at the lower power outputs. Therefore, the contribution of power output to the determination of optimal cadence appears to be very important, and represents one of the key differences between the research of Hagberg and colleagues (1981) and earlier work.

Some also regard the skill level and experience of the rider as important in the determination of optimal cadence. Since cyclists train at high pedal rates, it seems reasonable that they would be most efficient at those pedal rates as well. This phenomenon is referred to as contextual dependence (Wright & Shea, 1991), and it suggests that people perform motor tasks best under the contexts in which they have learned the tasks. In cycling, this has not been studied to any great extent, however. Böning, Gönen, and Maassen (1984) showed that the physiological responses of trained cyclists and untrained subjects did not differ in relation to cadence; the two groups showed similar quantitative and qualitative responses to changes in pedal rate. We (Coast, Cox, & Welch, 1986) found that the perceived exertion was lowest at a slightly higher cadence than were the $\dot{V}O_2$ or the heart rate values. Part of this difference could be explained by the contextual-dependent learning effect of training at high pedal rates. Recent work by Marsh and Martin (1993) also argued against experience influencing optimal cadence. Therefore, efforts should probably be concentrated in other areas, to be described.

The differences in the use of the cycle ergometer versus the bicycle on a treadmill may also contribute to an artificial difference in the determined optimal pedal rate. Gregor, Broker, and Ryan (1991) suggest that this may be part of the reason why Hagberg and coworkers (1981) were able to find higher optimal pedal rates than were other researchers. While this may be a factor in the differences seen, studies in our laboratory using wind-load simulators with subjects' bicycles mounted on them showed pedal rate optima comparable to those found on the cycle ergometer. This, however, is only preliminary data, and further studies need to be conducted to evaluate the possible differences between the two testing modes.

All of the work cited thus far has used heart rate or oxygen consumption as the indicator of optimal pedal rate, with the assumption that the most economical pedal rate from the standpoint of these whole body metabolic factors is the optimum pedal rate. This assumption, then, places the primary importance in cycling optimization on the ability of the cardiovascular and respiratory systems to deliver oxygen to the muscles and the ability of the muscles to use that oxygen to produce energy. This is, indeed, a critical factor in events demanding near-maximal power outputs, and will be discussed later in the chapter. However, a number of other considerations may be important in pedal rate optimization. One issue that many cyclists raise is that pedaling at slow cadences hurts the knees and legs. This may be the case because at a constant power output, pedal force and cadence are inversely related, and pedaling at low rates requires high muscle forces. Therefore, a factor related to muscle and joint stress may be important in determining optimal pedal rate.

Biomechanical Optimization Estimates

The group led by M.L. Hull at the University of California-Davis has been active in the biomechanical examination of cadence. They reasoned that one of the factors that should be optimized during cycling is the effort and fatigue of the muscles propelling the rider. If such is the case, the combination of muscle stresses and joint torques should be at a minimum at the optimal pedal rate (Redfield & Hull, 1986a). Using force and angular data measurements from a pedal transducer, these investigators calculated that joint moments for the hip and knee were minimal at a cadence of about 105 rpm, very similar to the pedal rates used by competitive cyclists. This finding led them to the conclusion that whole body energetics, as measured by VO_2, were not very important in the selection of an optimal cadence. They further showed that when muscle stresses were added into the equation, the results were similar, with calculated pedal rate optima at 95 to 100 rpm (Hull, Gonzalez, & Redfield, 1988).

The work of Hull and his group has implicated the muscles and joints in pedal rate optimization. Others who have worked on this topic have used the concept of internal work to evaluate cadence (Kaneko, Yamazaki, & Toyooka, 1979; Widrick, Freedson, & Hamill, 1992). Internal work is the change in the total (potential + translational kinetic + rotational kinetic) energy of the limb segments across time (Widrick, Freedson, & Hamill, 1992), or the energy used in moving the limbs. This factor may be important because the legs move more times at higher cadences, and thus more energy gets used just to move the legs before any external work is accomplished. Because the work of moving the legs increases with increased pedal rate, the total work of cycling (external + internal) is not the same at different pedal rates. When these two work measurements are summed, the total power output increases with increased pedal rate, even though the external power stays constant. Under these conditions, the cadence at which the $\dot{V}O_2$ is lowest at a constant external power output is different from the optimal cadence measured when external power is used alone. Widrick and colleagues (1992) estimated the optimal pedal rate to be approximately 80 to 100 rpm at external power outputs of 50 to 150 W; again these cadences are similar to those used by competitive cyclists.

From most of the biomechanical studies, it appears that optimal cadence is high and that cyclists who use pedal rates of 100 rpm and higher are using muscle work or muscle and joint stress and strain as the key factor in optimization of pedal rate. Such an optimization technique makes good sense in certain instances, perhaps particularly in long events, where muscle fatigue becomes an important factor in finishing a race, let alone finishing it strongly. It may also be important in events in which rapid acceleration is needed and the force required to accelerate in a high gear might be greater than the force the muscle is capable of producing. We will discuss this later in the chapter.

Perceived Exertion

The arguments about which factors may be important in optimizing pedal rate have centered on rather narrow categories thus far—metabolic rate and muscle and joint stress. It can be logically argued that these two elements probably are the two most important variables we need to consider when choosing a cadence; but is there a measurement we can make that takes both of these factors into account? One possible method is to use perceived exertion. This technique, developed by Borg (1970), uses a scale from 6 to 20 (newer ones use 1 to 10) with written cues next to the numbers to let subjects evaluate how physically difficult a task is. Perceived exertion is generally thought to reflect metabolic (cardiovascular and respiratory) exertion as well as muscle exertion.

Several investigators have evaluated the relationship between perceived exertion and pedal rate, with differing results. Stamford and Noble (1974) asked trained subjects ($\dot{V}O_2$max = 61.7 ml $\cdot$ kg^{-1} $\cdot$ min^{-1}) to ride a cycle ergometer at a constant power output using pedaling rates of 40, 60, and 80 rpm. They found no difference in heart rate, $\dot{V}O_2$, or ventilation, but did find that perceived exertion was highest at 40 rpm and lowest at 60 rpm. They concluded that perceived exertion did not necessarily follow metabolic cost but that limb feedback might have had an input into the rating. Although their finding of a similar metabolic cost at different pedal rates is different from that of other investigators (Dickinson, 1929; Eckermann & Millahn, 1967; Hagberg, Mullin, Giese, & Spitznagel, 1981), it must be noted that few studies have shown large differences between the metabolic costs at 40, 60, and 80 rpm. Most found that large cost increases begin above 80 rpm. Therefore, the report by Stamford and Noble (1974) of similar metabolic responses should not be considered problematic.

Lollgen, Ulmer, Gross, Wilbert, and Meding (1975) found that both trained and untrained subjects preferred higher cadences, as judged by the perceived exertion, and that the preferred cadence increased as the power output increased. In a study from our laboratory (Coast, Cox, & Welch, 1986), the minimum perceived exertion occurred at a slightly higher pedal rate than did the minimum $\dot{V}O_2$ or heart rate during cycling at an average power output of slightly less than 300 W (85% $\dot{V}O_2$max). While the perceived exertion tended toward a higher pedal rate than did the $\dot{V}O_2$, it was still not optimized at levels as high as those used by cyclists on a routine basis.

Taken together, these studies indicate that in certain cases, perceived exertion may track very closely to the metabolic rate, while in other cases it more closely approximates the strain in the legs. Thus perceived exertion may be a good indicator of both central and peripheral exertion, as has been suggested. To some extent, this summation of peripheral and central signals is what really happens during a cycling event. You will see riders often go to a very high gear and a slightly lower pedal rate when they are in front of the pack or attempting to catch up to the peloton, maybe in an attempt to optimize central (metabolic) exertion. Yet when riders are in the middle of the pack, they will often shift to a slightly lower gear and "spin" more, maybe in an attempt to lessen fatigue in the legs or soreness in the hips and knees.

Can We Optimize Cadence?

Again, the optimization of pedal rate appears to be a rather complicated process, with the demands of the legs and those of the cardiovascular and respiratory systems coming into conflict. It has been common to think of optimization in terms of efficiency. Strictly speaking, efficiency is simply the ratio of the useful work performed to the energy used to perform that work. This is referred to as gross efficiency (Gaesser & Brooks, 1975):

$$\text{Gross efficiency} = \frac{\text{Work done}}{\text{Energy used}} \times 100.$$

(5.1)

To improve our gross efficiency, we could decrease the energy used to perform a task and thus perhaps increase the amount of time we could work before fatiguing. This is what many people think of when they think of improved efficiency and is similar to the concept of efficiency ratings for automobiles, that is, the idea that the efficient car gets more miles to the gallon of gasoline. However, if we increase the work done without increasing the energy used, we will also increase efficiency. Therefore, anything that improves efficiency is important in cycling optimization. When we change the pedal rate and raise or lower the $\dot{V}O_2$, we are changing efficiency. This is because $\dot{V}O_2$, which is the main indicator we use to measure energy production (1 L $O_2 \approx 5$ kcal), changes while the external power output remains constant. All of the studies cited thus far, by measuring $\dot{V}O_2$ or heart rate during cycling at a constant speed or power output, essentially measured gross efficiency. As we saw earlier, most of the studies have found that the lowest $\dot{V}O_2$ (highest efficiency) tends to occur at a pedal rate of about 50 to 60 rpm, with some studies showing most efficient cadences at an rpm as high as 80.

There are other estimates of efficiency, however, that reflect more than simply the energy input of a subject and the work that subject can perform. One common efficiency estimate is termed *work efficiency* (Gaesser & Brooks, 1975). The equation for work efficiency is

$$\text{Work efficiency} = \frac{\text{Work done}}{\text{Energy used} - \text{Energy used at 0 load}} \times 100.$$

(5.2)

This estimate of efficiency takes into consideration the energy we use to just move the legs, by subtracting that from the total energy used during the exercise task. In this way, work efficiency accounts for some or all of the internal work. Many researchers believe that work efficiency more closely approximates the efficiency of the muscles doing work by eliminating the energy used to maintain the body and move the limbs and including only the energy needed to perform useful work. Several investigators have specifically examined the effect of pedal rate on work efficiency versus gross efficiency. Garry and Wishart (1931), in addition to calculating the gross efficiency, also subtracted the cost of no-load cycling and found that the minimal energy cost of pedaling at a constant power output went from about 50 rpm to approximately 90 rpm. When data from our laboratory (Coast & Welch, 1985) are reworked to take into account the cost of unloaded cycling, the findings are similar. Rather than optimal pedal rates of 50 to 80 rpm, the minimum energy cost is in the range of 90 to 110 rpm. Analogous results can also be derived from other studies if the cost of unloaded pedaling is known. This has been done in Figure 5.1 for a number of studies.

The low point on the lines in the upper graph ranges from about 40 to 80 rpm. This is as discussed earlier; the oxygen consumption (gross

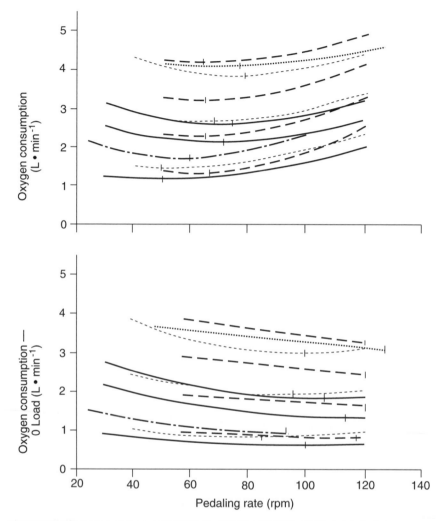

Figure 5.1 Oxygen consumption versus pedal rate from several studies. The upper graph shows oxygen consumption, an indicator of gross efficiency. The lower graph is the oxygen consumption after the oxygen cost of unloaded pedaling is subtracted, indicating work efficiency. The vertical marks indicate the minima, or most efficient, cadences. — — from Banister and Jackson (1967); ------ from Coast and Welch (1985); —··— from Garry and Wishart (1931); ············from Hagberg, Mullin, Giese, and Spitznagel (1981); and ———— from Seabury, Adams, and Ramey (1977).

efficiency) is optimal at relatively low pedal rates. In addition, it is fairly clear that at the higher oxygen consumption levels, which indicate higher power outputs, the optimal pedal rate is higher. The lower graph reflects the oxygen consumption after removal of the $\dot{V}O_2$ related to unloaded cycling; this is equivalent to the calculation of work efficiency. The minimum points are at much higher pedal rates—80 to 120 rpm and above. The optimal cadences are also not as closely related to the energy cost of the task as are the optimal pedal rates obtained using gross efficiency.

If, as suggested by past investigators, the gross efficiency is a good indicator of whole body stress, and the work efficiency is a good indicator of muscle work and stress, then one could expect that the difference between gross and work efficiency might explain the differences between what the cyclists do and what the researchers say. An explanation along these lines would be the following:

For events in which the concern is to maximize the power output for a specific amount of time, we would choose to optimize using gross efficiency (estimated by $\dot{V}O_2$ or heart rate). The prototypical event for such an approach would be the 40-km time trial. In this event, the goal of the rider is to maintain the highest possible speed for approximately 1 hr. The duration of the time trial dictates that the event is aerobic in nature, and the strategy for a successful performance dictates that the rider does not speed up and slow down repeatedly over the course of the race. Therefore, the limiting factor becomes the maximal ability to deliver and use oxygen ($\dot{V}O_2$max) and the highest percentage of $\dot{V}O_2$max at which the rider can perform for the duration of the ride. A study by Coyle et al. (1991) showed that elite cyclists could ride for 40 km at approximately 85 to 90% $\dot{V}O_2$max. From the figure, we see that if pedal rate is increased from 80 rpm to an rpm of 100 to 110, the oxygen consumption increases by as much as 5 to 10%. This would be unacceptable to a person already riding at 90% of $\dot{V}O_2$max. Therefore, time trial pedal rate might be optimized by gross efficiency.

On the other hand, for events in which we would have a lower power output for a longer period of time, or in which accelerating is important, it might be best to optimize using work efficiency or a combination of the two measurements. In such a case the limiting factor for a highly trained cyclist will not be the $\dot{V}O_2$max, but rather fatigue of the muscles and the ability to react to situations (corners, breakaways, etc.) and accelerate quickly enough to not get dropped. In these cases, the stress on the muscles and joints and the forces that the muscles must exert are critical factors, and pedal rate might be optimized by work efficiency, which seems to take muscle activity into consideration.

Optimizing Cadence in the Real World

These arguments may make some sense academically, but how do they work in the real world of cycling and bicycle racing? In the real world, cyclists do not ride a cycle ergometer at a constant pedal rate and a constant power output for a specified amount of time so that $\dot{V}O_2$ or heart rate can be measured. In the real world there are hills, wind, rough roads, and other riders, all altering the power that we must exert to maintain a constant speed, or alternatively, the speed we can maintain if we keep a constant power output. Yet there is some evidence that cyclists may optimize differently in the different situations of a time trial and a mass-start road race or criterium. The time trial is notable as an event in which riders use very high gears. In the 40-km time trial, times of 51 min and less are now relatively commonplace at the national level, and times in the range of 47 min are not unheard of. At the same time, front chainrings of 54 or more teeth and rear cogs of 13 or fewer teeth are generally the gears of choice for the flat straight sections of the race. These combinations result in low pedal rates, as can be seen in Table 5.1.

With only one exception, all of these cadences, using common gearing, fall at rates lower than those commonly considered optimal in bicycling, and are consistent with the concept that the optimal cadence is related to the power output of the riders. Exceptions to these examples can easily be found in certain time trial riders, but many successful time trial riders do pedal at these rates. One reason the optimal pedal rates in laboratory experiments agree with those used in the time trial is probably that tests performed in the laboratory mimic time trials in many

Table 5.1 Common Gears and National Level Times for the 40-km (24.83 mile) Time Trial

Finish time and average speed (min mph kph)			Gear used (Front teeth Rear teeth)		Pedal rate (rpm)
52	28.6	46.2	54	12	79.2
			54	13	85.8
50	29.8	48.0	55	12	80.9
			54	13	89.2
48	31.0	50.0	55	12	84.2

Note. All pedal rates have been calculated assuming a rear wheel with a 27-in. (68.58 cm) diameter. The choice of gearing used for calculations was that of the author on the basis of literature and communication with riders. The equation used to calculate average pedal rate is:

$$\frac{\text{Average pedal}}{\text{rate (rpm)}} = \frac{\text{Distance (miles)} \times 63360 \text{ (in./mile)} \div \text{race time (min)}}{\text{Wheel circumference (in.)} \times \text{\# front teeth} \div \text{\# rear teeth}}$$

ways. Typical American time trials are raced on out-and-back courses with relatively few corners or hills. This course layout lends itself to the maintenance of a constant high power output and presents few interruptions that would necessitate changing gears or pedal rates; this situation is similar to those seen in laboratories, where riders are often asked to pedal at a constant power output for a certain period of time while physiological variables are measured. Thus we may optimize on the basis of whole body $\dot{V}O_2$ and external power output, as has been demonstrated most often in the laboratory.

What about cases in the real world where higher pedal rates may be optimal? As we have seen, according to the work efficiency criterion, high pedal rates should be optimal in cases where muscle forces or joint stresses would be high, such as races with many cycles of acceleration and deceleration. Alternatively, high cadences might also be optimal in situations in which specific muscle fatigue could be a factor in exercise limitation. Such would be the case in a race of long duration, where the absolute power output is not as high because riders work in groups or work at a slower speed than during shorter races; but the use of lower pedal rates with higher gears might cause undue stress and fatigue in races lasting longer than the typical 1 hr of a 40-km time trial and render the rider unable to perform well toward the end of the race. This, too, is a common occurrence in racing. The races in which higher cadences are used are the criteriums and road races. In these races, the riders have high gears when they need them but commonly work in a lower gear and at a higher pedal rate. For example, a rider averaging 25 mph using a 54×17 gear (common during a race) would pedal at 98 rpm. The advantage of using a higher cadence in these cases may lie in the decreased leg fatigue, as advocated by a number of researchers, or it might be that the higher cadence and lower gear allow for a more rapid acceleration out of corners or in response to attacks during a race. These cases are more difficult to mimic in the laboratory in order to get objective data, however. Most estimates of efficiency rely on the sustained production of energy and performance of work, and not intermittent periods of high and low power output. This is an area that needs to be explored further, possibly with the use of a combination of physiological and biomechanical methods to obtain a simultaneous measurement for optimization.

Directions for Future Research

Clearly, the study of pedal rate optimization, and of cycling optimization in general, has not progressed to a point where we know what an optimal pedal rate is or even what the critical factors are for determining optimal cycling cadence. From this brief review it should be obvious that both metabolic cost and muscle and joint strain or fatigue play a role. Advocates of both aspects of this optimization question have placed their data in the literature and have arrived at two (or more) answers about the optimal pedal rate.

Future work may be able to combine these techniques. The concept of optimization modeling in cycling has been discussed clearly by Gregor, Broker, and Ryan (1991), with the emphasis on evaluation of joint and muscle force and stress as performed by Hull's group. With the sophisticated modeling techniques of today, it should be possible to add metabolic cost data to the joint moment and muscle stress data to further narrow the estimates we can make. When this is done, it may be possible to predict how a rider will react in a training ride with few hills or corners versus a criterium race with four corners per kilometer, among many other situations.

From there, methods should be developed to test these models in the laboratory. The combination of metabolic and biomechanical optimization techniques, as well as understanding of the physical properties of pendulum motion that might be adopted by swinging limb segments, has been adapted to walking and running stride length and frequency with encouraging results (Holt, Hamill, & Andres, 1991). Cycling research may need to employ some of these techniques in cadence optimization. For cycling, new equipment allows cyclists to ride their own bicycles on trainers that are capable of both measuring the power output and changing the power requirements at various intervals. Instruments such as these, already in use in some laboratories (see Coyle et al., 1992), may be the principal tool for sport-specific laboratory testing of cyclists in the future.

When these techniques have been developed, applications may be made to the other areas popular in cycling. Two areas that may provide useful bases for study are cycle touring and off-road riding. Cycle touring is characterized by relatively long periods of riding at slower speeds (compared to racing). However, the load on the bicycle necessitates the output of more power to accomplish the task than would be required on an unloaded bicycle. Off-road riding and racing are relatively new in the sport of cycling, but are rapidly growing. The demands in this sport incorporate brief bursts of high-intensity effort with long "grinding" uphill climbs. Techniques are beginning to be developed to test off-road riding in a controlled laboratory setting (Berry, Woodard, Dunn, Edwards, & Pittman, 1993). Therefore these are areas into which cycling research in general and optimization techniques specifically need to be expanded.

References

Banister, E.W., & Jackson, R.C. (1967). The effect of speed and load changes on oxygen intake for equivalent power outputs during bicycle ergometry. *International Zeitschrift fur angewandte Physiologie,* **24**, 284-290.

Benedict, F.G., & Cathcart, E.P. (1913). *Muscular work.* Washington, DC: Carnegie Institute. (Publication #187)

Berry, M.J., Woodard, C.M., Dunn, C.J., Edwards, D.G., & Pittman, C.L. (1993). The effects of a mountain bike suspension system on metabolic energy expenditure. *Cycling Science,* **5**, 8-14.

Böning, D., Gönen, Y., & Maassen, N. (1984). Relationship between work load, pedal frequency, and physical fitness. *International Journal of Sports Medicine,* **5**, 92-97.

Borg, G. (1970). Perceived exertion as an indicator of somatic stress. *Scandinavian Journal of Rehabilitative Medicine,* **2**(3), 92-98.

Cathcart, E.P., Richardson, D.T., & Campbell, W. (1924). Studies in muscle activity. II. The influence of speed on the mechanical efficiency. *Journal of Physiology,* **58**, 355-361.

Coast, J.R., Cox, R.H., & Welch, H.G. (1986). Optimal pedalling rate in prolonged bouts of cycle ergometry. *Medicine and Science in Sports and Exercise,* **18**, 225-230.

Coast, J.R., & Welch, H.G. (1985). Linear increase in optimal pedal rate with increased power output in cycle ergometry. *European Journal of Applied Physiology,* **53**, 339-342.

Coyle, E.F., Feltner, M.E., Kautz, S.A., Hamilton, M.T., Montain, S.J., Baylor, A.M., Abraham, L.D., & Petrek, G.W. (1991). Physiological and biomechanical factors associated with elite endurance cycling performance. *Medicine and Science in Sports and Exercise,* **23**, 93-107.

Dickinson, S. (1929). The efficiency of bicycle-pedalling, as affected by speed and load. *Journal of Physiology,* **67**, 242-255.

Eckermann, P., & Millahn, H.P. (1967). Der einfluß der drezahl auf die herzfrequenz und die sauerstoffaufnahme bei konstanter leistung am fahrradergometer [The effect of pedalling rate on heart rate and oxygen uptake with constant power on the bicycle ergometer]. *International Zeitschrift fur angewandte Physiologie,* **23**, 340-344.

Gaesser, G.A., & Brooks, G.A. (1975). Muscular efficiency during steady-rate exercise: Effects of speed and work rate. *Journal of Applied Physiology,* **38**, 1132-1139.

Garry, R.C., & Wishart, G.M. (1931). On the existence of a most efficient speed in bicycle pedalling, and the problem of determining human muscular efficiency. *Journal of Physiology,* **72**, 425-437.

Gregor, R.J., Broker, J.P., & Ryan, M.M. (1991). The biomechanics of cycling. *Exercise and Sport Science Reviews*, **19**, 127-169.

Gueli, D., & Shephard, R.J. (1976). Pedal frequency in bicycle ergometry. *Canadian Journal of Applied Sport Science*, **1**, 137-141.

Hagberg, J.M., Mullin, J.P., Giese, M.D., & Spitznagel, E. (1981). Effect of pedaling rate on submaximal exercise responses of competitive cyclists. *Journal of Applied Physiology*, **51**, 447-451.

Holt, K.G., Hamill, J., & Andres, R.O. (1991). Predicting the minimal energy costs of human walking. *Medicine and Science in Sports and Exercise*, **23**, 491-498.

Hull, M.L., Gonzalez, H.K., & Redfield, R. (1988). Optimization of pedalling rate in cycling using a muscle stress-based objective function. *International Journal of Sport Biomechanics*, **4**, 1-20.

Kaneko, M., Yamazaki, T., & Toyooka, J. (1979). Direct determination of the internal work and the efficiency in bicycle pedalling. *Journal of the Physiological Society of Japan*, **41**, 68-69.

Lollgen, H., Ulmer, H.V., Gross, R., Wilbert, G., & Meding, G.V. (1975). Methodical aspects of perceived exertion rating and its relation to pedaling rate and rotating mass. *European Journal of Applied Physiology*, **34**, 205-215.

Marsh, A.P., & Martin, P.E. (1993). The association between cycling experience and preferred and most economical cadences. *Medicine and Science in Sports and Exercise*, **25**, 1269-1274.

Redfield, R., & Hull, M.L. (1986a). On the relation between joint moments and pedalling rates at constant power in bicycling. *Journal of Biomechanics*, **19**, 317-329.

Redfield, R., & Hull, M.L. (1986b). Prediction of pedal forces in bicycling using optimization methods. *Journal of Biomechanics*, **19**, 523-540.

Seabury, J.J., Adams, W.C., & Ramey, M.R. (1977). Influence of pedalling rate and power output on energy expenditure during bicycle ergometry. *Ergonomics*, **20**, 491-498.

Stamford, B.A., & Noble, B.J. (1974). Metabolic cost and perception of effort during bicycle ergometer work performance. *Medicine and Science in Sports*, **6**, 226-231.

Widrick, J.J., Freedson, P.S., & Hamill, J. (1992). Effect of internal work on the calculation of optimal pedaling rates. *Medicine and Science in Sports and Exercise*, **24**, 376-382.

Wright, D.L., & Shea, C.H. (1991). Contextual dependencies in motor skills. *Memory and Cognition*, **19**, 361-370.

Cycling Optimization Analysis

Steve A. Kautz, PhD • Maury L. Hull, PhD

Biomechanists and cyclists alike have long been interested in determining the optimal equipment adjustment for a cyclist. Whereas some studies have addressed this question experimentally, this chapter reviews a theoretical technique called analytical optimization that has been used in an attempt to determine the answer. Analytical optimization studies in cycling have used mathematical models of pedaling to systematically investigate the contribution to cycling performance of different biomechanical variables, either alone or in combination.

The concept of a motion cycle—the repetitive motion of the legs during steady state pedaling—is central to understanding the potential for improvements in cycling performance through optimization analyses. The path of the foot and its instantaneous velocity along that path determine the motion cycle. Thus, geometric variables adjusted in the setup of the bicycle-rider system, such as seat height, and variables associated with the angular velocity of the crank, such as cadence, affect the motion cycle.

Several geometry variables related to the bicycle affect the kinematics of the leg during pedaling, and hence the biomechanics of cycling. Crank arm length, seat height, seat tube angle, pedal platform height, and longitudinal foot position on the pedal affect cycling biomechanics because the geometry of the cyclist-bicycle setup practically determines the joint angle trajectories at the hip and knee (the trajectory of the knee joint is the time history of the amount that the knee is flexed as the crank completes one revolution). Nordeen and Cavanagh (1976) found "fairly good agreement" between measured and predicted trajectories of both the hip and knee angles for four subjects (maximum differences about 7°) using simulations based on the geometry of the cyclist-bicycle setup. Thus, the range of motion of the ankle and the anatomical constraints of the leg effectively limit the extent to which hip and knee angle trajectories can vary, and the cyclist largely establishes the kinematics of the legs during seated cycling by adjusting the geometry variables during equipment setup. Optimization studies seek to determine the optimal equipment setup.

In addition to bicycle geometry, foot path and foot velocity may also lend themselves to further optimization. Although infinite alternatives exist for the path and velocity of the foot, if attention is restricted to the case where the foot travels in the conventional circular path, then the potential optimization variable becomes the foot velocity. Foot velocity may be either constant during the cycle or continuously varying. For constant velocity, the cadence is the primary variable for optimization, whereas the instantaneous velocity can be optimized when the velocity is varying. Although a variety of mechanisms might vary the foot velocity during the cycle, the simplest is the chainring geometry, which induces variations in the angular velocity of the crank arm. While this mechanism constrains the range of practical velocities, its advantages of mechanical simplicity and light weight are appealing.

Chainring geometry alters cycling mechanics by affecting the higher-order kinematics (velocity and acceleration) of pedaling, such as peak knee extension velocity during the downstroke at a particular average cadence. The large bicycle-rider system inertia results in a relatively constant rear wheel angular velocity during steady state cycling, and, as a result, the changing instantaneous chainring radius causes crank angular velocity fluctuations. Therefore, how fast the hip and knee joints extend and flex for a given average cadence is determined predominantly by the instantaneous chainring radius profile. The complex musculoskeletal geometry of the legs, as well as the internal dynamic properties of the muscles that cause the movement, suggests that a noncircular chainring shape might improve cycling performance relative to a circular chainring.

The first step in the search for increased performance using analytical optimization methodologies is to derive a mathematical model of cycling. Most studies have focused on steady state endurance cycling, similar to a time trial, where the cyclist remains seated. For such an analysis, the mathematical model commonly used represents the legs as planar five-bar linkages where the links are defined as the crank arm, foot, shank, thigh, and a fixed link connecting the crank center and the hip joint center (Figure 6.1). Frictionless hinge joints at the hip, knee, ankle, and the bottom bracket are assumed to connect the links.

Analytical Optimization Approaches

There are two principal approaches to analytical optimization in cycling, dependent on whether the mathematical model is formulated through use of the inverse or the forward dynamics equations of motion. An inverse dynamics-based model uses the observed pedaling motion and pedal forces (considered here as "outputs" of our cycling leg system) as input data to calculate the net joint torques (considered here as the "inputs" that produce the motion) developed by the muscles, whereas a forward dynamics-based model directly uses the net joint torques (the "inputs") to calculate the pedaling motion ("output") that would result (Figure 6.2). A net joint torque quantifies the torque (tendency of an applied force to cause rotation about a specified axis) produced by all structures spanning a particular joint axis. Net joint torques indicate predominantly the active torque produced by muscular forces when away from the extremes of the joint range of motion, where forces created by ligaments and other passive structures may

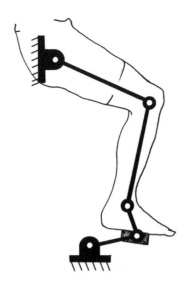

Figure 6.1 Sagittal view of five-bar linkage model of leg commonly used in optimization analyses. Links are the crank, foot, shank, thigh, and bicycle (fixed link connecting hip and crank center). The foot link is an imaginary line connecting the ankle and pedal spindle, and not the actual foot segment. The model assumes that the motion is constrained to one plane, that the hip is fixed, and that the knee joint cannot extend past the straight leg position.

create significant passive torques (Andrews, 1982). For example, the net joint torque at the knee mainly represents the active muscular effort that is trying to cause either flexion or extension at the knee. Thus, the net joint torques are important quantities because they provide one of the only biomechanically quantifiable noninvasive measures of the underlying muscular effort.

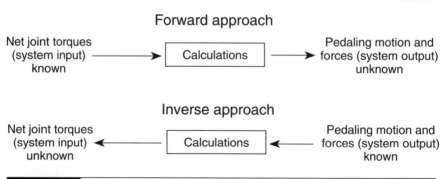

Figure 6.2 Forward versus inverse dynamics approaches to optimization.

Inverse Dynamics-Based Techniques

Most analytical optimization studies of cycling have used an inverse dynamics-based technique. Inverse dynamics-based optimization analyses require four separate empirical relationships from experimental data:

1. The higher-order crank kinematics (angular velocity and acceleration) as a function of crank angle (often simplified by assuming constant crank angular velocity)

2. The pedal kinematics (angle, angular velocity, and angular acceleration) as a function of crank angle

3. The applied pedal force as a function of crank angle

4. The position of the hip joint center as a function of crank angle (usually simplified by assuming a fixed hip joint center)

Using these relationships, geometric variables (like crank length) and biomechanical variables (like cadence) are systematically varied and the required net joint torques are calculated (this provides an estimate of the necessary muscular effort).

For example, an inverse dynamics-based optimization of seat height would be performed as follows (Figure 6.3). An initial guess for the seat height would be made. Then the kinematics of the pedaling motion would be calculated from the mathematical model of pedaling using that seat height, in conjunction with the anthropometric parameters, geometry of the bicycle, and empirical relationships for crank and pedal kinematics and hip joint position. Next the net joint torques would be calculated by using the kinematics of the legs and the empirically determined pedal forces. Then the cost would be evaluated through use of the cost function (a cost function ascribes a cost to the performance so that performances can be compared and the best performance found). In this example, the cost function would be derived from the net joint torques because these provide some estimate of muscular effort. Finally, an optimization algorithm would calculate a next guess for seat height, repeating these steps until the seat height resulting in minimum cost was found.

Forward Dynamics-Based Techniques

In addition to inverse dynamics-based optimization techniques, dynamic optimization techniques have been used in cycling studies. The main difference is that dynamic optimization is a forward dynamics approach. In cycling, the dynamic optimization problem is to find the

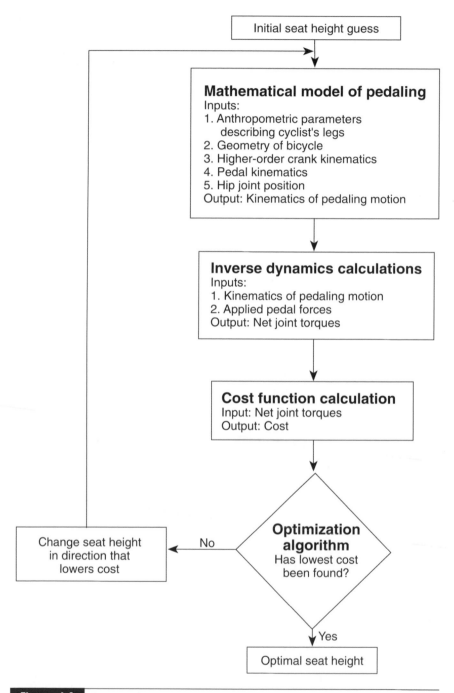

Initial seat height guess

Mathematical model of pedaling
Inputs:
1. Anthropometric parameters
   describing cyclist's legs
2. Geometry of bicycle
3. Higher-order crank kinematics
4. Pedal kinematics
5. Hip joint position
Output: Kinematics of pedaling motion

Inverse dynamics calculations
Inputs:
1. Kinematics of pedaling motion
2. Applied pedal forces
Output: Net joint torques

Cost function calculation
Input: Net joint torques
Output: Cost

Optimization algorithm
Has lowest cost been found?

Change seat height in direction that lowers cost

No

Yes

Optimal seat height

Figure 6.3 Inverse dynamics-based optimization.

optimal joint torques so that the crank completes one steady state revolution at the proper cadence at minimal cost (Figure 6.4). For the case of optimizing seat height just considered, the dynamic optimization problem would be performed as follows. An initial guess of the seat height and net joint torques would be made. Next the kinematics of the pedaling motion would be calculated from the forward dynamics model of pedaling using the seat height and net joint torques, in conjunction with the anthropometric parameters, geometry of the bicycle, and an empirical relationship for the hip joint position. Then the cost would be evaluated through use of the cost function. Finally, an optimization algorithm would calculate a next guess for seat height and net joint torques, repeating the steps described until the seat height resulting in minimum cost was found that did not violate the constraints. Checking for constraint violation to determine whether the steady state pedaling condition was achieved is usually performed within the optimization algorithm, as most algorithms have been programmed to handle constrained optimization problems. Therefore, the major difference between the two techniques is that the dynamic optimization approach can eliminate the need for empirical relationships for the crank and pedal kinematics and the applied pedal force.

Definition of Cost Function

The concept of the cost function is fundamental to understanding analytical optimization. A cost function is a mathematical expression that rates the performance of the pedaling movement by assigning a numerical value. Thus, a movement that has a lower value of the cost function is considered to produce a superior performance. The most physically meaningful measure of endurance cycling performance would be the time to complete a time trial on a given course under standardized conditions, because completing the same course in a faster time after adjusting a variable would clearly provide experimental verification of improved performance. Since such a measure of performance is not practical for theoretical studies, the cost function must try to rate the overall performance in a different manner. Cost functions based on observations of a single revolution of pedaling are usually used to evaluate the cycling performance because endurance cycling is assumed to be a steady state activity in which one revolution can suitably represent the overall performance.

A combined physiological and biomechanical study of cycling showed that the absolute rate of oxygen consumption at lactate threshold ($\dot{V}O_2$ at LT) was the best predictor of performance for a sample of national and

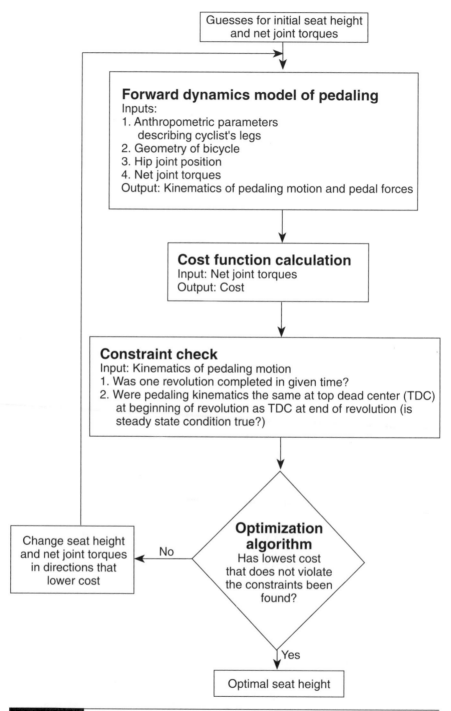

Figure 6.4 Forward dynamics-based optimization.

state level 40-km time trialists (Coyle et al., 1991). Although the cyclists were able to ride above $\dot{V}O_2$ at LT during a 1-hr laboratory simulated time trial, the correlation of $\dot{V}O_2$ at LT with performance implied that there was a maximum energy expenditure rate for the cyclist that was related to $\dot{V}O_2$ at LT. Assuming a maximum energy expenditure rate, improved efficiency (external work done/energy consumed) would lead directly to increased performance. Unfortunately, efficiency is very difficult to predict in human movements (Cavanagh & Kram, 1985) in large part because of the problems in measuring the mechanical work associated with muscular effort and its corresponding energetic cost. However, a suitable measure of efficiency would be a prime candidate for a cost function (optimization problems can easily be formulated to find a maximum performance instead of a minimum).

Optimization studies of endurance cycling have predominantly used cost functions derived from the net joint torques. As mentioned previously, a net joint torque indicates the torque produced by muscular effort away from the extremes of the joint range of motion. The cost function in the first optimization study was the sum of the squares of the net joint torques of the leg (Redfield & Hull, 1986a). The net joint torques were squared because then positive and negative values could not cancel, and squaring the terms in the cost function is a commonly used approach that makes the optimization problem easier to solve than a similar approach such as taking the absolute values.

A cost function based on muscular stress (muscle force divided by cross-sectional area), derived from the work of Crowninshield and Brand (1981), was used in a subsequent optimization study (Redfield & Hull, 1986b). Muscular stress is an appealing quantity on which to base a cost function because it is related to the capacity of each individual muscle for generating force, in that the stress in a larger muscle is lower than the stress in a smaller muscle when both create the same force. Muscular stress was calculated from the net joint torques by an algorithm that lumped muscles into functional groups reflecting muscle usage in cycling. Since many muscles in the leg are capable of producing force, there is no unique solution for the muscle force distribution causing a given set of net joint torques. The algorithm avoided the indeterminate muscle force distribution problem by limiting the number of muscles within the leg that were considered and by requiring fixed relationships between those that were considered (Redfield & Hull, 1986b). The muscular stress-based cost function predicted measured pedal forces and joint torques better than the joint torque-based cost function of Redfield and Hull (1986a).

Because the muscular stress-based and joint torque-based cost functions yielded similar predictions of optimal cadence, subsequent studies used a joint torque-based cost function to greatly simplify computations within the optimization. However, the torque-based cost function included only the torques at the hip and knee because experience showed that fatigue in the thigh muscles was a limiting factor in cycling. Hull and Gonzalez (1988) claimed that the hip and knee torque-based cost function was physiologically based and that it indicated muscle fatigue because of the direct relationship between the joint torque and the muscular stresses. The torques were squared because muscle fatigue was shown to be related to the muscle stress raised to a power between 1.5 and 5 (Crowninshield & Brand, 1981).

A torque-based cost function would seem to have received further validation in a study by Marshall, Wood, and Jennings (1989), who compared seven different cost functions during a portion of the walking cycle (while this differs from pedaling, it is a motion in which minimizing effort is thought to be similarly important). Citing the work of Williams and Cavanagh (1983), which emphasized accounting for differences between the costs of positive and negative work in evaluating power flow, Marshall and colleagues (1989) evaluated a torque-based cost function where the joint torques of the hip, knee, and ankle were reduced by a scale factor of one third whenever a joint torque represented negative work. This torque-based cost function was compared to cost functions based on several other quantities: total energy, the derivative of acceleration (jerk), linear acceleration of the head, muscle power at joints, and muscle power transfer. The investigators found that the torque-based cost function performed best. However, they cited the ability of other cost functions to better predict different aspects of the kinematics as a possible indication of multiple performance criteria acting simultaneously.

McLean and Lafortune (1991b) performed an experimental study of torque-based cost functions during cycling. They experimentally determined the cadence at which oxygen consumption measurements yielded the highest gross efficiency for a 200 W power output. They then compared this cadence to the cadence that gave the lowest value for five different torque-based cost functions:

1. Sum of the squared hip, knee, and ankle torques
2. Sum of the squared hip and knee torques
3. Sum of the squared hip torques
4. Sum of the squared knee torques
5. Sum of the squared ankle torques

The cadence that gave the lowest value of the sum of the squared knee torques (80.4 rpm) was the only one that was not different from the cadence that gave the highest gross efficiency (81.3 rpm). Thus, McLean and Lafortune (1991b) suggest that minimizing knee torque minimizes the physiological cost of cycling.

Conventional Motion Cycle

Inverse dynamics-based analytical optimization studies have investigated optimal cadence and nearly all of the variables related to the geometry of the bicycle. These investigations have studied the effects of single variables as well as interactions between multiple variables.

Optimization of Cadence

The first variable investigated in analytical optimization studies was cadence (Hull, Gonzalez, & Redfield, 1988; Redfield & Hull, 1986a). The analysis assumed that the velocity of the crank was constant, and representative relationships for the pedal kinematics and the pedal force were determined. The power output was kept constant by a simple linear scaling law that decreased the magnitude of the pedal force when the cadence increased. Then an inverse dynamics-based optimization routine varied the cadence and calculated the net joint torques. This procedure was repeated until the minimum value of the cost function was found at the optimal cadence. The cost functions used—the minimum of the squared joint torques and the minimum of the square of the muscular stress—were those described earlier. For the case of pedaling at 200 W, the prediction of optimal cadence was between 95 and 100 rpm for both the muscular stress-based and the joint torque-based cost functions. Neither study directly investigated changes in the optimal cadence as the power level changed, although Redfield and Hull (1986a) suggested that the optimal cadence might be expected to vary directly with work rate because of characteristic changes in the joint torques with increasing cadence.

Confidence in the analytical optimization technique increased because the predicted optimal cadence matched cadences commonly selected by endurance cyclists. Accordingly, further studies were undertaken to determine the relationship between geometric variables and cycling performance.

Multivariate Optimization Studies

All of the analytical optimization studies of geometric variables included cadence as a variable to be optimized because of its importance to cycling biomechanics. As a result, all of the studies were multivariate—meaning that more than one variable was optimized at the same time. For a hypothetical example of finding the optimal combination of crank arm length and cadence, an intuitive picture can be drawn to illustrate how a multivariate optimization is performed (Figure 6.5). For each crank length-cadence combination there is an associated cost. These costs can be represented as the height above the plane defined by the values of cadence and crank length. Thus, a surface is defined that represents the cost. The optimization algorithm would estimate the shape of this cost function surface and systematically move from the initial guess to the minimum point. While it is difficult to visualize what a cost surface would look like in higher dimensions, solving the optimization problem is mathematically similar in larger problems with multiple variables.

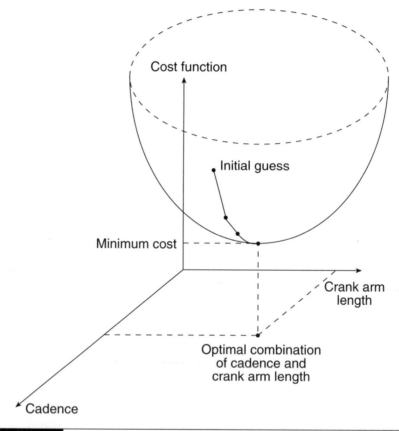

Figure 6.5 Diagram of multivariate optimization.

Multivariate problems illustrate the power of analytical optimization techniques: With these techniques, in contrast to experimental methods, the interaction between variables can be determined in a straightforward manner. The interaction between cadence and other variables is of practical importance for a cyclist with a preferred cadence near the extremes of the normal range. This is so because the optimal value of a variable, say crank length, may differ depending on whether a cyclist prefers to spin at 75 or 100 rpm.

The first multivariate study was an investigation of the optimal crank length-cadence combination (Hull & Gonzalez, 1988). The researchers found that a combination of a 170-mm crank and 100-rpm cadence corresponded closely to the cost function (derived from hip and knee torques) minimum for endurance cycling at 200 W. However, in cycling situations that deviated from 100 rpm, crank lengths of other than 170 mm produced cost function minima. In addition, the results showed that the cost function minimum was more strongly related to the cadence. The authors also examined how the size of the rider interacted with the results of the optimization. The interaction was substantial, and the cost function minimum for tall cyclists occurred at longer crank lengths and lower cadences than for short cyclists.

The combined effects of pedal platform height and cadence were also investigated in a study using analytical optimization techniques (Hull & Gonzalez, 1990). The study varied the pedal platform height relative to the pedal spindle axis over the range from 4 cm below to 4 cm above the pedal spindle axis. The cost function derived from the hip and knee torques was found to be minimized at the height of 2 cm above the pedal spindle axis for pedaling at 90 rpm. At 90 rpm the sensitivity of the cost function to pedal platform height changes was low, with the cost function increasing by only 2% over the variable range. The sensitivity of the cost function to pedal platform height increased as the cadence was varied: The minimum cost function corresponded to 4 cm below the pedal spindle axis for 60 rpm and to 4 cm above the pedal spindle axis for 120 rpm. Because of this interaction between pedal platform height and cadence, the cyclist should select a compromise height for the pedal platform that depends upon the individual's preferred cadence.

The most detailed analytical optimization study of geometric variables performed to date has been that of Gonzalez and Hull (1989). They investigated the relationship between performance, cadence, and four geometric variables (illustrated in Figure 6.6). The geometric variables were crank arm length, seat height, seat tube angle, and the longitudinal position of the foot. Once again, the effect of cyclist size on the optimization results was also investigated.

Gonzalez and Hull (1989) found large interactions between all variables for a cyclist of a given size, with changes in cadence affecting the cost function the most, followed by crank arm length, seat tube angle, and seat height. The effect of the longitudinal position of the foot on the cost function was inconsequential. Because the sensitivities of the crank length and the two seat position variables were similar, the authors recommended that equal care be given to making these three adjustments. When the size of the cyclist was varied, there were marked changes in the optimization results. In general, Gonzalez and Hull (1989) found that the optimal crank length, seat height, and longitudinal foot position increased with cyclist stature, whereas seat tube angle and

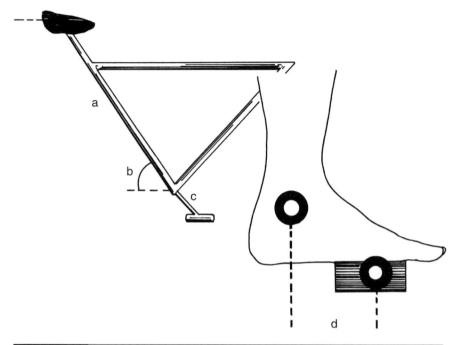

Figure 6.6 Four geometric variables that can be adjusted readily in conventional cycling: (a) seat height (from crank axis to hip axis), (b) seat tube angle, (c) crank arm length, and (d) foot position (longitudinal distance between ankle and pedal spindle).

cadence decreased. Table 6.1 lists the optimal parameter values for the optimal cadence and four other cadences (commonly selected cadences between 85 and 110 rpm) for cyclists of three different sizes. Therefore, a cyclist of a particular stature with a particular preferred cadence can get a sense for the optimal parameters and how they would change with cadence.

In conclusion, inverse dynamics-based analytical optimization studies have revealed complicated interactions between nearly all of the relevant geometry variables, as well as interactions with the size and preferred cadence of the cyclist. Therefore, it is important that the setup of the bicycle be tailored to the individual.

Unconventional Motion Cycle

Despite the technical advances in bicycle design witnessed during the 20th century, endurance cyclists use a bicycle drive system that has remained essentially unchanged. The power generated by the cyclist at

Table 6.1 Four Variable Optimization Results for Given Cadences and Anthropometric Variations

	Short cyclist	Average cyclist	Tall cyclist
Given cadence (rpm)	95	90	85
Crank arm length (m)	0.193	0.191	0.185
Seat tube angle (°)	81.6	78.4	74.9
Seat height (m)	0.696	0.773	0.858
Foot position (m)	0.130	0.143	0.156
Moment cost function value (N²m²)	41,481	48,053	58,442
Given cadence (rpm)	100	95	90
Crank arm length (m)	0.182	0.178	0.173
Seat tube angle (°)	80.7	77.6	74.5
Seat height (m)	0.705	0.784	0.868
Foot position (m)	0.130	0.143	0.156
Moment cost function value (N²m²)	40,560	47,982	57,176
Given cadence (rpm)	105	100	95
Crank arm length (m)	0.171	0.167	0.161
Seat tube angle (°)	80.0	77.0	74.0
Seat height (m)	0.714	0.793	0.876
Foot position (m)	0.130	0.143	0.156
Moment cost function value (N²m²)	39,766	47,095	56,262

(continued)

Table 6.1 *(continued)*

	Short cyclist	Average cyclist	Tall cyclist
Given cadence (rpm)	110	105	100
Crank arm length (m)	0.161	0.157	0.151
Seat tube angle (°)	79.3	76.5	73.4
Seat height (m)	0.722	0.801	0.876
Foot position (m)	0.130	0.143	0.156
Moment cost function value (N^2m^2)	39,090	46,405	55,819
Optimal cadence (rpm)	124	115	102
Crank arm length (m)	0.140	0.140	0.148
Seat tube angle (°)	78.3	75.7	73.2
Seat height (m)	0.737	0.804	0.876
Foot position (m)	0.130	0.143	0.156
Moment cost function value (N^2m^2)	37,908	45,809	55,784

Reprinted from Gonzalez and Hull (1989).

the pedals is still transmitted to the back wheel by a crank arm turning a circular chainring.

However, the circular chainring has not been without its competitors. In the late 19th century an American bicycle sprint champion, Major Taylor, used an elliptical chainring (Miller & Ross, 1980). And in the past decade the Shimano Biopace noncircular chainring was widely used. The obvious question is whether there is a noncircular chainring shape that would improve cycling performance. Researchers have investigated this performance question with respect to both maximal power and endurance cycling.

Cost Functions

The three main studies cited for noncircular chainring analyses have all used different cost functions. Miller and Ross (1980) analyzed maximum power cycling (sprinting), so the maximized cost function was the average power applied to the cranks during one revolution. Hull, Kautz, and Beard (1991) analyzed endurance cycling by minimizing the total mechanical work (as defined by the internal work hypothesis) required for one revolution. Kautz (1992) also analyzed endurance cycling, with the squared sum of the joint torques being the minimized cost function.

Maximum Power

Several of the studies on noncircular chainrings have attempted to maximize the power produced by the pedaling movement to facilitate brief periods of high power requirement. While the goals of endurance cycling are very different from those of maximal power generation, the maximal power studies have potential applications to sprinting, hill climbing, and mountain biking.

In a study that considered rowing motions as well as cycling motions, Harrison (1970) varied the motion cycle to investigate maximizing human power. He increased periods of constant velocity in the motion cycle, but despite theoretical predictions, statistically significant increases in power output did not result. He also found no difference in power output between a circular chainring and an elliptical chainring with the crank mounted parallel to the minor axis of the ellipse.

Miller and Ross (1980) developed a noncircular chainring design method to maximize power applied to the back wheel. The method consisted of empirically modeling the maximum muscular torque developed about the center of the crank by first measuring the maximum torque a cyclist generated about a stationary crank as a function of crank angle and then subtracting from this measurement the component of the crank torque due to the weight of the legs. The resulting relationship of torque versus crank angle was assumed to decrease hyperbolically with increasing crank velocity (Miller & Ross, 1980) due to the force-velocity relationship for contracting muscle. The force-velocity relationship for contracting muscle is a well known relationship that results because of the way that muscles generate force; more force can be generated at low shortening velocities than at higher shortening velocities. Thus, Miller and Ross (1980) defined a relationship in which developed muscular torque was a function of the crank angle and angular velocity. The empirical relationship was combined with a mathematical model that determined the dynamic torque about the crank due to the weight and inertia of the legs, yielding an equation for the maximum applied torque as a function of crank angle and angular velocity. Then the optimization routine determined the theoretical crank angular velocity profile that maximized the average power for one cycle.

Figure 6.7 shows the determined theoretical crank angular velocity profile. The crank angular velocity was decreased near the center of the traditional power phase (90°). Miller and Ross (1980) modified the determined theoretical profile so that a chainring could physically implement the desired crank angular velocity profile. Figure 6.7 also shows the theoretically optimal crank angular velocity profile after the problem was constrained so that a chainring could actually reproduce the desired crank angular velocity profile. Notice that constraining the

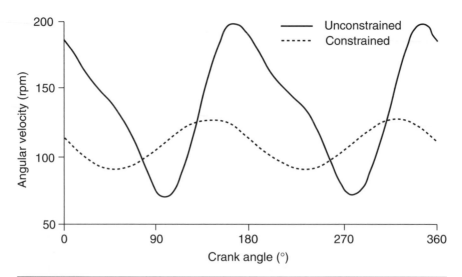

Figure 6.7 Theoretical crank angular velocity profiles determined by Miller and Ross (1980) for maximum power cycling when crank angular velocity variation is unconstrained and when crank angular velocity variation is constrained.

velocity variation caused a phase shift in the crank angular velocity profile. Figure 6.8 shows the chainring shape that implements the constrained crank angular velocity profile. The crank arm was mounted to the chainring as shown (Figure 6.8) so that the minimum velocity would occur when the crank arm was near 60° and maximum velocity would occur near 150° (crank arm is shown in the 90° position).

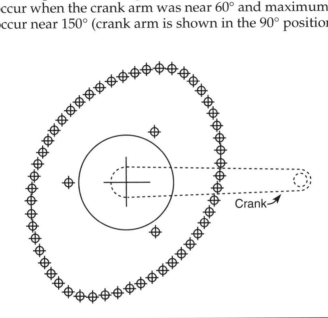

Figure 6.8 Chainring shape for constrained profile in Figure 6.7. Reprinted from Miller and Ross (1980).

Minimum Mechanical Work

The inverse dynamics-based analytical optimization method was used to design a chainring to increase mechanical efficiency during endurance cycling (Hull, Kautz, & Beard, 1991). The chainring design tested a definition of mechanical efficiency based on the internal work hypothesis (Pierrynowski, Winter, & Norman, 1980; Winter, 1979): Internal work was defined as the sum of the absolute changes in the total mechanical energy of the cyclist's legs and total work was defined as the sum of the internal and external work (where external work is predominantly work done in overcoming aerodynamic forces, gravity forces, or both, in conventional cycling). If the definition of total mechanical work resulting from the internal work hypothesis was correct, then reducing energy changes could result in total work reductions of up to 20% for a given power output at common endurance cycling cadences of 90 rpm.

Hull and colleagues (1991) developed a design methodology to synthesize a desired total mechanical energy profile and applied the method to keep the total mechanical energy constant throughout the cycle, thereby eliminating internal work as defined in previous studies (Pierrynowski, Winter, & Norman, 1980; Winter, 1979). As defined in these earlier studies, reducing internal work would increase efficiency. The methodology consisted of using equations describing the kinematics of the legs in conjunction with an experimentally determined reference pedal angle profile to derive the total mechanical energy as a function of crank angular velocity at each point in the crank cycle. Then the crank angular velocity profile that kept the total mechanical energy of the rider's legs constant throughout the cycle was calculated.

The theoretical angular velocity profile that was found to eliminate internal work for an example subject is shown in Figure 6.9 in comparison to the actual angular velocity profile provided by an elliptical chainring that reduced internal work (RIW). Periods of minimal crank angular velocity occur during the power stroke. Figure 6.10 shows the chainring shape for RIW.

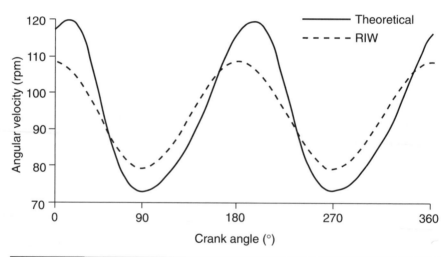

Figure 6.9 Comparison of the constant total energy angular velocity profile for an example subject and the angular velocity profile of an elliptical chainring that reduced internal work (RIW). The RIW profile did not duplicate the constant total energy profile, being lower in velocity variation and different in shape. As a result, the profile did not eliminate internal work although it did reduce it from that seen with a circular chainring. Adapted from Hull, Williams, Williams, and Kautz (1992).

Dynamic Optimization

Kautz (1992) developed a dynamic optimization approach to noncircular chainring design. The method allowed changes in the applied pedal

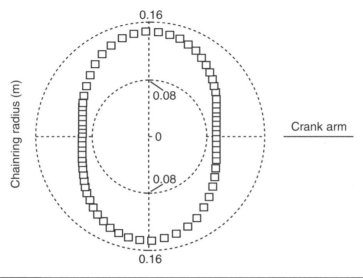

Figure 6.10 Polar plot of chainring shape for RIW profile.

forces to occur as a natural consequence of the velocity variations induced by the noncircular chainring shape, thereby eliminating the requirement to empirically determine the applied pedal force as a function of crank angle as in inverse dynamics-based optimizations.

The principal step in the dynamic optimization of chainring shape was deriving the mathematical model of cycling in a form such that the inputs were the crank angular velocity at top dead center and the joint torques at the hip, knee, and ankle for each leg throughout the cycle, and the outputs were the accelerations of both legs and the crank as well as the pedal forces. To relate the input torques to the proper accelerations, Kautz (1992) modeled pedaling on an ergometer, where work is done against a frictional load. Thus, the shape of the chainring appeared in the equations in the mathematical model that related the joint torques to the acceleration of the crank at each position in the crank cycle. Then the dynamic optimization treated the chainring shape function as an input and found the combination of chainring shape and joint torques that produced the lowest cost function for one revolution while requiring the initial and final crank velocities to be the same, as in steady state cycling. Similarly to what is done in inverse dynamics-based optimization, Kautz (1992) assumed a reference pedal angle versus crank angle relationship within the model. However, this assumed relationship is not required by the dynamic optimization, and Kautz (1992) discussed alternative formulations that could eliminate the assumption.

The theoretical angular velocity profile derived by Kautz (1992) is shown in Figure 6.11. A polar plot of the chainring radius as a function of crank position appears in Figure 6.12, allowing the chainring shape to be visualized. Notice that if such a chainring were manufactured, then the theoretical crank velocity would not result because of the concave sections of the chainring. Kautz (1992) recommended constraining the allowable angular velocity variations in any future studies.

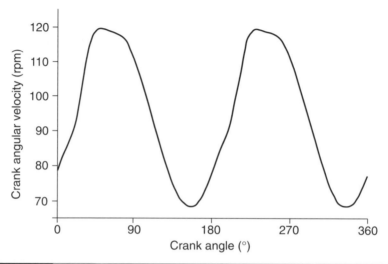

Figure 6.11 Angular velocity profile determined for endurance cycling by Kautz (1992).

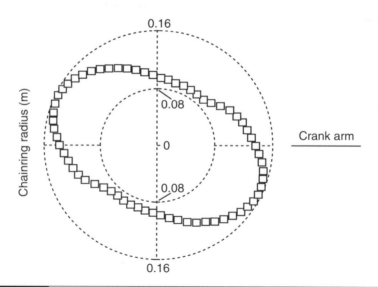

Figure 6.12 Polar plot of chainring shape associated with angular velocity profile determined for endurance cycling by Kautz (1992).

This study provided the first dynamic simulation in which pedaling with a noncircular chainring exhibited improved endurance performance relative to optimal pedaling with a circular chainring. The example dynamic optimization of chainring shape resulted in a theoretical cost decrease of 1.4% when the sum of the joint torques squared was used as the cost function. While convergence difficulties limited confidence in obtaining the globally optimal solution, the chainring shape optimization is well suited for use in an iterative design process.

Comparing the chainrings determined by the maximum power study and the endurance cycling dynamic optimization reveals that different tasks may imply very different chainring shapes. The two chainrings are out of phase, meaning that they are nearly opposite shapes. As a result, even if the endurance chainring were successful for steady state pedaling at 90 rpm, it might be ineffective for sprinting during a road race. Thus, it is possible that noncircular chainrings will be useful only for very specific tasks. For instance, one chainring might be used for sprinting while another one might be needed for steady state pedaling as in a time trial, where changes in speed are minimal. Possibly the circular chainring will remain as the popular choice for road racing because of its versatility in handling all situations that arise during this type of event. However, this discussion is speculative, and experimental verification of the optimization analyses results is needed.

Of the three chainring shapes determined in the studies described, only the work of Hull, Kautz, and Beard (1991) has been tested experimentally. Hull, Williams, Williams, and Kautz (1992) listed the experimental conditions that they felt were required to adequately assess the human performance:

1. Adequate sample of trained cyclists
2. Equipment representative of cycling
3. A test protocol duplicating the power output and cadence of high-performance cycling
4. A test protocol that minimized the influence of training and biological variation

Using these criteria, Hull and coworkers (1992) investigated oxygen consumption during cycling using a circular chainring, the Shimano Biopace noncircular chainring, an elliptical chainring (based on the work of Hull, Kautz, & Beard, 1991) that reduced internal work (RIW), and the RIW chainring turned 100° out of phase so that the major axis was similar to that of the Biopace (10° ahead of the crank arm) and internal work was increased relative to circular. The elliptical chainrings produced an angular velocity variation of 27% relative to peak angular velocity assuming constant rear wheel velocity. Hull and colleagues (1992) were unable to show statistically significant differences between chainrings with respect to the measured oxygen consumption at a given work rate. However, a consistent trend was that the circular chainring had the lowest values, followed by RIW. The conclusion was that neither the Biopace nor the RIW chainring increased efficiency in cycling relative to a circular chainring (however, long-term adaptations to the chainrings were not investigated to determine whether more than 10 min of pedaling was needed to "learn" to use the noncircular chainrings). In additional work, Kautz, Hull, and Neptune (1994) showed that the theoretical basis of the internal work hypothesis was not adequate for use as a cycling efficiency measure. In fact, muscular mechanical energy expenditure was shown to increase, even though internal work decreased, with the RIW chainring.

Recommendations for Further Study

Improving the theoretical basis for the cost functions used in optimization analyses is the single most important step needed to increase the utility of the method for cycling studies. Theoretical studies need to address the implications of the force-length and force-velocity relationships of the individual muscles involved in cycling. In addition, theoretical studies need to more fully integrate the wealth of knowledge of cycling energetics resulting from exercise physiology studies. It will be important for biomechanists and physiologists to collaborate to determine how to appropriately assess human performance in cycling, and to provide the experimental techniques necessary to attempt to validate the results of optimization analyses. The results from experimental studies of different cost functions, like those cited earlier by Marshall, Wood, and Jennings (1989) and McLean and Lafortune (1991b), also need to be integrated with the theoretical work.

With respect to the current optimization techniques, the pedal force scaling required by inverse dynamics-based optimizations is the most pressing concern. Currently, an inherent assumption of inverse dynamics-based optimization analyses is that the kinematics of the pedal do not change substantially as the variables assume different values and that the pedal force does not change differently than predicted by the linear scaling law. However, recent studies have shown that the pedal force profile as well as the pedal kinematics varies systematically as a function of cadence (McLean & Lafortune, 1991a; Sanderson, 1991). Thus, a theoretical basis is needed to predict changes in the applied pedal force under parameter variation.

Kautz and Hull (1993) developed a theoretical framework for explaining observed pedal forces. Muscular forces accelerate the legs while the foot-pedal connection constrains the resulting movement so that the foot follows a circular path about the crank axis. Consequently, pedal forces not only reflect muscular activity, but also depend upon weight and inertia forces. As a result, the applied pedal force is not independent of the dynamics of the cycling movement. Thus the dynamic effects of the pedaling movement upon the applied pedal force need to be evaluated; if substantial changes from the given reference profile exist, then the appropriate pedal force needs to be used in an inverse dynamics-based optimization approach.

The dynamic optimization technique based on the forward dynamics approach is promising for cycling analysis. As computer power becomes cheaper and more accessible, these types of large problems will be more easily addressed. The reduced number of assumptions necessary for forward dynamics-based optimization as compared to inverse dynamics-based optimization makes it an appealing option.

A logical next step with the dynamic optimization approach would be to include the unique physiological and anatomical aspects of human muscles. This would require introducing models of the individual muscles into the mathematical model of pedaling. Then instead of joint torques, neural activation signals would be the input to the model. While this would greatly increase the complexity of the model, it would also make the model more realistic; it would allow more sophisticated cost functions to be used that would reflect known relationships of muscle—like force and velocity, force and length, and force and activation. For instance, the force-velocity relationship of muscle is probably important to chainring design because the energetic cost of muscular action and the peak force of muscular contraction both depend upon the velocity of shortening. Work investigating the optimization of power production during cycling using a forward dynamics model with individual muscles has recently been presented in abstract form (van den Bogert, 1994; van den Bogert & Van Soest, 1993).

In conclusion, a solid foundation for performing optimization analyses in cycling exists. With future studies ascertaining the important determinants of cycling performance, it should be possible to address in detail the trade-offs necessary in order for individual cyclists to find their optimal bicycle setup.

References

Andrews, J.C. (1982). On the relationship between resultant joint torques and muscular activity. *Medicine and Science in Sports and Exercise*, **14**, 361-367.

Cavanagh, P.R., & Kram, R. (1985). The efficiency of human movement—a statement of the problem. *Medicine and Science in Sports and Exercise*, **17**, 304-308.

Coyle, E.F., Feltner, M.E., Kautz, S.A., Hamilton, M.T., Montain, S.J., Baylor, A.M., Abraham, L.D., & Petrek, G.W. (1991). Physiological and biomechanical factors associated with elite endurance cycling performance. *Medicine and Science in Sports and Exercise*, **23**, 93-107.

Crowninshield, R.D., & Brand, R.A. (1981). A physiologically based criterion of muscle force prediction in locomotion. *Journal of Biomechanics*, **14**, 793-801.

Gonzalez, H., & Hull, M.L. (1989). Multivariable optimization of cycling biomechanics. *Journal of Biomechanics*, **22**, 1151-1161.

Harrison, J.Y. (1970). Maximizing human power output by suitable selection of motion cycle and load. *Human Factors*, **12**, 315-329.

Hull, M.L., & Gonzalez, H. (1988). Bivariate optimization of pedalling rate and crank arm length in cycling. *Journal of Biomechanics*, **21**, 839-849.

Hull, M.L., & Gonzalez, H. (1990). The effect of pedal platform height on cycling biomechanics. *International Journal of Sport Biomechanics*, **6**, 1-17.

Hull, M.L., Gonzalez, H., & Redfield, R. (1988). Optimization of pedalling rate in cycling using a muscle stress-based objective function. *International Journal of Sport Biomechanics*, **4**, 1-20.

Hull, M.L., Kautz, S.A., & Beard, A. (1991). An angular velocity profile in cycling derived from mechanical energy analysis. *Journal of Biomechanics*, **24**, 577-586.

Hull, M.L., Williams, M., Williams, K., & Kautz, S.A. (1992). Physiological response to cycling with both circular and non-circular chainrings. *Medicine and Science in Sports and Exercise*, **24**, 1114-1122.

Kautz, S.A. (1992). *Biomechanics of pedaling with non-circular chainrings in cycling*. Unpublished doctoral dissertation, Biomedical Engineering Group, University of California-Davis.

Kautz, S.A., & Hull, M.L. (1993). A theoretical basis for interpreting the force applied to the pedal in cycling. *Journal of Biomechanics*, **26**, 155-165.

Kautz, S.A., Hull, M.L., & Neptune, R.R. (1994). A comparison of muscular mechanical energy expenditure and internal work in cycling. *Journal of Biomechanics*, **27**, 1459-1467.

Marshall, R.N., Wood, G.A., & Jennings, L.S. (1989). Performance objectives in human movement: A review and application to the stance phase of normal walking. *Human Movement Science*, **8**, 571-594.

McLean, B.D., & Lafortune, M.A. (1991a). Influence of cadence on mechanical parameters of pedalling. In R.N. Marshall, G.A. Wood, B.C. Elliott, T.R. Ackland, & P.J. McNair (Eds.), *Proceedings of XIIIth*

International Congress of Biomechanics (pp. 102-104). Perth, Australia: The University of Western Australia, Department of Human Movement Studies.

McLean, B.D., & Lafortune, M.A. (1991b). Optimum pedalling cadence determined by joint torque parameters and oxygen cost. In R.N. Marshall, G.A. Wood, B.C. Elliott, T.R. Ackland, & P.J. McNair (Eds.), *Proceedings of XIIIth International Congress of Biomechanics* (pp. 100-102). Perth, Australia: The University of Western Australia, Department of Human Movement Studies.

Miller, N.R., & Ross, D. (1980). The design of variable ratio chain drives for bicycles and ergometers—application to a maximum power bicycle drive. *Journal of Mechanical Design*, **102**, 711-717.

Nordeen, K.S., & Cavanagh, P.R. (1976). Simulation of lower limb kinematics during cycling. In P.A. Komi (Ed.), *Biomechanics V-B* (pp. 26-33). Baltimore: University Park Press.

Pierrynowski, M.R., Winter, D.A., & Norman, R.W. (1980). Transfers of mechanical energy within the total body and mechanical efficiency during treadmill walking. *Ergonomics*, **23**, 147-156.

Redfield, B., & Hull, M.L. (1986a). On the relationship between joint moments and pedalling rates at constant power in bicycling. *Journal of Biomechanics*, **19**, 317-329.

Redfield, B., & Hull, M.L. (1986b). Prediction of pedal forces in bicycling using optimization methods. *Journal of Biomechanics*, **19**, 523-539.

Sanderson, D.J. (1991). The influence of cadence and power output on the biomechanics of force application during steady-rate cycling in competitive and recreational cyclists. *Journal of Sports Sciences*, **9**, 191-203.

van den Bogert, A.J. (1994). Optimization of cycling performance using computer simulation. In L. Blankevoort & J.G.M. Kooloos (Eds.), *Abstracts of the Second World Congress of Biomechanics* (p. II-135a). Nijmegen, The Netherlands: Stichting World Biomechanics.

van den Bogert, A.J., & van Soest, A.J. (1993). Optimization of power production in cycling using direct dynamics simulations. *Proceedings of the 4th International Symposium on Computer Simulation in Biomechanics* (pp. BMG2-14-BMG2-17). Paris: Montlignon.

Williams, K.R., & Cavanagh, P.R. (1983). A model for the calculation of mechanical power during distance running. *Journal of Biomechanics*, **16**, 115-128.

Winter, D.A. (1979). A new definition of mechanical work done in human movement. *Journal of Applied Physiology*, **46**, 79-83.

7

Cycling Biomechanics

Jeffrey P. Broker, PhD • Robert J. Gregor, PhD

Scientists have long been attracted to the study of cycling. This attraction is attributable, in part, to the ease with which the cycling task can be used in a laboratory setting to evaluate human performance. The attraction is bolstered by a strong interest in the sport of cycling in general and in the unique function of human-machine systems in particular. Today, interest in cycling, the evolution of cycling equipment, and the continued use of cycling to study human performance have sustained the advancement of cycling-related research, and new concepts and ideas continue to emerge.

This chapter presents some of the more recent scientific findings related to the biomechanics of cycling. Our focus will begin at the pedal, where important interactions between the cyclist and bicycle occur. We will briefly discuss the evolution of clipless bicycle pedals in a biomechanical context and describe recent advancements in instrumented pedal designs. Our discussion of pedals will then move to the latest research in pedal loading, addressing the new concept of fundamental pedaling dynamics, the relationship between pedal torsion and knee injuries, pressure distribution within the cycling shoe, and the pedaling mechanics of disabled cyclists. Next, we will turn to characteristics of the engine, or cyclist. We will present recent findings regarding the sources of mechanical energy to the rider-bicycle system, leg muscle activation patterns, power produced at the joints of the lower leg, and the uniqueness of two-joint muscles in distributing energy within the cycling system. We will conclude with a brief discussion of directions for future research.

The Pedal: A Critical Rider-Bicycle Interface

The bicycle pedal has received considerable attention within the scientific community, presumably because the pedal is the site where energy is transferred from the rider to the bicycle and also because pedal motion and pedal loading largely establish how a cyclist's legs move and are stressed during pedaling. Of particular interest to researchers in recent years have been the engagement between the shoe and pedal, the forces and torques produced at the shoe-pedal connection, and pedaling "effectiveness." Before we consider these issues, however, a brief review of recent bicycle pedal evolution is in order.

Evolution of the Clipless Bicycle Pedal

The advantages of using rigid-sole cycling shoes and a secure engagement of the shoe to the bicycle pedal are rather obvious when one considers the need for efficient transport of energy from the cyclist's foot to the pedal. Rat-trap or quill-style pedals in combination with stiff cycling shoes, used for so many years on racing circuits, were the products of this thinking.

Track riders were particularly interested in the quality and security of the shoe-pedal interface, and often "double-strapped" their shoes to the pedals. These riders were also sensitive to bicycle weight and pedal clearance above the banked track surface and began to experiment with homemade methods of securing (e.g., nailing or screwing) their shoes to the pedals or pedal spindles.

In preparation for the 1984 Olympics, U.S. engineers designed and fabricated a titanium pedal platform that offered a light-weight, aerodynamic pedal design, which effectively eliminated the toe clip and strap by securing the shoe directly to the pedal. Soon thereafter, similar "clipless" pedal designs emerged on the retail cycling market. The emergence was led by the ski binding manufacturer Look, followed later by Cyclebinding, AeroLite, Addidas/Manalo, Pedalmaster, Keywin, Sampson, Shimano, and Mavic, to name a few. These manufacturers offered cyclists a myriad of new pedals that connected rigidly to the shoe, allowed for easy exit and entry, weighed less, permitted greater bicycle lean angle, were more aerodynamic, and eliminated the pressure of the toe strap upon the top surface of the foot.

Proper shoe-cleat alignment and its control during pedaling became an issue in the evolution of clipless pedals in the late 1980s. Specifically, Jean Beyl, inventor of the Look clipless pedal, suggested that rigidly fixing a cyclist's foot to the pedal may place undesirable stresses on the knee during pedaling and therefore that a pedal system should provide "float," or rotational allowance of the shoe relative to the pedal. As an outgrowth of these concerns, Beyl created the Time pedal system, called Bioperformance, which permitted 15° of free rotation and approximately 0.4 in. of lateral foot motion (Gregor & Wheeler, 1994). Popularity of the new floating clipless pedals grew rapidly, and other clipless pedal manufacturers quickly responded by adding float features to their pedal systems.

Looking back over the evolution of the clipless pedal, it appears that few objective biomechanical data were used in the design and development of the new pedal systems. Questions concerning function of the new pedal systems typically followed their development and introduction—for example, what are the effects of pedal float, engagement angulation, and cleat placement on skeletal loading, transmission of power to the pedal, and cycling performance? The need for a systematic scientific evaluation of critical rider-bicycle interface components was apparent and, motivated by the lack of objective available data, biomechanists were drawn into the evaluation of shoe-pedal systems.

Instrumented Bicycle Pedals

The principal tool used by biomechanists to observe and evaluate shoe-pedal interface dynamics became the instrumented bicycle pedal. Instrumentation employed specifically to measure forces between a cyclist and the pedals was actually available late in the 19th century (Sharp, 1896/1977). The specially designed pedal described by Sharp contained springs mounted between two plates that deflected in response to load during pedaling and caused a marker to scribe a force trace on a strip of circulating paper mounted below the pedal. His data (in graphical format) showed perpendicular force components similar to those recorded by the various high-tech instrumented pedals used today. While this early account illustrates the long-standing interest in cycling-induced loads, only recently have advancements in instrumented bicycle pedals and their applications emerged.

Instrumented bicycle pedals capable of completely measuring the forces and moments (torques) applied to the pedal were first introduced by Hull and Davis (1981). The Hull and Davis pedals employed strain gauges (foil-like elements that exhibit a change in resistance to electrical current when deformed) to measure normal (perpendicular), tangential (fore-aft), and medial-lateral (side to side) forces applied to the pedal surface, plus the moment, or torsion, produced between the foot and pedal about an axis passing vertically through the pedal. Hull and Davis suggested that elimination of medial-lateral loads and torsion about the vertical pedal axis would be beneficial in reducing cycling-related knee injuries, and thus they may have provided the first scientific rationale for floating pedal designs.

Piezoelectric force pedals designed to fully characterize shoe-pedal interface dynamics were introduced by Broker and Gregor (1990). Piezoelectric pedals contain encased crystals that, when deformed under load, exhibit a change in electrical charge proportional to the applied load. Piezoelectric pedals offer the advantage over strain gauge pedals of higher frequency response to applied loads, simpler calibration, and minimal cross sensitivity (meaning that loads applied in one direction do not affect the measurement of loads applied in another direction).

The pedal developed by Broker and Gregor (1990) has been used to evaluate the effect of athlete position on pedaling kinetics, to provide pedaling mechanics feedback to cyclists in a training environment, and to provide force data required to calculate joint moments (torques) and mechanical energy flow through the lower limb and to the pedal. Additionally, the Broker and Gregor (1990) piezoelectric pedal was modified (Wheeler, Gregor, & Broker, 1992) to permit the exchange of pedal interface (Shimano nonfloating, Time floating, or toe clip) for evaluating the effects of different shoe-pedal interfaces on cycling mechanics (see Figure 7.1). A duplicate of the instrumented pedal system reported by Wheeler, Gregor, and Broker (1992) is currently employed at the U.S. Olympic Training Center to test, evaluate, and train U.S. national team cyclists.

Figure 7.1 Instrumented piezoelectric bicycle pedal described by Wheeler, Gregor, and Broker (1992). The shoe-pedal interface can be adapted to provide toe clip, clipless fixed, or clipless float compatibility.

New Research Into Pedal Loading

Although early pedal loading research primarily sought to describe the forces and torques that arise between the foot and pedal during cycling, more recent research has focused on preferred or optimal pedaling technique and the relationship between shoe-pedal interface loads and cycling-related injuries. Of particular importance to cyclists and scientists should be the latest findings concerning a revised interpretation of pedal force effectiveness, pedal torsion and the effect of pedal float on knee pain, pressure on the foot during pedaling, and the unique pedaling mechanics of disabled cyclists.

Force Effectiveness Reviewed. The forces cyclists apply to bicycle pedals are commonly used to characterize pedaling technique. These forces are typically measured and subsequently described in component terms. The normal force component acts perpendicular to the pedal surface, and the tangential force component acts along the surface of the pedal (in the fore-aft direction). If the pedal angle is known, the normal and tangential components can be resolved into "effective" and "ineffective" components (Figure 7.2). The effective component acts perpendicular to the bicycle crank and thus is responsible for powering the bicycle. The ineffective component acts parallel to the crank and thus acts only to compress or lengthen the crank.

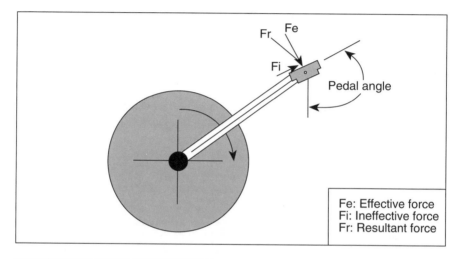

Fr Fe
Fi
Pedal angle

Fe: Effective force
Fi: Ineffective force
Fr: Resultant force

Figure 7.2 Effective (Fe) and ineffective (Fi) components of pedal loading. The effective component acts to drive the bicycle crank, while the ineffective component acts to lengthen or compress the crank.

Researchers have commonly used the effective force component to describe pedaling quality (Cavanagh & Sanderson, 1986; LaFortune & Cavanagh, 1983). This may be related largely to the direct relationship between the effective force profile and torque generation at the bicycle crank. Force effectiveness, displayed for one pedal as a function of crank angle in Figure 7.3, increases rapidly during the power phase (0° to 180°) and peaks shortly after the cranks pass horizontal (90°). Cyclists of all ability levels exhibit negative force effectiveness, that is, forces applied to the pedal that are perpendicular to the crank but in opposition to crank rotation, during recovery (180° to 360°) in steady state cycling. Cyclists correctly sense that they lift or pull up the leg during recovery; but they do not lift the leg as fast as the pedal is rising. Thus, the leg gets in the way of the pedal and, in a sense, the pedal helps lift the leg. The magnitude of the negative effective forces during recovery generally increases (gets more negative) as cadence increases (the pedal is rising

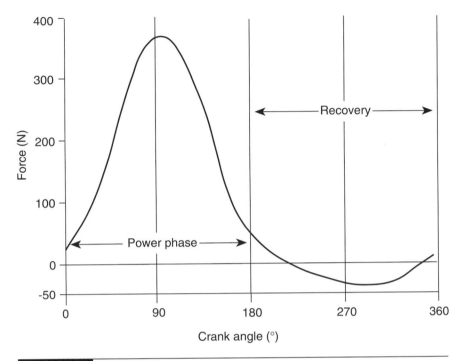

Figure 7.3 Force effectiveness patterns versus crank angle for a U.S. national team cyclist pedaling at 350 W, 90 rpm. Negative force effectiveness in recovery (180° to 360°) is typical, illustrating that the pedal acts to lift the foot and leg in this region.

faster). Effective forces during recovery are less negative (less counterproductive) and may even be positive during sprinting and climbing.

Elite cyclists generally show reduced negative force effectiveness during recovery compared to recreational cyclists (they are lighter on the pedals during recovery), and the region of recovery during which they exhibit these negative effective forces is typically smaller. This is usually achieved by the cyclist's generating positive crank torque, that is, positive effective force, early in recovery (past the bottom of the pedal cycle) and late in recovery (as the pedal approaches the top of the cycle). We have seen one elite cyclist (national team member) generate completely positive force effectiveness throughout recovery on one leg, but not the other, at a steady state test condition simulating a moderate-effort ride.

One-legged pedaling on a wind trainer and isolated periods of one-legged dominance during training appear to be good methods of developing lightness in recovery and positive effective forces early and late in recovery. Recognize, however, that recovery effectiveness does *not* necessarily reduce metabolic demand. Enhanced recovery phase effectiveness does reduce power demand on the opposite leg (in the first half of the pedal cycle) and represents a resource to draw on during high-level efforts.

In a study conducted by Browning (1991), effective force patterns (magnitude and timing) didn't change when elite iron man distance triathletes were moved between a conventional position (approximately 72° seat tube angle, hands on brake hoods), an aerodynamic position (approximately 72° seat tube angle, aero bars with elbow pads), and an advanced aerodynamic position (approximately 78° seat tube, aero bars with elbow pads). Browning concluded that aerodynamically motivated position changes may not compromise pedaling effectiveness as measured at the pedal.

Finally, effective force patterns (magnitude and timing) did not change when experienced cyclists were fitted with three different shoe-pedal interfaces: conventional toe clip pedals, fixed clipless (no-float) pedals, and floating clipless pedals (Wheeler, Gregor, & Broker, in press). These findings suggest that pedal float does not compromise the delivery of power to the pedal under steady state cycling conditions.

Fundamental Pedaling Dynamics and Force "Ineffectiveness."
For years, researchers have suggested that ineffective forces (those parallel to the crank) do no useful work and therefore represent wasted energy. A fault exists in this logic, and the fault becomes apparent when one considers that the fundamental dynamics of the spinning leg, foot, and pedal system generate forces (measurable at the pedal) independent of muscular work, or energy cost. For example, large downward-directed forces are applied to the pedal at the bottom of the pedal stroke (Figure 7.4a). These forces, classically defined as "ineffective" in that they act to lengthen the crank and do not assist in propelling the crank, are largely generated by the natural interaction between the pedal and the lower limb (as the pedal acts to support and change the direction of motion of the lower limb from downward to upward), and not by active muscular contractions. In fact, if a cyclist were to pedal in such a way that these forces were minimized or eliminated altogether, significant muscle work would be required—and no additional bicycle power would result.

In 1993, Kautz and Hull presented a method to separate the fundamental component of pedal loading from the measured pedal load. The fundamental component is generated by gravitational and inertial forces acting on the lower limb (nonmuscular in origin), which, because of the limb's connection to the crank, also acts on the pedal. Separation of the fundamental component of pedal loading from the measured pedal load requires the computation of joint torques and joint reaction forces, which in turn involves the complete description of the crank, foot, shank, and thigh kinematics (positions, velocities, and accelerations) throughout the pedal cycle.

The measured, fundamental (nonmuscular), and muscular components of pedal loading computed for an elite national team road cyclist pedaling at 400 W at 118 rpm are presented in clock diagram format in Figure 7.4a, 7.4b, and 7.4c, respectively. The measured pedal load (Figure 7.4a) portrays the typical downward loading of the pedal as it approaches bottom dead center, and the direction of this measured load opposes the direction of pedal motion during recovery. Also, the measured pedal loading at top dead center is directed nearly straight downward; this is commonly described as a "nonproductive" loading situation. The fundamental pedal loads shown in Figure 7.4b—arising solely

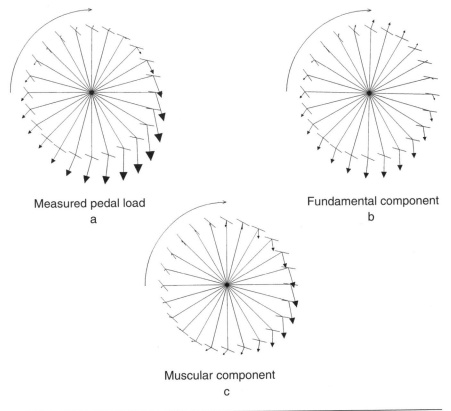

Measured pedal load
a

Fundamental component
b

Muscular component
c

Figure 7.4 Clock diagrams illustrating the measured (a), fundamental or nonmuscular (b), and muscular (c) components of pedal loading for an elite U.S. national team cyclist. The muscular and fundamental components, which sum to produce the measured force pattern, illustrate the separate effects of natural dynamics and active muscular contractions on pedal loading, respectively.

from the natural dynamics of the oscillating legs and their interaction with the pedals—clearly demonstrate that a substantial portion of the measured downward loading at the bottom of the pedal cycle (Figure 7.4a) is, in fact, not due to muscular actions. Furthermore, fundamental pedaling dynamics are responsible for the downward loading on the pedal as it rises in recovery (180° to 360°).

The muscular component of pedal loading (Figure 7.4c) represents more of what the cyclist perceives during pedaling. Notice that muscular actions work to drive the pedal rearward near bottom dead center and to lift the pedal during a large portion of recovery. Despite the actions of muscles, however, it is the fundamental (gravitational and inertial based) pedal dynamics that act to offset the muscular contributions in these regions—producing the seemingly "ineffective" pedal force characteristic so commonly described (Figure 7.4a). This particular cyclist does not generate significant forward-directed forces (measured or muscular based) at the top of the pedal cycle, and could benefit from improving this aspect of her pedaling.

As a final point, separation of the fundamental component of pedal loading from the measured load may permit a more genuine representation of "effective" and "ineffective" pedaling. As illustrated in Figure 7.4c, for example, the muscular-based portion of pedal loading (that which the cyclist can readily control) would be represented by an effective component (perpendicular to the crank) that is positive throughout most of the pedal cycle. What remain to be studied are the effects of such variables as training, fatigue, cadence, power output, skill level, and rider-bicycle geometry on the relationship between the fundamental, muscular, and measured components of pedal loading.

Pedal Torsion and Knee Injuries. Internal rotation of the tibia (e.g., counterclockwise rotation of the right leg when viewed from above) and knee valgus (a knock-kneed position) have been postulated to represent potentially injurious conditions for the knee in cycling (Francis, 1988; Sanderson, 1990). Furthermore, Francis (1986) and Hannaford, Moran, and Hlavac (1986) reported a positive relationship between the deviation from linearity of knee motion (when viewed from the front) and knee pain. These researchers experimented with orthotics and pedal cant to elicit more linear knee motion in cyclists.

In search of a more complete understanding of knee pain and its source in cycling, biomechanists employed instrumented bicycle pedals to examine the torsion generated at the shoe-pedal interface during pedaling. Torsion at the shoe-pedal interface arises as the foot in the shoe attempts to rotate about an axis perpendicular to the pedal surface (think of the release action of clipless pedals). Pedal torsion typically peaks midway through the power phase of the pedal cycle (downstroke) and is internally directed (Figure 7.5). In other words, the foot attempts to rotate inward relative to the pedal (heel moves out). During recovery (upstroke), torsion is externally directed but is lower in magnitude than the internally directed torsion during the power stroke.

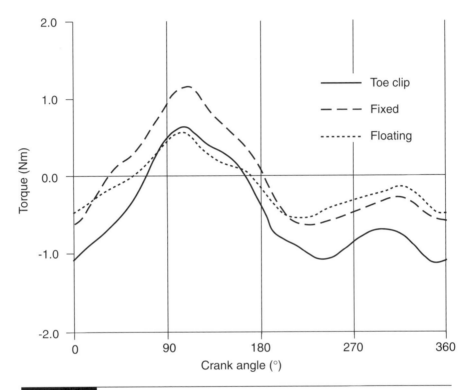

Figure 7.5 Mean applied pedal torsion patterns versus crank angle for toe clip, clipless fixed, and clipless floating shoe-pedal interface conditions ($N = 27$). Positive torsion represents internal applied torque, produced when the right foot attempts to rotate counterclockwise relative to the pedal when viewed from above. Adapted from Wheeler (1993).

Ruby, Hull, and Hawkins (1992) calculated knee loads from force pedal data, sagittal (progression) plane lower limb motions, and frontal (side to side) knee motion. These researchers reported the torsion applied about the axis perpendicular to the pedal surface was a primary contributor to a torsion induced at the knee about a parallel axis. Since this torsion at the shoe-pedal interface was known to be affected (and probably reduced) by the allowance for "float" within the pedal system, the authors suggested that the introduction of float into the pedal system may reduce the incidence of cycling-related knee injuries.

In a study by Wheeler (1993), pedal interface type was found to affect the magnitude of pedal torsion. Specifically, floating clipless pedals attenuated (i.e., reduced) the power phase torsion relative to fixed clipless and toe-clip designs. The attenuation decreased both the internal and external peak torsion (Figure 7.5). Furthermore, Wheeler discovered that experienced cyclists clinically diagnosed with overuse knee injuries exhibited distinctly different pedal torsion patterns. Chronic anterior knee pain subjects demonstrated exaggerated internally directed peak torques during the power phase, increased rates of torsional load generation, and a longer duration of the applied internal torsion. These results strongly suggest a link between pedal torsion and knee pain in cyclists.

Finally, recent studies conducted with U.S. national team cyclists at the Olympic Training Center revealed that tibial (lower leg) rotation in elite cyclists appears to have a very weak correlation with torsion measured at the pedal. Perhaps pronation and supination at the subtalar joint, which couple rotations of the tibia to motion within the foot, complicate the relationship between lower limb action and pedal torsional loading. A detailed investigation of skeletal motions in the lower limb in conjunction with pedal force and torsion measurements will be required to shed light on this important issue. Furthermore, the potential impact of bicycle angulation (e.g., during hill climbing) on pedal torsion and its relation to knee loading remains to be studied.

Pressure Distribution on the Foot During Pedaling.   Sanderson and Cavanagh (1987) used a specially designed insole with 256 separate force-measuring elements to evaluate the distribution of pressure on the bottom of the foot during cycling. They reported that the majority of pressure directed upon the foot was concentrated in the forefoot region, directly above the pedal spindle (particularly over the head of the first metatarsal and hallux, or big toe). In a subsequent study, Sanderson and Hennig (1992) measured the effect of shoe type on pressure distribution during steady state cycling and reported more evenly distributed pressure across the sole with the use of rigid cycling shoes as compared to running shoes. Increased power output, correlated with higher pedal forces, was reported to produce higher relative pressure in the anterior-medial foot structures (Hennig & Sanderson, 1992). These findings have rather obvious implications regarding both performance and foot injuries in cycling. Furthermore, in light of continual advancements in shoe-pedal system designs, further research on the pressures, forces, and torques induced at the interface between cyclist, shoe, and pedal are warranted.

Pedaling Mechanics of the Disabled Cyclist.   Disabled cyclists have received little attention in the cycling biomechanics literature, presumably because of the limited number of research facilities equipped to study the biomechanics of cycling and the difficulty in recruiting a significant number of similarly disabled cyclists. The opportunity to study the pedaling mechanics of disabled cyclists arose during a recent disabled-cycling camp conducted at the U.S. Olympic Training Center (April, 1993).

Three unilateral (single limb) below-knee amputee cyclists and six cerebral palsy cyclists were tested across various workloads at preferred cadence by means of a pair of piezoelectric-instrumented force pedals similar to those reported by Wheeler, Gregor, and Broker (1992). Pedaling mechanics for several disabled cyclists exhibited remarkable recovery phase effectiveness (180° to 360°). In fact, dominant (or natural) limb force effectiveness during recovery for the disabled cyclists was generally enhanced (i.e., less negative) relative to recovery force effectiveness patterns exhibited by national team members. It appears that significantly asymmetric musculoskeletal capabilities induced marked pedaling style adjustments in these athletes, illustrating the enormous potential for training-induced adaptations in all cyclists.

The three unilateral below-knee amputee cyclists did 183 to 232% more work at the pedals (at a total bicycle power of 250 W) with their natural limb than with their prosthetic limb. Force effectiveness patterns (Figure 7.6) revealed significantly lower peak values with the prosthetic limb, and the direction of force application at the pedals at the top and bottom of the pedal cycle (characterized by the magnitude of the effective force at 0° and 180°) was largely nonproductive. These data, the first to our knowledge describing the pedaling kinetics of disabled competitive cyclists, clearly expand our knowledge of cycling in general and indicate that more research is needed to understand this unique and growing cycling population.

The Cycling Engine

The relative dominance of the legs in providing energy to propel the bicycle during steady state cycling is obvious. The origin of mechanical energy within the legs, however, is less clear. Since the energetic demands on the lower extremity musculature have relevance to our understanding of muscle contributions to pedaling power, muscle fatigue, and muscle injury, a discussion of the demands on lower extremity muscles and their relationship to cycling energetics is warranted.

Muscle activation patterns measured in experienced cyclists (Ryan & Gregor, 1992) have been used to define independent roles for single- and two-joint muscles in the generation of power during cycling.

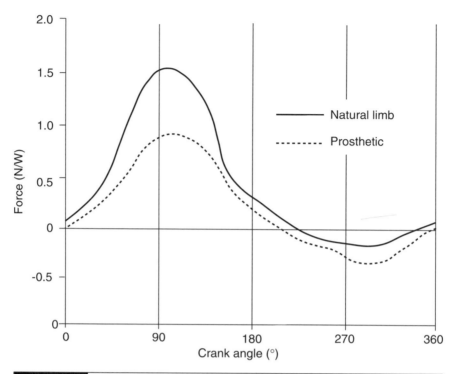

Figure 7.6 Mean effective force pattern versus crank angle for the natural and prosthetic limbs of unilateral (single limb) below-knee amputee cyclists ($N = 3$).

Specifically, Ryan and Gregor (1992) measured activity patterns (electromyography) in 10 lower extremity muscles in 18 experienced cyclists during steady state cycling (90 rpm, 250 W). The single-joint muscles monitored were gluteus maximus (crossing the hip), vastus lateralis, vastus medialis, and the short head of biceps femoris (crossing the knee), and soleus and tibialis anterior (crossing the ankle). Two-joint muscles monitored included the hamstrings (semimembranosus and semitendinosus, both crossing the hip and knee), the rectus femoris (crossing the hip and knee), and the gastrocnemius (crossing the knee and ankle). By analyzing their measured activation patterns in conjunction with previously reported joint torque profiles for the hip, knee, and ankle, these researchers suggested that single-joint muscles assume a relatively invariant role as primary power producers during cycling and that two-joint muscles act, with greater variability, as distributors of lower extremity energy. Muscle activity patterns for eight representative muscles among those monitored by Ryan and Gregor are shown in Figure 7.7.

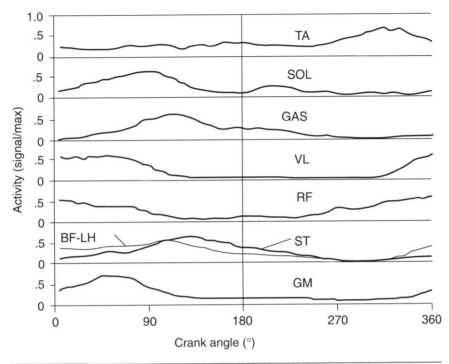

Figure 7.7 Muscle activation patterns for eight muscles of the leg monitored during steady state cycling. Muscles described include tibialis anterior (TA), soleus (SOL), gastrocnemius (GAS), vastus lateralis (VL), rectus femoris (RF), semitendinosis (ST), biceps femoris-long head (BF-LH), and gluteus maximus (GM). See text for description of the muscles and their roles in pedaling. Data from Ryan and Gregor (1992).

Another method of evaluating the contribution of different lower extremity muscles to cycling power involves a dynamic analysis of the rider-bicycle system, in which joint torques are computed for the hip, knee, and ankle during the pedal cycle. In this manner, the hip, knee, and ankle joints are imagined to be powered by hypothetical electric torque motors that vary in their contribution to system energy during the pedal cycle. Through observation of the operating characteristics of these hypothetical motors, an understanding of cycling system energetics emerges.

Broker and Gregor (1994), for example, calculated the joint powers developed at the hip, knee, and ankle (originating from hypothetical torque motors) for 12 junior national level cyclists pedaling at different cadences and work rates. These joint powers were computationally determined by multiplying the calculated instantaneous torque at a given joint by the respective joint angular velocity (Ingen Schenau &

Cavanagh, 1990). Joint powers determined in this study (Figure 7.8) indicated that all three joints generated energy throughout the first half of the pedal cycle. Peak power at the knee (250 W) was more than twice that observed at the hip and ankle (100 to 110 W). Additionally, the knee generated considerable power during recovery.

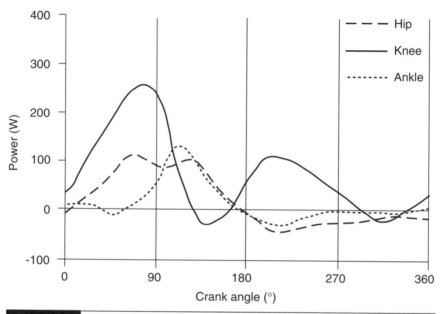

Figure 7.8   Mean joint power profiles for the hip, knee, and ankle versus crank angle for 12 junior national cyclists pedaling at 275 W, 90 rpm ($N = 12$). All three joints generate energy during the first half of the pedal cycle. During recovery, the knee generates energy while the hip and ankle absorb energy.

Several interesting concepts can be formulated from such an analysis. First, as indicated in Figure 7.8, power generated at each of the three joints is negative during portions of the pedal cycle. Negative power (or energy absorption) occurs when the torque developed by the muscles acting at a joint opposes the joint's direction of motion. At the knee, for example, a flexor torque is generated between 125° and 160° despite the fact that at this time in the pedal cycle the knee is extending (as the foot approaches the bottom of the pedal cycle). Similarly, energy is absorbed at the hip and ankle during portions of recovery as extensor torques (produced by the gluteals and hamstrings) and plantar flexor torques (produced by the calf muscles gastrocnemius and soleus) accompany hip flexion and ankle dorsiflexion, respectively. These actions, while seeming paradoxical, assist in delivering appropriately directed forces to the pedal and, perhaps more importantly, actually act to conserve mechanical energy (Broker & Gregor, 1994).

Second, integrating the joint powers with respect to crank angle (i.e., calculating the area under the power curves shown in Figure 7.8) provides the total amount of work (in joules) done at each joint. In this way, total joint contributions to cycling power are computed. For the test condition represented in Figure 7.8 (275 W, 90 rpm), for example, 63% of the energy developed at the joints was derived from action at the knee, 13% from the ankle, 17% from the hip; an additional 7% was associated with linear motion at the hip joint. The relatively low contributions at the hip and ankle were due to the significant regions of energy absorption (negative joint power) at these joints and the relatively low power developed at these joints during the power phase (when compared to the knee). A change in operating condition to higher cycling power resulted in a greater proportion of the energy coming from the hip and a lesser proportion from the knee.

A final concept derived from the dynamic analysis of cycling involves the use of joint powers to assess probable muscle and muscle group actions. Although beyond the scope of this chapter, the timing and magnitude of the joint powers can be used to estimate single- and two-joint muscle roles in powering the system. Using a computational method that accounts for anatomical features of specific muscles and muscle groups in the lower extremity, Broker (1991) suggested, not unlike Ryan and Gregor (1992), that single-joint muscles dominate in their contribution to powering a bicycle and also that two-joint muscles (specifically the hamstrings and gastrocnemius) may uniquely operate to (a) provide additional power to the bicycle and (b) distribute mechanical energy as needed between the hip, knee, and ankle to minimize unnecessary expenditure of energy during pedaling.

Directions for Future Research

Although the science of cycling has evolved considerably in recent years, the evolution of the sport threatens to outpace the supporting science. Biomechanists, engineers, and physiologists must work hard to continue unraveling the mysteries that remain unsolved, while adapting their questions to prevent changes in the sport from rendering their findings obsolete. The following are a few areas of research that, in our minds, deserve attention.

Radical Rider-Bicycle Geometries

During the 1992 Olympics in Barcelona, Chris Boardman (a British cyclist) rode a Lotus carbo-fiber monocoque bicycle that placed him in an unusually low, forward pedaling position. Boardman caught his competitor in the 4-km pursuit final—an unbelievable accomplishment at the elite level. Almost a year later, Graeme Obree (another British amateur) and Chris Boardman performed a series of assaults on the 1-hr distance record of 51.151 km (31.71 miles) set by Italian champion Francesco Moser in the thin air of Mexico City in 1984. Obree was the first to extend Moser's distance record, riding 51.596 km in an unusually large, 117-in. gear, on an awkward-looking bicycle in an extremely forward position (with his hands tucked against his shoulders). Boardman surpassed Obree's record 6 days later, pushing the mark to 52.270 km in the same forward position he had used to win the 1992, 4-km pursuit Olympic gold medal.

The accomplishments of Boardman and Obree may have literally changed the shape of cycling forever. Working creatively within the Union Cycliste Internationale's (UCI) rules for bicycle and componentry design, Boardman and Obree demonstrated the existence of alternative rider-bicycle positions that reduce aerodynamic drag without compromising critical elements of rider performance. More riders and bicycle designers will certainly follow the lead of Boardman and Obree. Furthermore, as UCI restrictions on bicycle designs change, one has to wonder what the bicycles of the next century will look like. Will a recumbent bicycle be raced in the 2000 or 2004 Olympics? The challenge falls upon the cycling scientific community to explore and interpret the effects of both mild and radical rider positional changes on the biomechanics of cycling.

Cycling Optimization

The accomplishments of Graeme Obree and Chris Boardman also exposed how little is known regarding "optimal" rider-bicycle systems. This lack of knowledge is surprising, particularly in light of the numerous studies that have specifically attempted to define optimal parameters of the rider-bicycle system (see Gregor, Broker, & Ryan, 1991). In summary, it appears that analytically or experimentally determined, superior rider-bicycle configurations and operating conditions (i.e., defined in terms of specific saddle height and fore-aft position, crank length, chainring shape, and cadence, etc.) have only marginally translated into "real world" results. Perhaps the task of cycling is much more complex than originally thought?

Continued research in the area of optimal cycling system definition is certainly needed. Limitations in previous optimization studies—for example, overly broad and unproven assumptions, limited input data, and low subject numbers—must be addressed. In light of the discrepancies between predicted (or laboratory) and real-world "optimal system" observations, the focus of further optimization studies may benefit from a shift to more athlete-specific optimal solution designs.

Injury Prevention

Injury prevention in cycling is a growing concern. As the cycling population expands, so do the number of cycling-related injuries. Recent shoe-pedal interface studies by Ruby, Hull, and Hawkins (1992) and Wheeler (1993) illustrate the type of research needed to identify critical interactions between rider and bicycle and their relationship with injury. A list of future biomechanical investigations designed to address the problem of injuries in cycling might include (a) the effects of modified cyclist positions (e.g., the forward aerodynamic position) on knee, back, and neck loads; (b) the effect of bicycle shock absorption systems on skeletal loading, fatigue, and injury; (c) the relationships between skeletal variations (e.g., leg length differences), bicycle setup (e.g., seat height, pedal system, crank length), and injury potential; and (d) the appropriate management of cycling injuries in general.

As new bicycle and component systems are developed, and as regulations concerning allowable geometries and safety features of racing and recreational bicycles continue to evolve, questions concerning cycling performance and injury potential under modified cycling conditions will arise. Biomechanists, physiologists, and engineers will be challenged with the task of addressing several of these questions; and the answers, as well as the scientific processes used to obtain them, promise to be very interesting.

References

Broker, J.P. (1991). *Mechanical energy management during constrained human movement.* Unpublished doctoral dissertation, University of California at Los Angeles.

Broker, J.P., & Gregor, R.J. (1990). A dual piezoelectric element force pedal for kinetic analysis of cycling. *International Journal of Sports Biomechanics,* **6**(4), 394-403.

Broker, J.P., & Gregor, R.J. (1994). Mechanical energy management in cycling: Source relations and energy expenditure. *Medicine and Science in Sports and Exercise,* **26**(1), 64-74.

Browning, R.C. (1991). *Lower extremity kinetics during cycling in elite triathletes in aerodynamic cycling.* Unpublished master's thesis, University of California at Los Angeles.

Cavanagh, P.L., & Sanderson, D.J. (1986). The biomechanics of cycling: Studies of the pedaling mechanics of elite pursuit riders. In E.R. Burke (Ed.), *Science of cycling* (pp. 91-122). Champaign, IL: Human Kinetics.

Francis, P.R. (1986). Injury prevention for cyclists: A biomechanical approach. In E.R. Burke (Ed.), *Science of cycling* (pp. 145-184). Champaign, IL: Human Kinetics.

Francis, P.R. (1988). Pathomechanics of the lower extremity in cycling. In E.R. Burke & M.M. Newsom (Eds.), *Medical and scientific aspects of cycling* (pp. 3-16). Champaign, IL: Human Kinetics.

Gregor, R.J., Broker, J.P., & Ryan, M.M. (1991). The biomechanics of cycling. *Exercise and Sport Sciences Reviews*, **19**, 127-169.

Gregor, R.J., & Wheeler, J.B. (1994). Biomechanical factors associated with shoe-pedal interfaces: Implications for injury. *Sports Medicine*, **17**(2), 117-131.

Hannaford, D.R., Moran, G.T., & Hlavac, H.F. (1986). Video analysis and treatment of overuse knee injury in cycling: A limited clinical study. *Clinics in Podiatric Medicine and Surgery*, **3**, 671-678.

Hennig, E.M., & Sanderson, D.J. (1992). In-shoe pressure distribution for cycling at different power outputs. In L. Draganich, R. Wells, & J. Bechtold (Eds.), *Proceedings of the Second North American Congress on Biomechanics* (pp. 251-252). Chicago: North American Congress on Biomechanics Organizing Committee.

Hull, M.L., & Davis, R.R. (1981). Measurement of pedal loading in bicycling—I. Instrumentation. *Journal of Biomechanics*, **14**, 843-855.

Kautz, S.A., & Hull, M.L. (1993). A theoretical basis for interpreting the force applied to the pedal in cycling. *Journal of Biomechanics*, **26**, 155-165.

LaFortune, M.A., & Cavanagh, P.R. (1983). Effectiveness and efficiency during bicycle riding. In M. Matsui and K. Kobayashi (Eds.), *Biomechanics VII-B: International series on sports science* 4B (pp. 928-936). Champaign, IL: Human Kinetics.

Ruby, P., Hull, M.L., & Hawkins, D. (1992). Three-dimensional knee loading during seated cycling. *Journal of Biomechanics*, **25**, 1195-1207.

Ryan, M.M., & Gregor, R.J. (1992). EMG profiles of lower extremity muscles during cycling at constant workload and cadence. *Journal of Electromyography and Kinesiology*, **2**(2), 69-80.

Sanderson, D.J. (1990, September). The biomechanics of cycling shoes. *Cycling Science*, 27-30.

Sanderson, D.J., & Cavanagh, P.R. (1987). An investigation of the in-shoe pressure distribution during cycling in conventional cycling shoes or running shoes. In B. Jonsson (Ed.), *Biomechanics X-B* (pp. 903-907). Champaign, IL: Human Kinetics.

Sanderson, D.J., & Hennig, E.M. (1992). In-shoe pressure distribution in cycling and running shoes during steady-rate cycling. In L. Draganich, R. Wells, & J. Bechtold (Eds.), *Proceedings of the Second North American Congress on Biomechanics* (pp. 247-248). Chicago: North American Congress on Biomechanics Organizing Committee.

Sharp, A. (1977). *Bicycles and tricycles.* Cambridge, MA: MIT Press. (Original work published 1896) van Ingen Schenau, G.T., & Cavanagh, P.R. (1990). Power equations in endurance sports. *Journal of Biomechanics, 23,* 865-881.

Wheeler, J.B. (1993). *Applied Mz moment patterns at the shoe/pedal interface: A biomechanical analysis of clip-less pedals, float features, and their implications for overuse knee injuries during cycling.* Unpublished master's thesis, University of California at Los Angeles.

Wheeler, J.B., Gregor, R.J., & Broker, J.P. (1992). A dual piezo-electric bicycle pedal with multiple shoe/pedal interface compatibility. *International Journal of Sports Biomechanics, 8,* 251-258.

8

Energy Expenditure During Cycling

James Hagberg, PhD • Steve McCole, MS

Energy expenditure is required in any movement where resistance or resistances must be overcome. In cycling, the energy expenditure required for different riding speeds is a complex function of a number of resistances, including frictional, rolling, and air resistances. To add further to the complexity, the contribution of these different resistances to the total resistance encountered varies with riding speed and numerous other environmental and mechanical factors.

Physics of Cycling

A critical consideration relative to the physics of cycling is that the total resistance to movement on a bicycle is a function of the square of the speed (Figure 8.1). Thus, doubling a rider's speed increases the total resistance to movement fourfold. In addition, there is a much greater increase in total resistance when a rider accelerates from 40 to 42 kph than in going from 20 to 22 kph.

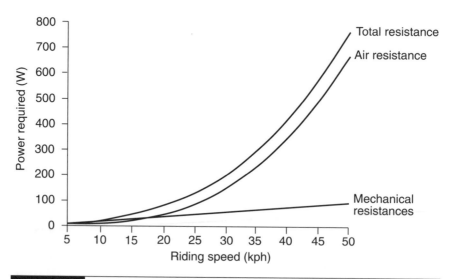

Figure 8.1 Mechanical, air, and total resistances across the range of speeds encountered by cyclists. These values are calculated based on a cyclist 75 kg in weight, 1.80 m² in body surface area, and 0.45 m² in frontal area in the upright position and a 9-kg bike.

Frictional Resistance

One component of the total resistance that cyclists encounter is the friction resulting from the mechanical components of the bicycle (DiPrampero, Cortili, Mognoni, & Saibene, 1979; Kyle, 1988; Pugh, 1974;

Sharp, 1896/1989; Sjogaard, Nielsen, Mikkelsen, Saltin, & Burke, 1986; Whitt, 1971; Whitt & Wilson, 1974). These resistances arise primarily from the drivetrain (frictional interaction between the chain and the chainring and freewheel gear) and within the wheel hubs. The power and energy expenditure required to overcome these resistances increases as a linear function of riding speed. However, these resistances are generally quite small in a well-maintained bicycle, and for the remainder of this discussion they will be considered as a unit with rolling resistance—a second mechanical component of the total resistance to movement.

Rolling Resistance

Rolling resistance is primarily a function of the resistance to movement resulting from the interaction between the bicycle tires and the road surface (DiPrampero, Cortili, Mognoni, & Saibene, 1979; Kyle, 1988; Pugh, 1974; Sharp, 1896/1989; Sjogaard, Nielsen, Mikkelsen, Saltin, & Burke, 1986; Whitt, 1971; Whitt & Wilson, 1974). The power and the energy expenditure required to overcome this factor is, again, a linear function of the cyclist's riding speed. However, rolling resistance can be decreased with smoother and harder road surfaces, larger-diameter wheels, higher tire pressure, and a number of other factors related to tire design (Kyle, 1986). Though lightweight racing tubular tires have the lowest rolling resistances, the performance characteristics of high-pressure clincher tires are nearly as good as those of midrange sew-up tires (Kyle, 1988). When frictional and rolling resistance are considered together as a total mechanical resistance, they account for the majority of the resistance to movement at slow cycling speeds (Figure 8.1). For example, at a 10-kph riding speed, frictional plus rolling resistances account for nearly 80% of the total resistance to movement. While the absolute amount of mechanical resistance increases with rider speed, the increase in air resistance is much greater and accounts for a disproportionate amount of the total resistance. Thus, at riding speeds of 20 and 40 kph, mechanical resistances account for only 46 and 18% of the total resistance, respectively.

Air Resistance

Air is the major resistance that must be overcome by cyclists riding at speeds usually encountered during racing and serious touring (Davies, 1980; Dill, Seed, & Marzulli, 1954; Kyle, 1979, 1988; Nonweiler, 1956; Pugh, 1974; Sharp, 1896/1989; Sjogaard, Nielsen, Mikkelsen, Saltin, & Burke, 1986; Whitt, 1971; Whitt & Wilson, 1974). At riding speeds greater than 20 kph, air resistance accounts for over half of the total resistance to movement encountered by the cyclist. Air resistance is the component of the total resistance that increases as the square of the rider's speed and is responsible for the exponential increase in total resistance as a function of a rider's speed. This exponential relationship results in the fact that at a 10-kph riding speed, air resistance accounts for less than 20% of the total resistance to movement encountered by the cyclist, whereas at 20 and 40 kph, air resistance increases to 54 and 82% of the total resistance, respectively (Figure 8.1).

Factors Influencing Energy Expenditure

Numerous factors can modify the air resistance riders encounter at speeds normally used during racing and serious touring. In this chapter we will discuss how riding speed, body position, drafting, and aerodynamic equipment can modify the air resistance of cyclists and hence their energy expenditure.

Wind Tunnel Studies

Most of the information concerning the resistances riders encounter during cycling has been derived from wind tunnel studies. In these studies the drag forces, and the resultant resistances, of the different components of total resistance can be quantified (Kyle, 1988, 1989, 1990, 1991a, 1991b; Nonweiler, 1956). However, the most valid test of aerodynamic benefits for cyclists is a reduction in energy expenditure while a cyclist is riding, as this is the physiological factor that cyclists must attempt to optimize. The ultimate goal of altering the aerodynamics of cyclists is to reduce their resistance and energy expenditure at a given speed, thus making it possible for them to ride longer at that speed, or to increase the speed they can achieve at a given energy expenditure, thereby making it possible for them to complete a given distance more rapidly. Energy expenditure is the critical physiological link between the physics and engineering aspects of reducing resistances to movement and improving performance. This interaction is important because numerous adjustments can be made to the equipment and position on the bike that will reduce the resistance to movement, but this may compromise the rider's physiological capacities. The final result could be that if the most aerodynamic position for a cyclist reduces his or her physiological capacities, performance may not improve.

Outdoor Measurements

Investigating the interaction between cyclists' aerodynamics and physiology requires making actual energy expenditure measurements on them as they ride outdoors. We developed a system a number of years ago to make such measurements for our studies funded by the U.S. Olympic Committee (McCole, Claney, Conte, Anderson, & Hagberg, 1990; Figure 8.2). The energy expenditure of cyclists riding their bicycles outdoors was measured by other investigators as far back as 1899 (Pugh, 1974; Zuntz, 1899), and our system was similar to those used previously (Adams, 1975; Dill, Seed, & Marzulli, 1954; Pugh, 1974; Swain, Coast, Clifford, Milliken, & Stray-Gunderson, 1987). A flexible fiberglass boom, from which the breathing valve was suspended, was extended forward at roughly a 45° angle from the roof of the cab of a small pickup truck (Figure 8.2). When the rider was connected to this system, he was in front and to the right of the truck so that the vehicle would have minimal impact on his aerodynamics. Riders performed the entire trial with a nose clip in place so that when they were connected to the system their expired gases were directed into low-resistance tubing that was suspended on the fiberglass boom and connected to a three-way valve in the back of the truck. Timed collections of each cyclist's expired gases were made into meteorological balloons over the last 3 to 4 min of 10-min trials; riders were in the experimental condition for the entire trial except

Figure 8.2 The system used to collect the cyclist's expired gases during riding outdoors on the roads. The flexible fiberglass boom from which the respiratory tubing and breathing valve are suspended is extended forward from the truck at about 45°. The three-way valve, wind speed indicator, and one meteorological balloon can be seen on the left side of the figure.

for a turnaround after approximately 3 to 4 min. Riders maintained the desired speed by using a calibrated cycle computer and recorded the time and distance during the expired gas collections to precisely quantify their speed. Wind speeds were also determined frequently during the expired gas collections so that alterations in headwinds and tailwinds could be factored into the final statistical analyses. A survey of the road where the trials were performed indicated that it had a total elevation change of less than 2 m over the 2,000-m section where the cyclists' expired gases were collected. No other substantive changes in elevation were evident anywhere along the course where the cyclists rode even prior to their connection to the system.

The collected expired gases were analyzed for oxygen and carbon dioxide content and their volume was measured so that the riders' oxygen consumption ($\dot{V}O_2$) could be calculated. $\dot{V}O_2$ was used in our studies to estimate energy expenditure because in all prolonged competitive events oxygen must be utilized to produce virtually all of the energy expenditure required to fuel the continued contractions of the active skeletal muscle. To determine the approximate number of kilocalories of energy expended per minute (a more familiar unit to many), multiply the $\dot{V}O_2$ values discussed in the following pages by 5.

Riders in these studies rode their own bicycles, except for people in the studies involving the aerodynamic bike. Riders in all studies used a standard set of control wheels on their bike (Mavic GEL 280 rims, Campagnolo 32-spoke hubs, double-butted spokes), except in the studies involving comparisons of different sets of wheels. All wheels had the same freewheels and tires (Vittoria Pro L 280-g slick sew-up racing tires), and tire pressure for all studies was standardized to 100 psi immediately before each trial. All cyclists rode with their hands on the dropped portion of the handlebars for the collection phase of each study and wore the same clothing and helmet in all trials. They also used the same gear for all trials except in studies of different riding speeds; they selected the gear they used as that most comfortable for them at that speed. To provide valid comparisons, all studies utilized a control trial under standard conditions on the same day the experimental trials were completed.

Riding Speed

Our first studies assessed the impact of different riding speeds on energy expenditure. The results indicated that we could make the best prediction of energy expenditure for individual riders when $\dot{V}O_2$ was expressed in units of liters per minute ($L \cdot min^{-1}$), or the liters of oxygen consumed per minute, as opposed to another frequently used way of expressing $\dot{V}O_2$, in units of milliliters of oxygen consumed per kilogram of body weight per minute (ml · kg^{-1} · min^{-1}). These results indicated an advantage that larger riders have on level grades. Although the total body $\dot{V}O_2$ of the larger riders was the same as that of smaller riders at the same speed, the larger riders would have more muscle mass to consume this O_2 and, hence, less of a physiological demand would be placed on each unit of their muscle mass. This phenomenon will be discussed later in the chapter.

During our studies we measured the $\dot{V}O_2$ required by riding speeds of 32, 37, and 40 kph. Our results are presented and compared to those of previous investigators in Figure 8.3. We did not see an exponential increase in $\dot{V}O_2$ as a function of riding speed because we studied only a limited range of riding speeds. However, when our data are combined with those from other studies to cover a wider range of riding speeds, it is clear that overall there is an exponential relationship between $\dot{V}O_2$ and riding speed. Thus, our measured energy expenditure data agree with previous hypothetical estimations and wind tunnel determinations indicating that energy expenditure increases exponentially with increasing riding speeds.

On the basis of data from nearly 100 trials in our study that were conducted under the same conditions, we derived an equation to predict the $\dot{V}O_2$ required for different riding speeds. In addition to riding speed, however, our analysis indicated that including both rider weight

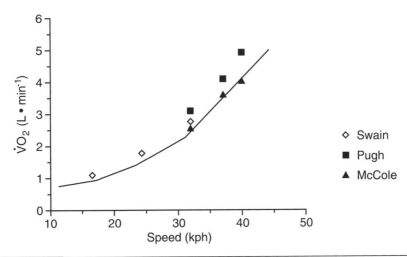

Figure 8.3 Comparison of the $\dot{V}O_2$ data from McCole and coworkers (1990), Pugh (1974), and Swain and coworkers (1987) for cyclists riding outdoors at different speeds. The solid line represents data from Whitt (1971) corrected to the body weight of the cyclists in our study using our derived body weight correction factor. Reprinted from McCole, Claney, Conte, Anderson, and Hagberg (1990).

and headwinds and tailwinds further improved our predictive accuracy. This analysis yielded the following equation:

$$\dot{V}O_2 = -4.50 + 0.17\ V_R + 0.052\ V_W + 0.022\ W_R,$$

$$(8.1)$$

where $\dot{V}O_2$ is in units of $L \cdot min^{-1}$, V_R is rider speed in kph, V_W is wind speed in kph (expressed as a positive number for a headwind, negative number for a tailwind), and W_R is rider weight in kilograms. This equation accounted for over 70% of the differences in $\dot{V}O_2$ observed among the various trials in our study. Thus, while this equation will not give a rider an absolutely precise value for $\dot{V}O_2$ under all conditions, it will provide a general estimate of a cyclist's energy expenditure, at least across the range of 32 to 40 kph utilized in this study. This equation also further substantiates the advantage larger riders have on level ground. Although the predicted $\dot{V}O_2$ increased with increasing rider weight at a given riding speed and headwind or tailwind, the increase is minimal if one considers the increased muscle mass the heavier rider would have with which to accomplish this only slightly higher level of energy expenditure.

Body Position

One simple and obvious method to decrease air resistance and hence energy expenditure is for cyclists to alter their position on the bike. The studies we have described were all conducted with the cyclists riding in a "racing" position, that is, with their hands on the dropped portion of the handlebars and with their backs relatively parallel to the ground. Thus, the riders in our studies had already reduced their effective frontal area and minimized their energy expenditure at any given riding speed. However, the information presented for power requirements in Figure 8.1 was based on a cyclist in an upright riding position. Thus, the effect of assuming a racing position on the bicycle can be determined by comparisons to these values (Table 8.1). A number of previous studies have determined that the racing position results in a 21% average reduction in effective rider frontal area compared to an upright body position (Nonweiler, 1956; Pugh, 1974; Whitt, 1971). This decrease in effective rider frontal area decreases the air resistance component of total resistance by the same fraction (Table 8.1). Therefore, assuming a racing position at slower riding speeds would have only a minimal effect on the power required. However, with increasing speed, the reduction in total power required would also approach 21% as air resistance becomes the major resistance to movement that must be overcome.

Table 8.1	Watts of Power Required to Overcome Air and Total Resistances in the Upright or Racing Position When Riding at Different Speeds

	Riding speed				
	10 kph	**20 kph**	**30 kph**	**40 kph**	**50 kph**
Upright position	23.6	79.4	199.1	415.0	759.3
Racing position	22.6	70.8	170.2	346.8	625.7
% Reduction	4%	11%	15%	17%	18%

Note. % Reduction is the reduction in total power required at that speed when going from the upright to the racing position.

Drafting

On the basis of our data on the energy cost of different riding speeds, our next goal was to assess the impact of drafting on energy expenditure. The benefit of drafting with respect to reducing air resistance and energy expenditure has been obvious to cyclists for nearly 100 years (Sjogaard, Nielsen, Mikkelsen, Saltin, & Burke, 1986). One early reference to the benefits of drafting is contained in the classic work by Sharp (1896/1989), who stated that two riders maintained a pace of nearly 45 kph for 4 hr, which he believed was beyond the power output capacity of a single rider because of "the decrease in the air resistance caused by the pace-makers in front" (p. 254). The benefits of drafting continue to be demonstrated in cycling events today. One graphic demonstration is that the world hour record set by Francesco Moser in 1984 under optimal aerodynamic conditions (high altitude and aero bike, wheels, components, and clothing), and its extension in 1994 by Graeme Obree to 52.713 km, represent paces that are maintained for roughly 2 hr by a number of top four-rider amateur teams in the 100-km team time trial at each year's world championships.

Our studies quantified the effect of drafting at the same three speeds used in our baseline energy expenditure studies—32, 37, and 40 kph. At 32 kph, the $\dot{V}O_2$ of riders drafting within 0.2 to 0.5 m of the rear wheel of a single rider in front of them was reduced by $18 \pm 11\%$ (mean ± standard deviation) compared to the value obtained when they were riding alone. At 37 and 40 kph the reductions were $28 \pm 10\%$ and $26 \pm 8\%$, respectively, both of which are greater than the reduction evident at 32 kph. Thus, it appears that the effect of drafting a single rider at speeds of 32 to 40 kph amounts to as much as 25 to 30% of the total required energy expenditure.

Data from Kyle (1979) indicate that air resistance was decreased by 38% in riders drafting at speeds ranging from 24 to 56 kph with the same wheel gap as that used in our studies. Since air resistance provides a different percentage of the total resistance cyclists encounter across this range of speeds, one would expect that at slow speeds this drafting effect would play less of a role in altering total resistance, and hence energy expenditure, while at higher speeds the difference in energy expenditure should asymptotically approach the 38% difference noted in air resistance. In fact, this is the case for Kyle's 1979 data, which show that drafting increases the energy expenditure savings from 7% at 10 kph to 32% at 50 kph (Table 8.2). Also, our data at 37 and 40 kph are consistent with those of Kyle at a speed of 40 kph (Table 8.2). However, at 32 kph we found much less of a drafting benefit than that calculated by Kyle from his air resistance reduction data (1979).

We also quantified the effects of different drafting formations on cyclists riding at 40 kph. We first studied the reduction in energy expenditure experienced by a rider drafting a line of 1, 2, or 4 riders (Figure 8.4). These results indicated that the reduction was approximately 27 ± 7% and was the same regardless of the number of cyclists in the pace line. The air resistance reduction measured by Kyle (1979) was also the same whether the rider followed 1, 2, or 3 other riders. We then quantified the reduction in energy expenditure resulting from riding at the back of a pack of cyclists. The pack consisted of 8 riders with 2 in the front row, 3 in the second row, and the experimental subject riding in the middle of a 3-rider third row. This subject experienced a 39 ± 6%

Table 8.2 Percentage Reductions in Energy Expenditure While Drafting at Different Speeds

	Riding speed				
	10 kph	**20 kph**	**30 kph**	**40 kph**	**50 kph**
Estimated reduction	7%	18%	26%	30%	32%
Measured reduction	−[1]	−[1]	18%[2]	27%	−[1]

Note. The estimated reductions are from Kyle (1979). The measured reductions in energy expenditure are from McCole, Claney, Conte, Anderson, and Hagberg (1990).

[1]Actual reductions in energy expenditure while drafting were not measured at these riding speeds.

[2]Actually measured while drafting at a riding speed of 32 kph.

reduction in energy expenditure while riding at 40 kph (Figure 8.4). Hence, it is little wonder why cyclists "sit in" in the pack; a lead rider could be working at maximal aerobic capacity ($\dot{V}O_2$max) while the rider "sitting in" in the pack would be working at only 60% of $\dot{V}O_2$max, a relative exercise intensity someone could maintain for hours without undue stress and fatigue.

Energy savings   Drafting formation

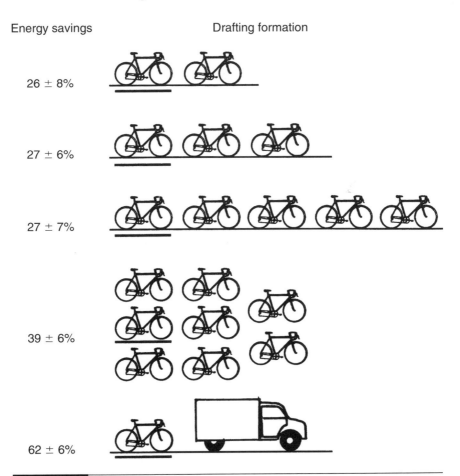

26 ± 8%

27 ± 6%

27 ± 7%

39 ± 6%

62 ± 6%

Figure 8.4 The energy reduction benefits of drafting in different formations. Reprinted from Hagberg and McCole (1990).

We also studied cyclists drafting a closed-bed pickup truck with the rear door raised above the rider's head. These results showed quite clearly the importance of air resistance at the high speeds cyclists encounter during competitive events, as energy expenditure was reduced by 62 ± 6% under these conditions (Figure 8.4). In other words, at

40 kph when riders were drafting a truck, their energy expenditure was only one third of that seen when they rode at that speed by themselves. These data also indicate quantitatively and experimentally that air resistance is the major component of the total resistance that cyclists must overcome when riding at speeds generally evident in competitive and serious touring events.

Aerodynamic Equipment

Another method of decreasing the air resistance of competitive and touring cyclists that has become very popular in the last decade is the use of numerous pieces of aerodynamic cycling equipment. In our studies we quantified the maximal effect achievable with aerodynamic cycling components available at the time by assessing the energy expenditure reductions associated with riding an aerodynamic bike. This bike had cow-horn handlebars and a down-sloping top tube, used a 24-in. front and a Wolber Record Discjet rear wheel (Table 8.3), and weighed 6.4 kg without wheels (compared to 6.6 to 7.0 kg for conventional bikes). The use of this bicycle resulted in a $7 \pm 4\%$ reduction in $\dot{V}O_2$ at a riding speed of 40 kph compared to the energy expended at this speed on a conventional road racing bicycle (see Figure 8.5). Data presented by Kyle (1988, 1991b) indicate that the design features incorporated into the aerodynamic bike would result in a 10% reduction in air resistance at a speed of 50 kph. At 40 kph the reduction in resistance would be somewhat less, and these changes affect only the air resistance component of total resistance. Thus, Kyle's results are probably not very much different from the 7% reduction in energy expenditure we observed with this bike. Thus, these data are consistent with those previously derived by others from wind tunnel studies of the reductions in resistances associated with aerodynamic bicycles.

We also assessed the effects of a number of different aerodynamic and disk wheel combinations (Table 8.3) on the energy expenditure of cyclists riding at 40 kph. These combinations ranged from fairly conventional wheels with aerodynamic spokes, rims, and nipples and minimal numbers of spokes to two sets of both front and rear disk wheels. Two sets of these wheels resulted in significant reductions in $\dot{V}O_2$ compared to the value obtained with the control set of wheels (Figure 8.5). The aerodynamic set of wheels with 16 spokes in the front and 18 in the rear reduced $\dot{V}O_2$ by $7 \pm 5\%$. These results also agree surprisingly well with the wind tunnel data of Kyle (1988, 1990, 1991b) indicating that resistance should have been reduced by roughly 8.5% at a speed of 50 kph. Assuming that this benefit, again, is somewhat less at the slower speed of 40 kph and that it represents a reduction in only the air resistance component of the total resistance, this 8.5% reduction in resistance

Table 8.3 Descriptive Information on the Wheel Combinations Used in the Studies of McCole, Claney, Conte, Anderson, and Hagberg (1990)

Wheels	Description	Wheel weight (kg)	
		Front wheel	Rear wheel
Control wheels	Campagnolo hub with 32 double-butted spokes, Mavic GEL 280 rims	1.025	1.550
Aero 16-18 wheels	Roval hubs, bladed spokes, 16-spoke front, 18-spoke rear, aerodynamic rims, recessed spoke nipples	1.075	1.525
Aero 24-32 wheels	Roval hubs, bladed spokes, 24-spoke front, 32-spoke rear, aerodynamic rims, recessed spoke nipples	1.110	1.525
Rear disk #1	Smooth enclosed rear disk wheel (Ambrosio)	–[1]	3.250
Rear disk #2	Same as control rear wheel except spokes covered by urethane-coated nylon sheet (Unidisk)	–[1]	1.675
Double disk #1	Epoxy composite disk bonded to aluminum rims with sealed hubs (HED disks)	1.350	1.740
Double disk #2	Flat composite honeycomb core between carbon fiber sheets, spun carbon fiber rims, and DuraAce hubs; 26-in. front wheel, 28-in. rear wheel (Wolber Record Discjet disks)	1.625	1.900
24-in. front	Radially spoked front wheel for aerodynamic bike	0.850	–[2]

Note. All weights were determined with tires on the wheels and the same freewheel on all the rear wheels.

[1]The control front wheel was used in combination with the rear disk wheels.

[2]The rear Wolber Record Discjet disk wheel was used in the aerodynamic bike studies.

Reprinted from McCole, Claney, Conte, Anderson, and Hagberg (1990).

would probably be reduced to somewhere close to the 7% reduction in total energy expenditure that we observed. The benefit that resulted from using the 16-18-spoke wheel set is also virtually the same as that resulting from the aerodynamic bike ($7 \pm 4\%$), a finding that is somewhat surprising. However, since our riders had not trained extensively on the aerodynamic bike before the study, we may not have maximized the benefit that could be achieved if the riders had felt more comfortable on it. Also, aerodynamic and energy expenditure benefits aside, the riders stated that the 16-18-spoke wheel set felt somewhat "mushy" during the rides and that they experienced a lot of wheel "flex" when accelerating.

One double-disk set of wheels also reduced energy expenditure by $3 \pm 4\%$; this value was relatively consistent among all of the cyclists and hence was statistically significant. However, even though winds were

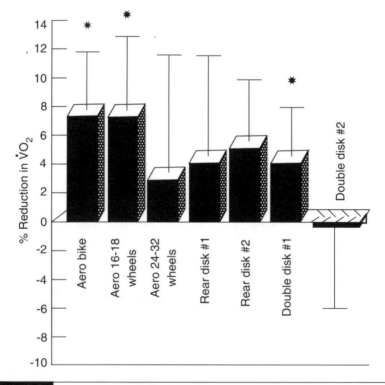

Figure 8.5 The energy reduction benefits of the aerodynamic bike and the different sets of wheels described in Table 8.3. The labels for the different wheel combinations are the same as in Table 8.3.

*Significant reduction in $\dot{V}O_2$ compared to that obtained when the cyclists used the control set of wheels on their own bikes. Reprinted from McCole, Claney, Conte, Anderson, and Hagberg (1990).

minimal during these trials, the riders reported that they had to concentrate more and perhaps expend some extra energy to steer and control their bikes when riding on both sets of double-disk wheels. The remaining sets of wheels also generally produced reductions in energy expenditure that averaged 1 to 4% compared to the value obtained with the control set of wheels; however, the reductions were not consistent enough to be statistically significant. These results agree well with the wind tunnel data of Kyle (1988, 1990, 1991a) showing that resistance reductions were generally in the range of 2 to 3% with similar sets of wheels.

Directions for Future Research

The methods we have used for measuring the energy expenditure of cyclists riding outside on the roads, at speeds similar to those encountered in competitive situations, have been employed previously by a number of investigators. Because of the logistical and technical problems inherent in performing these studies, it is difficult, if not impossible, to achieve variability as low as the 3 to 5% error values reported for laboratory determinations of $\dot{V}O_2$. Thus, unless an investigator has the capacity to study large numbers of cyclists, this methodology will not be useful for assessing differences in energy expenditure that would be in the range of only 1 to 5%. This problem is already evident in our studies of the benefits of the different set of wheels: One difference of 3% achieved statistical significance while another 4% average reduction in energy expenditure for a different set of wheels was not consistent enough to achieve statistical significance. Perhaps even more importantly, the 1 to 2% differences that could have tremendous performance implications in elite cyclists are virtually undetectable with this methodology. Thus, this limitation in sensitivity must be addressed when one attempts to apply this methodology to specific research questions.

On the other hand, the energy expenditure benefits resulting from a number of methods of altering cyclists' aerodynamics that undoubtedly have effects greater than 5%, have yet to be studied. One obvious set of studies must deal with forms of drafting different from those that we investigated. These might include larger packs, double pace lines, and echelons, for example. Additional possibilities for future studies are different sets of handlebars (ranging from standard to triathlon bars), the newer sets of wheels that have been developed (Trispoke, Aerospoke, Spinergy), and more recently developed aerodynamic bikes (Lotus, Corima, Zipp, GT). In addition, numerous other advances that are being made virtually continuously in the aerodynamics of cyclists and their equipment may have effects beyond the 5% lower limit detectable with this system.

Studies on the energy expenditure benefits of these new pieces of equipment and new techniques are critical for a complete understanding of the interactive effect between aerodynamics and the rider's physiology. This may become even more important in the future as more radical changes are made in the cyclist's position on the bike—changes that might eventually impair cyclists' physiological capacities and performance, despite substantial benefits in aerodynamic terms. One example that is tending in this direction is the rather radical changes in bike and cycling position used recently by Graeme Obree of Great Britain (Zinn, 1993). As is evident in Figure 8.6, his arms are under his chest with his chest resting on his hands, the handlebars are flat and narrower than conventional bars, and the bottom bracket has been narrowed so that his knees virtually touch each other. Such a riding position is beneficial only if the rider maintains the physiological capacities to take advantage of the aerodynamic benefits.

The other very real possibility is that energy expenditure studies can quantify the adaptations cyclists make over time to these new riding

Figure 8.6 New aerodynamic bike and cycling position of Graeme Obree.
Photo courtesy of Photosport International®.

positions. Any time an elite athlete's physiology or equipment is altered, a deterioration in performance will generally result unless the benefit associated with the change is substantial. However, the rider may well adapt physiologically over time to take advantage of an enhanced aerodynamic position. Thus, as adaptations are taking place, the energy expenditure of the rider may be decreasing as his or her physiology responds to the alteration in position. The possibility that this has occurred is suggested by reports that Graeme Obree and Chris Boardman were developing, and riding in, their new cycling positions (Figure 8.6) for a number of years before their breakthrough performances in 1993-1994 (Zinn, 1993). In addition, at age 42 Francesco Moser, after training to ride in the "Obree position," capitalized on the aerodynamic benefits by breaking his hour mark set 10 years previously and fell only 700 m short of the current world hour record.

Acknowledgments

The research by the authors that is described in this chapter was supported by grants from the U.S. Olympic Committee Sports Medicine Council. The authors also would like to thank Troxel West of California for the generous donation of the Wolber Record Discjet set of disk wheels. The authors also appreciate the ability to purchase the Roval wheel sets from William Lewis Imports of Pflugerville, Texas, and the HED disk wheels from HED Design of White Bear Lake, Minnesota, at cost. The authors would also like to thank the numerous graduate and undergraduate students who assisted in these studies and the cyclists who, usually willingly, gave of their early morning hours to take part in these studies. We are also grateful to Mike Cochran, the owner of Pedallers Bike Shop (Gainesville, Florida), and his staff for their mechanical and logistical support, without which these studies would have been impossible.

References

Adams, W.C. (1975). *Studies of metabolic energy expenditure in bicycling* (Rep. 75-2). Davis, CA: University of California, Department of Civil Engineering, College of Engineering.

Davies, C.T.M. (1980). Effect of air resistance on the metabolic cost and performance of cycling. *European Journal of Applied Physiology,* **45,** 245-254.

Dill, D.B., Seed, J.C., & Marzulli, F.N. (1954). Energy expenditure in bicycle riding. *Journal of Applied Physiology,* **47,** 320-324.

DiPrampero, P.E., Cortili, G., Mognoni, P., & Saibene, F. (1979). Equation of motion of a cyclist. *Journal of Applied Physiology*, **47**, 201-206.

Hagberg, J.M., & McCole, S.D. (1990). The effect of drafting and aerodynamic equipment on energy expenditure during cycling. *Cycling Science*, **2**(3), 20.

Kyle, C.R. (1979). Reduction of wind resistance and power output of racing cyclists and runners travelling in groups. *Ergonomics*, **22**, 387-397.

Kyle, C.R. (1986). Mechanical factors affecting the speed of a cycle. In E.R. Burke (Ed.), *Science of cycling* (pp. 123-136). Champaign, IL: Human Kinetics.

Kyle, C.R. (1988). The mechanics and aerodynamics of cycling. In E.R. Burke & M.M. Newsom (Eds.), *Medical and scientific aspects of cycling* (pp. 235-252). Champaign, IL: Human Kinetics.

Kyle, C.R. (1989). The aerodynamics of handlebars and helmets. *Cycling Science*, **1**, 22-25.

Kyle, C.R. (1990). Wind tunnel tests of bicycle wheels and helmets. *Cycling Science*, **2**, 27-30.

Kyle, C.R. (1991a). New aero wheel tests. *Cycling Science*, **3**, 27-30.

Kyle, C.R. (1991b). Wind tunnel tests of aero bicycles. *Cycling Science*, **3**, 57-61.

McCole, S.D., Claney, K., Conte, J-C., Anderson, R., & Hagberg, J.M. (1990). Energy expenditure during bicycling. *Journal of Applied Physiology*, **68**, 748-753.

Nonweiler, T. (1956). *Air resistance of racing cyclists* (Rep. No. 106). Cranfield, England: College of Aeronautics.

Pugh, L.C.G.E. (1974). The relation of oxygen intake and speed in competition cycling and comparative observations on the bicycle ergometer. *Journal of Physiology (Cambridge)*, **241**, 795-808.

Sharp, A. (1989). *Bicycles and tricycles: An elementary treatise on their design and construction*. Cambridge, MA: MIT Press. (Original work published 1896)

Sjogaard, G., Nielsen, B., Mikkelsen, F., Saltin, B., & Burke, E.R. (1986). *Physiology in bicycling*. Ithaca, NY: Mouvement Publications.

Swain, D.P., Coast, J.R., Clifford, P.S., Milliken, M.C., & Stray-Gunderson, J. (1987). Influence of body size on oxygen consumption during bicycling. *Journal of Applied Physiology*, **62**, 668-672.

Whitt, F.R. (1971). A note on the estimation of the energy expenditure of sporting cyclists. *Ergonomics*, **14**, 419-424.

Whitt, F.R., & Wilson, D.G. (1974). *Bicycling science*. Cambridge, MA: MIT Press.

Zinn, L. (1993, July 12). Shape of things to come? *VeloNews*, p. 53.

Zuntz, L. (1899). *Untersuchungen uber den Gaswechsel und Energieumsatz des Radfahrers* [An examination of gas exchange and energy metabolism in cyclists]. Berlin: Hirschwald.

9

Nutrition for Cycling

W. Michael Sherman, PhD

Proper nutrition is essential for good health. Physical activity increases the metabolism of nutrients that have been derived from foods to provide energy for muscular contraction. When people participate in physical activity (e.g., exercise), it is important to assure appropriate nutrient intake to at least maintain and possibly optimize the bodily levels of these nutrients to perform the required exercise task. Because the bodily carbohydrate reserves derived from the consumption of dietary carbohydrate are the primary determinants of endurance cycling capabilities, this chapter will focus on the interactions between carbohydrate in the diet, bodily carbohydrate reserves, and cycling performance.

Bodily Carbohydrate Stores

Bodily stores of carbohydrate are extremely limited compared to bodily stores of fat and protein. At the exercise intensities most often employed during training for cycling endurance and performance (> 90 min at > 70% $\dot{V}O_2$max) (Burke, Faria, & White, 1990), bodily carbohydrate reserves are the muscle's preferred fuel to provide the energy for muscle contraction (Saltin & Karlsson, 1971). Because bodily carbohydrate reserves are the preferred fuel and because those reserves are limited, exhaustion during endurance cycling exercise occurs when these reserves are reduced or severely depleted (Hermansen, Hultman, & Saltin, 1967; Hultman, 1978). Thus, to optimize adaptations to endurance training, it is sensible to undertake nutritional practices to assure sufficient reserves of bodily carbohydrate during every phase of training. Also, to optimize performance of a single cycling endurance event, it is shrewd to employ nutritional strategies to assure optimal performance. To meet these objectives, cyclists must not only learn to accurately monitor their carbohydrate intake; they must also learn which foods or beverages contain high amounts of carbohydrate, and they must learn how to consume these foods and beverages to attain the desired nutritional outcomes.

The bodily stores of carbohydrate that are broken down to provide the energy for muscular contraction during endurance cycling exercise are muscle glycogen and blood glucose. The muscle glycogen concentration is ~ 130 mmol · kg^{-1} in an endurance-trained cyclist consuming a diet containing 50% of energy from carbohydrate (Sherman, Costill, Fink, & Miller, 1981). As the intensity of cycling exercise increases, the rate of muscle glycogen degradation increases (Essen, 1977). Fatigue during endurance exercise often occurs coincidentally with a low muscle glycogen concentration (Hermansen, Hultman, & Saltin, 1967; Saltin &

Karlsson, 1971). Also, there is a strong association between the initial muscle glycogen concentration and the length of time that endurance exercise can be undertaken until fatigue (Ahlborg et al., 1967). Thus, cycling endurance training and performance capabilities should be optimized when the muscle glycogen concentration at the start of exercise is as high as can be attained.

The liver glycogen concentration is highly variable and can range between 80 and 400 mmol · kg^{-1} (Hultman, 1978). The blood glucose concentration represents the rate of glucose appearance in and disappearance from the blood stream. Endurance exercise at constant intensity produces a constant disappearance of glucose from the blood because muscle glucose uptake is constant (Ahlborg, Felig, Hagenfeldt, Hendler, & Wahren, 1974). During the later stages of exercise when the blood glucose concentration declines, the liver cannot produce blood glucose at a constant rate. The reduced rate of glucose production by the liver is due primarily to liver glycogen depletion (Ahlborg, Felig, Hagenfeldt, Hendler, & Wahren, 1974).

The muscle and liver glycogen concentrations are related to the amount of glycogen degraded during exercise, the time between exercise sessions, and the amount and form of dietary carbohydrate that is consumed between exercise sessions. It will be obvious from the following discussion that manipulating dietary carbohydrate intake can significantly influence the bodily carbohydrate stores and thereby influence cycling training and performance capabilities. Cyclists who wish to optimize their cycling capability should know when those "windows of opportunity" exist to positively influence bodily carbohydrate reserves.

What Do Endurance Athletes Really Eat?

While many endurance athletes contend that they consume a diet that is predominantly carbohydrate, a critical evaluation of the dietary practices of endurance athletes is less encouraging (Johnson et al., 1985). Elite male and female athletes typically consume diets that have less than the recommended dietary carbohydrate content (Grandjean, 1986). Presumably, daily ingestion of an adequate amount of dietary carbohydrate will "top off" bodily carbohydrate reserves between training sessions. The consequence of adequate daily carbohydrate intake should be an improved training capability that will translate into an improved performance capacity. Thus, cyclists should better educate themselves about the combinations of foods that will provide the proper quantity of dietary carbohydrate in the diet.

Daily Dietary Carbohydrate Consumption, Muscle Glycogen, and Performance

It has been known for a long time that there is a direct relationship between the quantity of dietary carbohydrate consumed and muscle and liver glycogen stores (Bergstrom, Hultman, & Roch-Norlund, 1972; Costill et al., 1981; Hultman, 1978). Because these bodily carbohydrate stores influence a cyclist's ability to train and perform optimally, the influences of consuming different amounts of carbohydrate on muscle glycogen and training and performance capabilities have been intensely studied. These studies have typically lasted for up to 10 days, while few studies have lasted up to 4 weeks.

The studies lasting up to 10 days have generally found that a moderate- or low-carbohydrate diet results in a lowered muscle glycogen concentration (Costill, Bowers, Branum, & Sparks, 1971; Costill et al., 1988; Kirwan et al., 1988; Pascoe et al., 1990; Sherman, Doyle, Lamb, & Strauss, 1993). However, there is not consistent and convincing evidence that the reduced muscle glycogen concentration produces a decrease in training or performance capabilities over this short period of time. For example, studies that suddenly roughly doubled overall training load when athletes consumed a moderate-carbohydrate (Costill, Bowers, Branum, & Sparks, 1971; Costill et al., 1988; Kirwan et al., 1988; Pascoe et al., 1990) or high-carbohydrate (Kirwan et al., 1988) diet, resulting in a 13 to 20% decline in muscle glycogen, respectively, reported no overall impairment in training or performance capabilities.

On the other hand, the results of the only study that has manipulated diet and exercise for longer than 10 days (Simonsen et al., 1991) suggest that chronic consumption of a moderate-carbohydrate diet probably begins to negatively affect training and performance capabilities after roughly 4 weeks. In this study athletes consumed either a moderate- or high-carbohydrate diet (5-10 g carbohydrate $\cdot$ kg body weight^{-1} $\cdot$ day^{-1}) for 4 weeks while undergoing 6 days per week of twice-daily intense training. The morning workouts were primarily aerobic conditioning, and the afternoon workouts were interval sets employing negative splits for 3 days and anaerobic performance tests for the other 3 days. One day during the week was for aerobic training and reassessment of maximal oxygen consumption.

During the 4 weeks of training, muscle glycogen remained constant (119 mmol $\cdot$ kg^{-1}) for the moderate-carbohydrate group, whereas it increased by 65% for the high-carbohydrate group. Interestingly, whereas performance had improved by 11% for the high-carbohydrate group, performance had deteriorated most for the moderate-carbohydrate group on the final day of training. Thus, it appears that chronic consumption of a high-carbohydrate diet facilitates a greater training capacity, whereas chronic consumption of a moderate-carbohydrate diet may produce suboptimal training and performance capabilities after roughly 4 weeks.

It is apparent from the preceding discussion that no study has clearly demonstrated a cause-and-effect relationship between chronically lowered muscle glycogen concentrations resulting from consumption of a moderate-carbohydrate diet and reduced training and performance capabilities. On the other hand, no studies have disproved the hypothesis that chronic consumption of a high-carbohydrate diet results in higher muscle glycogen concentrations and that this maintains or improves training and performance capabilities. In fact, only one study supports this hypothesis (Simonsen et al., 1991). Nevertheless, because a high-carbohydrate diet contributes to the maintenance of bodily carbohydrate reserves, it remains reasonable for cyclists to attempt to consume a diet that contains a high amount of carbohydrate providing between 8 and 10 g carbohydrate $\cdot$ kg body weight^{-1} $\cdot$ day^{-1}. This recommendation is consistent with the recommendation that the general population consume a high-carbohydrate–low-fat diet for overall health reasons.

Preexercise Carbohydrate Consumption

Even though cyclists know that a high-carbohydrate diet is the best diet to optimize training and performance capabilities, dietary practices or timing of training and performance, or both, often create the potential for suboptimal training sessions or performance. This observation has led to examination of the potential for preexercise carbohydrate feedings to influence cycling performance capabilities.

Although in the 1970s and 1980s athletes were advised to not consume carbohydrates during the hours before exercise, it is clear now that this recommendation is not correct. This initial advice was based upon the observation that during 30 min of exercise at 70% maximal aerobic capacity ($\dot{V}O_2$max), undertaken 45 min after ingestion of a solution containing 70 g of glucose, the blood glucose concentration declined significantly and carbohydrate oxidation and glycogen breakdown were increased (Costill et al., 1977). Because of the rapid decline in blood glucose, the increased degradation of muscle glycogen, and the higher rate of carbohydrate metabolism, it could be suggested that preexercise carbohydrate feedings would impair endurance performance as a result of an early depletion of bodily carbohydrate reserves. The potential negative effects of preexercise carbohydrate feedings on endurance performance were not determined in this study. Nevertheless, these effects of preexercise carbohydrate feedings on carbohydrate metabolism were generalized to a negative effect on performance (Costill & Miller, 1980), and consumption of carbohydrate during the hours before exercise was strongly discouraged.

More recent evidence, however, suggests that preexercise carbohydrate feedings have the potential to supplement the bodily carbohydrate reserves and potentially improve cycling training and performance capabilities. An interesting study by Coyle, Coggan, Hemmert, Lowe, and Walters (1985) required subjects to cycle at 70% $\dot{V}O_2$max for 4 hr after consuming 2 g carbohydrate $\cdot$ kg body weight[-1] 4 hr before exercise. Muscle glycogen degradation was not altered by consuming the preexercise carbohydrate foods (bagels and jelly), and the rate of carbohydrate oxidation was increased *only during the first 105 min of exercise*. Importantly, in spite of the initially greater rate of carbohydrate metabolism that might impair endurance performance, all the subjects were able to complete the prescribed exercise task.

Subsequently, the majority of published studies have reported that preexercise carbohydrate feedings improve cycling performance capabilities (Gleeson, Maughan, & Greenhaff, 1986; Neuffer et al., 1987; Okano et al., 1988; Sherman et al., 1989; Sherman, Peden, & Wright, 1991; Wright, Sherman, & Dernbach, 1990). These studies employed preexercise carbohydrate feedings ranging between 2 and 5 g of liquid carbohydrate $\cdot$ kg body weight[-1] that was consumed between 1 and 4 hr before exercise. The exercise tasks lasted between 90 min and 4 hr or until exhaustion and sometimes included time trials or simulated breakaways during the trials. All the studies employed constant-intensity exercise between 62 to 75% $\dot{V}O_2$max, while the time trials or breakaways required much higher exercise intensities for short periods of time. Most importantly, performance was consistently significantly improved by 10 to 18%. While it is conceivable that the preexercise carbohydrate feedings increased the muscle and liver glycogen stores before exercise, it is most likely that the preexercise carbohydrate feedings improved performance by maintaining a higher level of carbohydrate availability that allows a higher power output during the later stages of the exercise tasks.

Importantly, there are no reliable and adequately replicated published studies demonstrating that preexercise carbohydrate feedings impair endurance performance (Sherman, 1991). However, the studies that used feedings of carbohydrate 1 hr before exercise (Costill et al., 1977; Gleeson, Maughan, & Greenhaff, 1986; Sherman, Peden, & Wright, 1991) reported an initial decline in blood glucose during the first 30 min of exercise. In spite of this initial rapid decline in blood glucose, there were no reports of individuals sensitive to this "lowering of blood glucose" who had to stop exercising or reduce their exercise intensity.

Nevertheless, there are people who purportedly *are* sensitive to a lowering of blood glucose and who would fatigue when the blood glucose concentration declined; these people would not benefit from preexercise carbohydrate feedings. We do not know what factors are responsible for this individual sensitivity to the lowering of blood glucose.

Effects of Carbohydrate Feedings During Exercise

The majority of cycling training and performances are undertaken at exercise intensities that range between 70 and 85% $\dot{V}O_2$max. At these intensities, roughly 55 to 65% of the energy for muscle contraction is derived from the metabolism of carbohydrate and the remaining is derived from the metabolism of fat (Coyle, 1991). Accordingly, during the first 60 to 120 min of exercise at these intensities, muscle glycogen is the primary carbohydrate that is broken down to provide energy for muscle contraction; thereafter, blood glucose is the primary carbohydrate broken down to provide this energy (Coggan & Swanson, 1992). Because the liver glycogen stores are limited, without carbohydrate supplementation the blood glucose concentration will decline, and fatigue will occur when inadequate carbohydrate (muscle glycogen and blood glucose) is available to maintain the desired exercise intensity (shown in Figure 9.1) (Coyle, Coggan, Hemmert, & Ivy, 1986).

As Figure 9.1 demonstrates, consuming carbohydrate during cycling maintains or elevates the blood glucose concentration, and this significantly improves cycling endurance and performance capabilities (Coggan

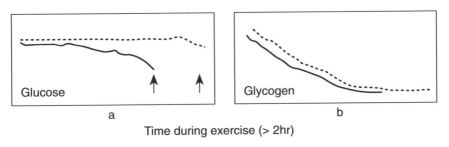

Figure 9.1 Blood glucose (a), muscle glycogen concentrations (b), and endurance time until fatigue (↑) during prolonged cycling endurance exercise (> 2 hr at > 70% $\dot{V}O_2$max) when either placebo (solid line) or carbohydrate-electrolyte (dotted line) solutions are consumed as recommended according to the text and in Table 9.1. Adapted from Coyle, Coggan, Hemmert, and Ivy (1986).

& Coyle, 1987, 1988; Coyle, Coggan, Hemmert, & Ivy, 1986; Coyle et al., 1983; Davis et al., 1988; Ivy, Costill, Fink, & Lower, 1979; Murray et al., 1987; Wright, Sherman, & Dernbach, 1991). However, carbohydrate ingestion must begin before there is a significant decline in bodily carbohydrate reserves. Also, appropriate amounts of carbohydrate must be consumed.

It is important to understand that even though carbohydrate feedings during exercise can improve cycling performance by delaying the decline in blood glucose, carbohydrate feedings during cycling exercise *cannot prevent fatigue*. There is an inevitable point in time at which the low muscle glycogen concentration in particular muscle fibers, the prevailing blood glucose concentration, and the inability of muscle fibers to metabolize other available fuels, in combination, contribute to muscular exhaustion. Notably, even when sufficient muscular and blood-borne fats are available, the maximal rate of fat metabolism cannot supply energy at a sufficient rate for most cyclists to maintain the desired pace and remain competitive when bodily carbohydrate stores are low.

Thus, the critical questions are: (a) When should carbohydrate be ingested during exercise? and (b) How much carbohydrate should be ingested during exercise? On the basis of current studies it appears that a cyclist should begin consuming carbohydrate as soon as possible after the start of exercise. Although carbohydrates may be consumed as foods, it is often necessary to prevent the negative effects of dehydration and thus they are typically consumed in liquid form as a carbohydrate beverage. In fact, most studies measuring the effects of carbohydrate ingestion on cycling performance have used liquid carbohydrate beverages. Relatively fewer studies have determined the ergogenic (work enhancing) effects of solid carbohydrate foods with and without fluid ingestion on cycling performance.

If dehydration is likely to occur during the training or performance activity, liquid carbohydrate supplementation should occur within the first 20 min of exercise. If dehydration is not likely to occur and thus fluid consumption early in exercise is not an objective, liquid carbohydrate supplementation must occur at least before the blood glucose concentration has begun to decline significantly (Coggan & Swanson, 1992).

During cycling at training and performance intensities, the blood glucose concentration usually begins to decline after about 2 hr of exercise. If carbohydrate and fluid supplementation are the objective (e.g., exercise is longer than 2 hr and dehydration is likely to occur), the liquid carbohydrate beverage should be consumed to provide about 40 to 60 g of carbohydrate per hour of exercise (Coggan & Swanson, 1992; Coyle, 1992). The concentration of the liquid carbohydrate beverage can range between 7 and 10% carbohydrate (weight/volume) for carbohydrate and fluid delivery to be optimized. Most carbohydrate-electrolyte beverages that are sold commercially have concentrations in this range (see Table 9.1).

If carbohydrate cannot be consumed until later in exercise (e.g., approximately 2 hr of cycling) but can be taken before the blood glucose concentration has begun to significantly decline, about 100 to 200 g of carbohydrate should be consumed as a single large feeding (Coggan & Coyle, 1989). The concentration of the liquid carbohydrate beverage should probably be 20% (weight/volume) so there is not a tremendous volume load under this circumstance. Most commercial carbohydrate beverages that are sold to replenish muscle glycogen during postexercise recovery have this concentration of carbohydrate (see Table 9.1). After ingestion of the large bolus of carbohydrate, a carbohydrate beverage should be consumed to provide about 40 to 80 g of carbohydrate per hour of exercise (Coggan & Swanson, 1992; Coyle, 1992).

In practice, cyclists consume both liquid and solid forms of carbohydrate during some cycling activities. Unfortunately, only one study has directly compared the effects of equivalent solid and liquid carbohydrate supplements on carbohydrate metabolism, fluid homeostasis, and performance capabilities. Lugo, Sherman, Wimer, and Garleb (1993) fed subjects 0.4 g carbohydrate · kg body weight[-1] 10 min before, and every 30 min during, 2 hr of cycling at 70% $\dot{V}O_2$max. The carbohydrate was provided in liquid form, solid form (with water to equal the volumes ingested for the liquid trial), and in combination (50% solid and 50% liquid). Blood glucose responses, total carbohydrate oxidation, and performance times were similar among the treatments. Thus, the results suggest that when equivalent amounts of fluid are consumed, carbohydrate can be ingested as either a liquid or a solid and that the consumed carbohydrate will be digested and absorbed at similar rates and will equally support muscle metabolism. It can be inferred, however, that solid forms of carbohydrate that are ingested without fluid would not be digested as quickly and thus would not as effectively support muscle metabolism or as effectively maintain hydration.

It is interesting to propose that combinations of nutritional strategies will produce potentially greater ergogenic effects than a particular nutritional strategy alone. Few studies have determined these combined effects, probably because of expense, time, the problem of subject compliance, and the difficulty in measuring performance outcomes of multiple interventions. Nevertheless, Wright, Sherman, and Dernbach (1991) sought to determine whether combining preexercise carbohydrate feedings with carbohydrate feedings during exercise would produce greater effects on endurance performance than only the preexercise feeding or the feedings during exercise. The 10 subjects in this study cycled at 70% $\dot{V}O_2$max until exhausted and performed break-away

Table 9.1 Selected Commercial Carbohydrate Beverages and Their Recommended Consumption

Beverage	Company	Carbohydrate concentration (%)	Volume of carbohydrates to consume each hour during exercise					
			40 g			60 g		
			mL	oz	# 8-oz cups	mL	oz	# 8-oz cups
Gatorade	Gatorade Worldwide Co.	6	667	24	3	1,000	36	4.5
Coca Cola	Coca Cola, USA	≈11	364	13	1.6	545	19	2.4
Orange Juice Apple Juice		≈15	267	10	1.2	400	14	1.8

Volume of carbohydrates to consume between 90 and 120 min of exercise

Beverage	Company	Carbohydrate concentration (%)	100 g			200 g		
			mL	oz	# 8-oz cups	mL	oz	# 8-oz cups
Gator-Lode	Gatorade Worldwide Co.	20	500	18	2.3	1,000	36	4.5

Volume of carbohydrates to consume immediately after exercise

Beverage	Company	Carbohydrate concentration (%)	1.5 g/kg/2 hr*			0.4 g/kg/15 min*		
			mL	oz	# 8-oz cups	mL	oz	# 8-oz cups
Gator-Lode	Gatorade Worldwide Co.	20	525	19	2.3	140	5	0.6

*Assuming a 70 kg person.

intervals every 40 min. Interestingly, combining preexercise carbohydrate feedings (5 g carbohydrate · kg body weight^{-1} 4 hr before exercise) with carbohydrate feedings during exercise (0.2 g carbohydrate · kg body weight^{-1} every 20 min [20% solution]) improved performance to a greater extent than either strategy alone (e.g., 80-min increase in endurance time for the combined trial and a 40-min increase in endurance time for either the preexercise feeding or the feeding during exercise trials, compared to a placebo trial). Thus, it is intriguing to propose that a combination of all the potentially ergogenic strategies using carbohydrates might produce an even greater ergogenic effect.

Carbohydrate Consumption After Exercise

Cyclists must often compete or train at regular intervals. Thus, it is important for them to employ nutritional strategies that will optimize the replenishment of bodily carbohydrate reserves during the rest interval between exercise sessions. Presumably the full restoration of bodily carbohydrate reserves during this rest interval will optimize training or performance capabilities, or both, during subsequent exercise sessions. Most studies have manipulated postexercise carbohydrate intake to determine the ideal postexercise carbohydrate feeding schedules to restore bodily carbohydrate reserves. However, few of those studies have determined whether the feeding schedules that maximize the restoration of bodily carbohydrate reserves also optimize the restoration of muscle function (e.g., training or performance capacity). Nevertheless, it seems reasonable to suggest that nutritional strategies producing greater restoration of bodily carbohydrate reserves will result in a greater restoration of muscle function than those strategies producing a smaller restoration of bodily carbohydrate reserves.

It appears that liver and muscle glycogen can be restored within 24 hr after glycogen-depleting exercise. This is true if between 9 and 16 g of carbohydrate · kg body weight^{-1} is consumed in the 24-hr period (Sherman & Lamb, 1988). The muscle glycogen level after 24 hr is also proportional to the amount of carbohydrate consumed, at least up to 600 g of carbohydrate per day (Costill et al., 1981). Importantly, when little (< 150 g carbohydrate) or no carbohydrate is consumed, the amount of glycogen in the muscle after 24 hr is low (Costill et al., 1981) because the rate of glycogen synthesis is low (< 3 mmol · kg^{-1} · hr^{-1}) (Ivy, Katz, Cutler, Sherman, & Coyle, 1988; MacDougall, Ward, Sale, & Sutton, 1977).

Although the influences of the type of exercise on nutritional manipulations to promote glycogen restoration have not been extensively studied, it has been suggested that less dietary carbohydrate is necessary to restore muscle glycogen after intense interval cycling exercise. It seems that consuming *only* 5 g carbohydrate · kg body weight^{-1} · day^{-1} may restore muscle glycogen in a 24-hr period after intense interval cycling exercise (MacDougall, Ward, Sale, & Sutton, 1977). However, before this recommendation is accepted, similar additional studies should be conducted to affirm this possibility.

Because different carbohydrates produce different blood glucose and insulin responses, some have suggested that the carbohydrates that produce the greatest and most sustained elevations of blood glucose and insulin might better restore muscle glycogen over 24 hr of recovery. One recent study (Keins, Raben, Valeus, & Richter, 1990) found no difference in muscle glycogen concentrations after consumption of meals containing primarily simple versus complex carbohydrates 20, 32, and 44 hr after glycogen-depleting exercise. On the other hand, Burke, Collier, and Hargreaves (1993) suggested that foods that produce a high blood glucose concentration (high glycemic index) will stimulate the most rapid restoration of muscle glycogen in a 24-hr period. When the diet contained 10 g carbohydrate · kg body weight^{-1} · day^{-1} of either high or low glycemic index foods, the high glycemic index foods produced a 47% larger storage of muscle glycogen. Thus, it appears that a diet containing foods with a high glycemic index may facilitate a greater restoration of muscle glycogen in 24 hr. Unfortunately, this study did not determine whether or not the greater restoration of muscle glycogen also facilitated better recovery of muscle function. Table 9.2 provides a listing of foods with high and moderate glycemic indexes.

Because of the sometimes short rest intervals between back-to-back endurance activities, studies have been conducted to determine the optimal timing, amount, type, and form of carbohydrate ingestion to facilitate the greatest glycogen synthesis over a 4- to 6-hr period. When no carbohydrate is consumed immediately after exercise, the rate of glycogen synthesis is low (3.2 mmol · kg^{-1} · hr^{-1}) (Ivy, Katz, Cutler, Sherman, & Coyle, 1988). If carbohydrate is consumed 2 hr after exercise the rate of synthesis can be slightly increased (4 mmol · kg^{-1} · hr^{-1}). However, if carbohydrate is ingested beginning immediately after exercise or even before exercise ceases, the rate of glycogen synthesis will be ≥ 6 mmol · kg^{-1} · hr^{-1}. Thus, if possible, carbohydrate ingestion should begin immediately after glycogen-depleting endurance exercise.

When carbohydrate is consumed immediately after exercise and at 2-hr intervals, the rate of muscle glycogen synthesis is 6 mmol · kg^{-1} · hr^{-1} when between 0.35 to 1.5 g carbohydrate · kg body weight^{-1} is consumed at those times (Blom, Hostmark, Vaage, Kardel, & Maehlum, 1987; Ivy, Katz, Cutler, Sherman, & Coyle, 1988; Ivy, Lee, Brozinick, & Reed, 1988;

Table 9.2 Sources of Moderate and High Glycemic Index Foods (Coyle, 1991)

Food group	Food item	Glycemic index	Serving size for 50 g carbohydrate (g)
Cereals	Bagel	High	89
	Rice (whole grain)	High	196
	White bread	High	201
	Spaghetti/macaroni	Moderate	198
	Oriental noodles	Moderate	370
Breakfast cereals	Cornflakes	High	59
	Shredded wheat	High	74
	Oatmeal	Moderate	69
Biscuits/confectionery	Plain cracker	High	66
	Whole wheat biscuits	High	76
	Sponge cake	Moderate	93
	Oatmeal biscuits	Moderate	79

Vegetables		
Sweet corn	High	219
Potato (instant)	High	310
Sweet potato	Moderate	249
Potato chips	Moderate	100
Fruit		
Raisins	High	78
Banana	High	260
Orange (1g)	Moderate	600
Grapes (green)	Moderate	310
Sugars		
Honey	High	67
Corn syrup	High	63

Foods with a glycemic index of 60 to 85 are classified as moderate, whereas foods with a glycemic index > 85 are classified as high; 28 g is roughly 1 oz.

Reed, Brozinick, Lee, & Ivy, 1989) (see Table 9.1). Interestingly, it appears possible to double the rate of glycogen synthesis when much more carbohydrate is consumed at more frequent intervals. Doyle, Sherman, and Strauss (1933) fed subjects 0.4 g carbohydrate · kg body weight^{-1} at 15-min intervals after glycogen-depleting exercise. This feeding schedule produced a rate of glycogen synthesis that was between 8 and 11 mmol · kg^{-1} · hr^{-1} (Table 9.1). However, this study requires replication to confirm this high rate of glycogen synthesis.

Several studies have examined the effects of the type of carbohydrate and the form of carbohydrate on the rate of muscle glycogen synthesis. When 0.7 g · kg body weight^{-1} of glucose or sucrose is provided immediately and at 2-hr intervals after exercise, the rate of muscle glycogen synthesis is twice that seen with an equivalent amount of fructose (Blom, Hostmark, Vaage, Kardel, & Maehlum, 1987). Also, when equal amounts of carbohydrate are consumed as a liquid or as a solid (1.5 g carbohydrate · kg body weight^{-1} immediately after and at 2-hr intervals), the rate of muscle glycogen synthesis is identical (Reed, Brozinick, Lee, & Ivy, 1989). Thus, it appears that glycogen synthesis in the short term can be stimulated equally by either liquid or solid carbohydrate that contains either glucose, sucrose, or a combination of the two. Fructose, on the other hand, may facilitate a more rapid recovery of liver glycogen (Nilson & Hultman, 1974).

Summary

The preceding discussion has highlighted the manipulations of dietary carbohydrate that can be undertaken during training, during the pre-event phase, during the activity, and during recovery from the activity in order to facilitate maintenance or recovery of the critically important bodily carbohydrate reserves. The phases of training and performance, dietary carbohydrate manipulations, mechanisms of action, and performance effects of those dietary manipulations are summarized below. If implemented properly, they have the potential to improve endurance cycling training and, presumably, favorably alter cycling performance.

Training phase

- **Rationale**: Athletes don't consume enough carbohydrate.
- **Procedure**: Consume 8-10 g carbohydrate · kg body weight^{-1} · day^{-1}.
- **Carbohydrate store affected**: Should optimize levels of both muscle glycogen and liver glycogen.

- **Performance effect**: Improve training and performance capabilities by delaying the point in time at which low bodily carbohydrate stores produce fatigue.

Pretraining or competition phase

- **Rationale**: Athletes often compete after an overnight fast that lowers liver glycogen; athletes often train or compete with inadequate carbohydrate intake.
- **Procedure**: Consume 1-5 g carbohydrate · kg body weight^{-1} between 4 to 1 hr before the start of exercise; the source of carbohydrate should be tolerable by the athlete.
- **Carbohydrate store affected**: Should increase liver and muscle glycogen stores slightly but may provide a source of carbohydrate that is absorbed during exercise.
- **Performance effect**: Improve training or performance capabilities by between 11-14% in those individuals who are not sensitive to the initial lowering of blood glucose that might occur within the first 15-20 min of exercise.

Training or competition phase

- **Rationale**: To maintain the blood glucose concentration and maintain the bodily fluid levels to offset dehydration.
- **Procedure**: Consume a carbohydrate-electrolyte beverage that is 6-10% at a rate to provide 40-80 g of carbohydrate · hr^{-1}; if consumption is delayed, consume 100-200 g carbohydrate from a carbohydrate beverage that is 20% before 2 hr of exercise and then follow the above schedule.
- **Carbohydrate store affected**: Maintains or elevates the blood glucose concentration; offsets the negative effects of sweating by maintaining the bodily fluid levels; may reduce the rate of muscle glycogen usage during interval-like cycling activities.
- **Performance effect**: May improve cycling endurance capability by up to 1 hr; may maintain the ability to undertake repeated breakaways.

Postexercise recovery phase

- **Rationale**: Produce a rapid recovery of both muscle and liver glycogen stores.

- **Procedure**: Consume at least 1.5 g carbohydrate · kg body weight^{-1} immediately and every 2 hr after exercise; alternatively, if tolerable, consume 0.4 g carbohydrate · kg body weight^{-1} every 15 min for as long as possible beginning immediately after exercise.
- **Carbohydrate store affected**: Stimulates glycogen synthesis between 5-6 mmol · kg^{-1} · hr^{-1}; alternatively, may stimulate glycogen synthesis up to 8-11 mmol · kg^{-1} · hr^{-1}.
- **Performance effect**: Facilitate rapid recovery of muscle glycogen between repetitions of activity on a single day; although presumed, the recovery of muscle glycogen doesn't assure recovery of muscle function.

Directions for Future Research

Studies should be conducted that unequivocally clarify the ways in which the muscle glycogen concentration and the glycogen concentration of muscle fiber types interrelate with the etiology of fatigue. Additional studies should evaluate the effects on cycling performance of consuming carbohydrate in its various forms and of consuming combinations of various forms of carbohydrates under varied environmental conditions. The effects of consuming carbohydrates with various glycemic indexes on bodily carbohydrate reserves, exercise metabolism, and performance require additional research. Future research should, to the extent possible, simulate actual cycling events for more "ideal" generalizability of the results to the sport of cycling.

Acknowledgment

Thanks to David Morris, MS, for his helpful comments in the preparation of this chapter.

References

Ahlborg, G., Bergstrom, J., Brohult, J., Ekelund, L-G., Hultman, E., & Maschio, G. (1967). Human muscle glycogen content and capacity for prolonged exercise after different diets. *Foersvarsmedicin*, **3**, 85-99.

Ahlborg, G., Felig, P., Hagenfeldt, L., Hendler, R., & Wahren, J. (1974). Substrate turnover during prolonged exercise in man: Splanchnic and leg metabolism of glucose, free fatty acids, and amino acids. *Journal of Clinical Investigation*, **53**, 1080-1090.

Bergstrom, J.L., Hultman, E., & Roch-Norlund, A.E. (1972). Muscle glycogen synthase in normal subjects: Basal values, effect of glycogen depletion by exercise and of a carbohydrate-rich diet following exercise. *Scandinavian Journal of Clinical Laboratory Investigation*, **29**, 231-236.

Blom, P.C.S., Hostmark, A.T., Vaage, O., Kardel, K.R., & Maehlum, S. (1987). Effect of different postexercise sugar diets on the rate of glycogen synthesis. *Medicine and Science in Sports and Exercise*, **19**, 491-496.

Burke, E.R., Faria, I.E., & White, J.A. (1990). Cycling. In T. Reilly, N. Secher, P. Snell, & C. Williams (Eds.), *Physiology of sports* (pp. 173-213). New York: Chapman & Hall, E. & F.N. Spon.

Burke, L.M., Collier, G.R., & Hargreaves, M. (1993). Muscle glycogen storage after prolonged exercise: Effect of glycemic index of carbohydrate feedings. *Journal of Applied Physiology*, **75**, 1019-1023.

Coggan, A.R., & Coyle, E.F. (1987). Reversal of fatigue during prolonged exercise by carbohydrate infusion or ingestion. *Journal of Applied Physiology*, **63**, 2388-2395.

Coggan, A.R., & Coyle, E.F. (1988). Effect of carbohydrate feedings during high-intensity exercise. *Journal of Applied Physiology*, **65**, 1703-1709.

Coggan, A.R., & Coyle, E.F. (1989). Metabolism and performance following carbohydrate ingestion late in exercise. *Medicine and Science in Sports and Exercise*, **21**, 59-65.

Coggan, A.R., & Swanson, S.C. (1992). Nutritional manipulations before and during endurance exercise: Effects on performance. *Medicine and Science in Sports and Exercise*, **24**, S331-S335.

Costill, D.L., Bowers, R., Branum, G., & Sparks, K. (1971). Muscle glycogen utilization during prolonged exercise on successive days. *Journal of Applied Physiology*, **31**, 834-838.

Costill, D.L., Coyle, E.F., Dalsky, G., Evans, W., Fink, W., & Hoopes, D. (1977). Effects of elevated plasma FFA and insulin on muscle glycogen usage during exercise. *Journal of Applied Physiology*, **43**, 695-699.

Costill, D.L., Flynn, M.J., Kirwan, J.P., Houmard, J.A., Mitchell, J.B., Thomas, R., & Park, S.H. (1988). Effects of repeated days of intensified swim training on muscle glycogen and swimming performance. *Medicine and Science in Sports and Exercise*, **20**, 249-254.

Costill, D.L., & Miller, J.M. (1980). Nutrition for endurance sport: Carbohydrate and fluid balance. *International Journal of Sports Medicine*, **1**, 2-14.

Costill, D.L., Sherman, W.M., Fink, W.J., Maresh, C., Whitten, M., & Miller, J.M. (1981). The role of dietary carbohydrates in muscle glycogen resynthesis after strenuous running. *American Journal of Clinical Nutrition*, **34**, 1831-1836.

Coyle, E.F. (1991). Timing and method of increased carbohydrate intake to cope with heavy training, competition and recovery. *Journal of Sports Science*, **9** (Suppl.), 29-52.

Coyle, E.F. (1992). Benefits of fluid replacement with carbohydrate during exercise. *Medicine and Science in Sports and Exercise*, **24**, S324-S330.

Coyle, E.F., Coggan, A.R., Hemmert, M.K., & Ivy, J.L. (1986). Muscle glycogen utilization during prolonged strenuous exercise when fed carbohydrate. *Journal of Applied Physiology*, **61**, 165-172.

Coyle, E.F., Coggan, A.R., Hemmert, M.K., Lowe, R.C., & Walters, T.J. (1985). Substrate usage during prolonged exercise following a preexercise meal. *Journal of Applied Physiology*, **59**, 429-433.

Coyle, E.F., Hagberg, J.M., Hurley, B.F., Martin, W.H., Ehsani, A.A., & Holloszy, J.O. (1983). Carbohydrate feedings during prolonged strenuous exercise can delay fatigue. *Journal of Applied Physiology*, **55**, 230-235.

Davis, J.M., Lamb, D.R., Pate, R.R., Slentz, C.A., Burgess, W.A., & Bartoli, W.P. (1988). Carbohydrate-electrolyte drinks: Effects on endurance cycling in the heat. *American Journal of Clinical Nutrition*, **48**, 1023-1030.

Doyle, J.A., Sherman, W.M., & Strauss, R.H. (1993). Effects of eccentric and concentric exercise on muscle glycogen replenishment. *Journal of Applied Physiology*, **74**, 1848-1855.

Essen, B. (1977). Intramuscular substrate utilization during prolonged exercise. *Annals of the New York Academy of Sciences*, **301**, 30-44.

Gleeson, M., Maughan, R.J., & Greenhaff, P.L. (1986). Comparison of the effects of preexercise feedings of glucose, glycerol, and placebo on endurance and fuel homeostasis in man. *European Journal of Applied Physiology*, **55**, 6645-6653.

Grandjean, A.C. (1986). Nutrition for swimmers. *Clinical Sports Medicine*, **5**, 65-76.

Hermansen, L., Hultman, E., & Saltin, B. (1967). Muscle glycogen during prolonged severe exercise. *Acta Physiologica Scandinavica*, **71**, 129-139.

Hultman, E. (1978). Liver as a glucose supplying source during rest and exercise with special reference to diet. In J. Parízková & V.A. Rogozkin (Eds.), *Nutrition, physical fitness & health* (pp. 9-30). Baltimore: University Park Press.

Ivy, J.L., Costill, D.L., Fink, W.J., & Lower, R.W. (1979). Influence of caffeine and carbohydrate feedings on endurance performance. *Medicine and Science in Sports and Exercise*, **11**, 6-11.

Ivy, J.L., Katz, A.L., Cutler, C.L., Sherman, W.M., & Coyle, E.F. (1988). Muscle glycogen synthesis after exercise: Effect of time of carbohydrate ingestion. *Journal of Applied Physiology*, **64**, 1480-1485.

Ivy, J.L., Lee, M.C., Brozinick, J.T., & Reed, M.J. (1988). Muscle glycogen storage after different amounts of carbohydrate ingestion. *Journal of Applied Physiology, 65,* 2018-2023.

Johnson, A., Collins, P., Higgins, I., Harrington, D., Connolly, J., Dolphin, C., McCreery, M., Brady, L., & O'Brian, M. (1985). Psychological, nutritional, and physical status of Olympic road cyclists. *British Journal of Sports Medicine, 19,* 11-14.

Kiens, B., Raben, A.B., Valeus, A-K., & Richter, E.A. (1990). Benefit of dietary simple carbohydrates on the early postexercise glycogen repletion in male athletes. *Medicine and Science in Sports and Exercise, 22,* S88. (Abstract)

Kirwan, J.P., Costill, D.L., Mitchell, J.B., Houmard, J.A., Flynn, M.G., Fink, W.J., & Beltz, J.D. (1988). Carbohydrate balance in competitive runners during successive days of intense training. *Journal of Applied Physiology, 65,* 2601-2606.

Lugo, M.J., Sherman, W.M., Wimer, G.S., & Garleb, K. (1993). Metabolic responses when different forms of carbohydrate energy are consumed during cycling. *International Journal of Sports Nutrition, 3,* 398-407.

MacDougall, D., Ward, G.R., Sale, D.B., & Sutton, J.R. (1977). Muscle glycogen repletion after high-intensity intermittent exercise. *Journal of Applied Physiology, 42,* 129-132.

Murray, R., Eddy, D.E., Murray, T.W., Seifert, J.G., Paul, G.L., & Halaby, G.A. (1987). The effect of fluid and carbohydrate feedings during intermittent cycling exercise. *Medicine and Science in Sports and Exercise, 19,* 597-604.

Neuffer, P.D., Costill, D.L., Flynn, M.G., Kirwan, J.P., Mitchell, J.B., & Houmard, J. (1987). Improvements in exercise performance: Effects of carbohydrate feedings and diet. *Journal of Applied Physiology, 62,* 983-988.

Nilson, L.H., & Hultman, E. (1974). Liver and muscle glycogen in man after glucose and fructose infusion. *Scandinavian Journal of Clinical and Laboratory Investigation, 33,* 5-10.

Okano, G.H., Takeda, H., Morita, I., Katoh, M., Mu, Z., & Miyake, S. (1988). Effect of preexercise fructose ingestion on endurance performance in man. *Medicine and Science in Sports and Exercise, 20,* 105-109.

Pascoe, D.D., Costill, D.L., Roberts, J.A., Davis, J.A., Fink, W.J., & Pearson, D.R. (1990). Effects of exercise mode on muscle glycogen restorage during repeated days of exercise. *Medicine and Science in Sports and Exercise, 22,* 593-598.

Reed, M.J., Brozinick, J.T., Lee, M.C., & Ivy, J.L. (1989). Muscle glycogen storage postexercise: Effect of mode of carbohydrate administration. *Journal of Applied Physiology, 66,* 720-726.

Saltin, B., & Karlsson, J. (1971). Muscle glycogen utilization during work of different intensities. In B. Pernow & B. Saltin (Eds.), *Muscle metabolism during exercise* (pp. 289-300). New York: Plenum Press.

Sherman, W.M. (1991). Carbohydrate feedings before and after exercise. In D.R. Lamb & M.H. Williams (Eds.), *Perspectives in exercise science and sports medicine: Ergogenics* (pp. 1-34). Indianapolis, IN: Brown & Benchmark.

Sherman, W.M. (1992). Recovery from endurance exercise. *Medicine and Science in Sports and Exercise,* **24,** S336-S339.

Sherman, W.M., Brodowicz, G., Wright, D.A., Allen, W.K., Simonsen, J.C., & Dernbach, A.R. (1989). Effects of 4-h preexercise carbohydrate feedings on cycling performance. *Medicine and Science in Sports and Exercise,* **21,** 598-604.

Sherman, W.M., Costill, D.L., Fink, W.J., & Miller, J.M. (1981). The effect of exercise and diet manipulation on muscle glycogen and its subsequent use during performance. *International Journal of Sports Medicine,* **2,** 114-118.

Sherman, W.M., Doyle, J.A., Lamb, D.R., & Strauss, R.H. (1993). Dietary carbohydrate, muscle glycogen, and exercise performance during 7 d of training. *American Journal of Clinical Nutrition,* **57,** 27-31.

Sherman, W.M., & Lamb, D.L. (1988). Nutrition and prolonged exercise. In D.R. Lamb & R. Murray (Eds.), *Perspectives in exercise science and sports medicine: Prolonged exercise* (pp. 213-280). Indianapolis, IN: Benchmark.

Sherman, W.M., Peden, M.C., & Wright, D.A. (1991). Carbohydrate feedings 1 h before exercise improves cycling performance. *American Journal of Clinical Nutrition,* **54,** 866-870.

Simonsen, J.C., Sherman, W.M., Lamb, D.R., Dernbach, A.R., Doyle, A.J., & Strauss, R.H. (1991). Dietary carbohydrate, muscle glycogen and power output during rowing training. *Journal of Applied Physiology,* **70,** 1500-1505.

Wright, D.A., Sherman, W.M., & Dernbach, A.R. (1991). Carbohydrate feedings before, during, or in combination improve cycling endurance performance. *Journal of Applied Physiology,* **71,** 1082-1088.

10

Resistive Exercises for Off-Road Cycling

Ronald P. Pfeiffer, EdD, ATC • Shane R. Johnson, MS

Resistive exercise, commonly known as strength training, has been gaining acceptance within the competitive cycling community as an exercise mode capable of increasing muscular strength, endurance, and power (Burke, 1992; Newton, 1986; Radcliffe, 1992). Recent research supports the notion that increases in lean tissue mass and muscular strength can improve cycling performance (Marcinik et al., 1991). As a result of increased pressure to be competitive at the national and international levels, specific resistive exercise protocols have been developed for the competitive road and track cycling communities (Newton, 1986). However, only one recommended protocol for resistive exercise training for the off-road cyclist has been published to date (Pfeiffer, 1993).

Movement-Oriented Approach to Program Design

Development of a year-round strength training program for the competitive off-road cyclist was facilitated by incorporating the movement-oriented approach to program planning as developed by Harman, Johnson, and Frykman (1992). This approach to selecting appropriate exercises includes an analysis of the movements specific to a given sport. With the aid of videotape, film, and still photography, the coach can identify and catalog the various joint and muscle actions required in a particular sport. Once these are identified, specific strength training exercises, which match closely the movements involved in the actual sport, can be selected. Thus, the strength training program focuses on the specific needs of the sport while avoiding exercises that are too general to be of value. The movement-oriented approach to sport analysis includes the identification of the muscle groups involved in the primary movements as well as the specific types of contraction, that is, static, dynamic concentric, or dynamic eccentric. Static contractions occur when opposing muscles contract in an effort to stabilize a bone or joint. No visible movement occurs during static contractions. A dynamic contraction involves visible movement at one or more joints; the concentric variety involves a shortening of the muscle, whereas the eccentric type involves contraction while the muscle length is actually being increased by the resistance (McArdle, Katch, & Katch, 1991). In cycling, for example, the muscles that control the movements of the bones of the shoulder often contract in a static way in order to keep the shoulder from moving up or down during climbing and descending, particularly on rough surfaces. The triceps muscle, the primary elbow extensor, often contracts concentrically when supporting the weight of the upper body against the handlebars, or in the case of riding on steep descents, is often contracting eccentrically when absorbing the forces from the front wheel on rough terrain. In that regard, the triceps muscle and the elbow act as the body's own, built-in, shock absorbers.

Physiologic Demands of Off-Road Cycling

The precise physiological demands of competitive off-road cycling have yet to be ascertained. Competitions at major events often include a timed hill climb, timed downhill, dual slalom, observed trials, circuit race, and cross-country races. Each format requires different types of skills and has unique fitness requirements. For example, the timed downhill event requires great bike-handling skills and total body strength with less emphasis on aerobic ability, whereas the timed hill climb, circuit race, and cross-country events place more emphasis on the aerobic system. The majority of competitors across all age groups and ability levels participate in the cross-country events, which are followed in popularity by the timed downhill. The following is a brief analysis of the demands of off-road bicycle racing.

Aerobic Power

The aerobic system of energy production is the dominant energy system utilized in events that last more than a few minutes. Since the typical NORBA (National Off-Road Bicycle Association) cross-country race may have a duration in excess of 2 hr, a heavy emphasis is placed on the aerobic system. In addition, races often include total elevation changes in excess of several thousand feet per event.

Anaerobic Power

The anaerobic systems of energy production are the dominant systems utilized in events that have a short duration with a very high intensity. In essence, the demands of the event exceed the body's ability to supply enough oxygen. Virtually all types of off-road cycling events include anaerobic components. For example, both the cross-country and circuit races typically include steep climbs as well as sprinting (when passing slower riders), which will require anaerobic efforts.

Muscle Strength and Endurance

Upper body strength is essential for controlling the bicycle during high-speed descents as well as during technically demanding sections of race courses. A high level of muscle endurance is required within the lower extremities because of the highly repetitive nature of cycling.

Lower Extremity Power

As just mentioned, in both the cross-country and circuit events the rider must have the ability to produce sudden, explosive efforts in order to negotiate steep climbs, sprint, or pass a slower rider. A rider lacking explosive power risks losing ground to his or her opponents on every lap of a given event.

Motor Skill

In order to be competitive in a NORBA event, the rider must be able to operate the bicycle at speeds in excess of 30 mph, often on steep, highly technical single-track trails. In addition, the rider is often required to avoid obstacles such as ruts, rocks, and logs.

Muscle Strength, Power, and Endurance Demands of Off-Road Cycling

When viewed even casually, it is obvious that riding a bicycle places unique demands on the muscles of the upper extremities, trunk, and lower extremities. The following sections will cover the muscle strength, power, and endurance demands that off-road cycling places on each of these areas.

Lower Extremities

The muscles of the lower extremity and the pelvic region are easily recognized as those components of the body that actually provide the force to the pedals, thus propelling the bicycle. Unlike road cycling, however, off-road cycling generally involves pedaling at lower cadences combined with frequent, high-intensity bursts of cadence increases, required for climbing steep grades or sprinting. As such, off-road cycling places unique demands on the athlete, with an emphasis on the development of power in the lower extremities. These muscles have been identified as composing the *power zone*, that is, the primary source of strength and power in any athletic-type movement (O'Shea, 1985). Although important, *muscle strength* (maximum amount of force generated in a single task or repetition) alone is of little value in endurance type of sports. Endurance sports place a continuous stress on the body and, in the case of off-road bicycle racing, may last for several hours. Thus, *muscle endurance*, the ability to exert force for many repetitions, is much more important. Fortunately for the cyclist, muscle endurance within the muscles of the power zone is developed primarily through training on the bicycle. To be competitive at even the regional level, an off-road cyclist must spend an average of 15 to 18 hr per week training on the bicycle (Pfeiffer, 1994).

An equally vital performance component for the off-road cyclist is *muscle power*, which is the muscular strength a limb can generate in a given movement multiplied by the limb velocity during the movement (O'Shea, 1985). For the off-road cyclist, muscle power equates into the ability to exert maximum effort for steep climbs, a major component in most cross-country courses, as well as for sprinting to pass slower riders or at the finish of an event. As mentioned earlier, these specific aspects of off-road racing involve short bursts of high-intensity, anaerobic effort. Muscle power can be likened to the turbo-boost of the Formula 1 race car. An off-road cyclist lacking adequate muscle power will lose ground to the opposition whenever confronted with a steep climb or sprint.

Exercise physiologists have concluded that a highly effective method of developing muscle power is through specialized strength training programs in the off-season. These programs emphasize the development of power by incorporating the lifting of weights at relatively high velocities associated with rapid acceleration of the resistance (Harman, 1994; Hedrick, 1993; Young, 1993). This type of training has been found to have a direct effect on the muscle fiber size as well as on the athlete's ability to activate muscle fibers for a given task. The ability to activate large numbers of muscle fibers is known as motor-unit recruitment. A motor unit is defined as "all the muscle fibers innervated by one motor nerve" (Guyton, 1986, p. 131). Research has shown that specific types of strength training can improve the ability to generate large amounts of force rapidly by increasing one's ability to recruit motor units.

Upper Extremities and Trunk

While it is obvious that the energy to turn the pedals of a bicycle comes from the lower extremities, for the competitive cyclist it is just as obvious that the muscles of the upper extremities and trunk are also very active during riding. The upper extremities and trunk serve a variety of functions, including maintaining an aerodynamic body position, absorbing shocks, and bracing against the handlebars so that maximum force can be applied to the pedals. According to the laws of basic physics, for every action there is an equal and opposite reaction. Accordingly, every time a cyclist applies force to the pedals, an equal amount of force pushes back against the cyclist. This force can result in unnecessary body movements on the bicycle unless the cyclist is able to transmit these forces through the upper extremity to the handlebars.

Strength training programs for the muscles of the upper extremities and trunk should focus on the development of muscle strength and muscle endurance. Thus in order to be effective, training programs for these body regions must incorporate different types of lifting protocols from those used for the lower extremity. Strength training for the upper body and trunk needs to place less emphasis on high-velocity movements and more emphasis on repeated, endurance types of movements, consisting of more repetitions in each set of exercises. The objectives of the strength training program are to

1. improve strength and endurance of the upper extremity and trunk muscles,
2. improve lower extremity muscle power,
3. integrate the resistive exercise component with other components within the total training program, and
4. achieve a design that will be effective yet not discourage the athlete from assimilating the protocol into the normal training routine.

Movement Analysis of Off-Road Cycling

The movement-oriented approach to sport analysis incorporates practical forms of skill analysis that can be used in the field, away from the biomechanics laboratory. For example, portable, battery-operated videotape recorders (camcorders) can be used virtually anywhere to produce high-resolution, real-time images of an activity. Filming of a typical NORBA cross-country event is quite easy, and all aspects of a given race, that is, seated climbing, standing climbing, descending, riding on the flats, and sprinting, can be captured on film for later analysis. It is advisable to film so as to produce several different views of the same action, for example, for seated climbing to get views from the back, front, and side. In this way, all critical muscle groups and joints can be viewed. In addition, videotape can be reviewed frame by frame or in slow motion for identification of joint and muscle actions. It is also sometimes helpful to have the rider assist in the interpretation of the film.

It is critical that such an analysis be completed by someone with the expertise to identify joint and muscle actions by the correct kinesiological terminology, for example, abduction of the glenohumeral (shoulder) joint or flexion (eccentrically) of the elbow. Although a precise biomechanical analysis is essential in order to quantify joint moments (forces and velocities), such a procedure is not necessary to obtain a qualitative analysis from which to develop a strength training program.

Although the number of unique body and joint positions may be nearly infinite in a sport as demanding and complex as off-road cycling, the vast majority fall into one of three categories: level ground riding, uphill riding (climbing), and downhill riding (descending).

Rider position and the muscle forces required are unique for each of these categories. Thus, the resistive exercises recommended in this program are based upon the needs unique to each. It should be noted that within each category, different body positions may be utilized; there are two basic positions for each category, that is, seated (on the saddle) and standing (off the saddle). As a general rule, riders remain seated unless they are exerting a relatively greater amount of force as in performing a steep climb, sprinting, or descending, in which case they usually stand. Joint positions and motions for seated versus standing positions on the bicycle are considerably different.

In order to facilitate the identification of specific body and joint positions and subsequent muscle group involvement, the analysis will begin with the upper extremities and trunk.

Upper Extremities and Trunk

The following section details the kinesiologic interpretation of our photographic and videotape analysis of off-road riding under racing and training conditions. A complete review of muscle and joint action is followed by specific recommendations for resistive exercises. Exercise descriptions are contained in the appendix at the end of this chapter.

Shoulder Girdle

- Analysis revealed that while riding on level terrain, as well as during climbing, the rider is alternately pulling the shoulder girdle on each side of the body in a backward (posterior) direction. This action is known as shoulder girdle *retraction* (adduction).

    Muscles involved: rhomboids and the trapezius (Barham & Wooten, 1973).

    Recommended strength training exercise: seated row.

- Riding in the standing position either on level terrain or during climbing involves the action at the shoulder girdle known as *elevation*.

    Muscles involved: upper trapezius, levator scapulae, and the rhomboids (Barham & Wooten, 1973).

    Recommended strength training exercise: shoulder shrug.

- During riding on downhill terrain (descending), the shoulder girdle muscles are active in *protraction* (abduction).

   Muscles involved: (eccentric contraction) serratus anterior, pectoralis minor, and pectoralis major (Barham & Wooten, 1973).

   Recommended strength training exercise: bench press or incline press.

Shoulder (Glenohumeral) Joint

The shoulder joint and related musculature are very active in all phases of off-road cycling.

- When the rider was in the seated position, riding on level and uphill terrain, the main action was observed to be *transverse abduction* (horizontal extension).

   Muscles involved: (concentric contraction) posterior deltoid, teres major, teres minor, infraspinatus, and latissimus dorsi (Barham & Wooten, 1973).

   Recommended strength training exercise: seated row.

- When standing and riding uphill, the rider was seen pulling backward at the shoulder in a movement known as *extension*.

   Muscles involved: (concentric contraction) posterior deltoid, teres major, latissimus dorsi, pectoralis major (sternal fibers), and triceps brachii (long head) (Barham & Wooten, 1973).

   Recommended strength training exercise: lat pull (shoulder width, pronated grip). This exercise also benefits the elbow flexors.

- When the rider was descending, the analysis revealed that the shoulder joint was active in *transverse adduction* (horizontal flexion).

   Muscles involved: pectoralis major, anterior deltoid, subscapularis, coracobrachialis, and the short head of the biceps brachii (Barham & Wooten, 1973). Due to the nature of descending, the movement is executed using eccentric contractions of the listed muscles. Riders interviewed reported that when descending they felt as if they were pushing the handlebars away from their chests. This was especially true during riding on steep downhill terrain or on exceptionally rough terrain.

   Recommended strength training exercises: bench press or incline press.

- During climbing, especially when in the standing position on steep ascents, another action identified at the shoulder joint was *flexion*. This was especially apparent with riders who were using handlebar extensions, which essentially project out at approximately a 90° angle from the long axis of the handlebars. These devices seem to give the rider an improved biomechanical position in order to better apply force to the bicycle when climbing steep terrain.

> **Muscles involved:** anterior deltoid, pectoralis major (clavicular portion), coracobrachialis, and the short head of the biceps brachii (Barham & Wooten, 1973).
>
> **Recommended strength training exercise:** front raise.

- Although pure abduction of the shoulder joint was not identified as a movement directly related to riding, the seated overhead press is recommended as an exercise in order to ensure muscle balance around this extremely complex joint.

Elbow Joint

The elbow joint and related musculature serve as the linkage between the rider and the bicycle in order to effect a fluid transmission of muscle force to the vehicle, especially during riding on level terrain and during climbing.

- When the cyclist is descending, the role of the elbow appears to be akin to that of a shock absorber, smoothing the often abrupt and severe ground reaction forces that the rider receives through the handlebars.

- Analysis revealed that during riding on level terrain and during climbing the action at the elbow is *flexion*.

> **Muscles involved:** biceps brachii, brachialis, and brachioradialis. The contraction type is concentric the majority of the time, interspersed with brief periods of static contractions.
>
> **Recommended strength training exercise:** standing barbell curl.

- Analysis of descending revealed that the elbow was active in resisting flexion by way of eccentric contractions of the elbow *extensors*. This enables the elbow to absorb ground reaction forces received from the front suspension of the vehicle. Even with the addition of a mechanical suspension system such as shock absorbers, considerable energy is still delivered to the upper extremity through the front suspension system.

> **Muscles involved:** triceps brachii and the anconeus (Barham & Wooten, 1973).
>
> **Recommended strength training exercises:** bench press or incline press.

Wrist Joint and Fingers

As with all the joints of the upper extremity, those of the wrist and fingers are very active during all aspects of off-road cycling. With the vast array of handlebar types and configurations and consequent hand-wrist positions available to the rider, the number of discrete hand-wrist positions is nearly infinite.

- Analysis revealed that regardless of specific components or riding styles, virtually all hand-wrist positions consisted of the wrist being held in *neutral* position, combined with *flexion* of the fingers as they gripped the handlebars.

   Muscles involved: (static contractions) flexor-pronator and the extensor-supinator groups. These groups comprise the bulk of the forearm musculature along with the muscles of the fingers and thumb. Gripping with the hand is accomplished through the combined efforts of the finger and thumb flexors (flexor digitorum superficialis, flexor digitorum profundus, flexor pollicis longus) found in the forearm (extrinsics) as well as the smaller finger and thumb flexors (intrinsics) found within the hand (Barham & Wooten, 1973).

   Recommended strength training exercise: wrist curl. This single exercise provides activity for all the muscles involved in off-road cycling, from the forearm into the hand.

Trunk (Low Back and Abdomen)

When the cyclist was viewed from the side, it became obvious that the positions of the trunk during riding are determined by the interaction of a variety of factors including frame geometry, seat height, top tube length, and handlebar type and height.

- All these factors aside, however, the trunk was found to remain in a state of sustained *flexion* during nearly all aspects of seated riding. This did not change regardless of whether the rider was climbing, riding on level terrain, or descending. Only when the rider assumed a standing position on the pedals did trunk position change significantly, essentially becoming more upright. However, it should be noted that even when the rider was standing, there was a slight amount of trunk flexion. Because of gravitational force, the position of trunk flexion is maintained through both static and eccentric contractions of the trunk extensors as well as the gluteals and the hamstrings.

   Muscles involved: known collectively as the erector spinae; continuous from the low back (lumbar) region up to the base of the skull (cervical region). Given that riders may be in a flexed position for periods of time exceeding 2 hr, depending upon the race, it is not surprising that low back fatigue and pain are common complaints.

Recommended strength training exercise: back hyperextension.

* Although the trunk extensors were identified as the active muscles during riding, it is important to note that training the abdominal muscles (trunk flexors) is also valuable, particularly for the prevention of low back problems. Both the erector spinae and the abdominals work to stabilize the position of the pelvis, which is critical to the health of the low back.

  Muscles involved: rectus abdominus, internal and external obliques, and the transverse abdominus; should be thought of as the antagonists to the erector spinae.

  Recommended strength training exercises: for the abdominal muscles, crunches *or* bent-knee sit-ups.

Lower Extremities

Unlike the upper extremities and trunk, the lower extremities not only must be able to sustain force (muscle endurance), but also must be able to generate considerable power for climbing and sprinting. Strength training can be utilized effectively in the latter part of the off-season training program to develop or improve lower extremity power. Initially, the resistive exercises for the lower extremities are designed to achieve what has been called anatomical adaptation (Bompa, 1990). Anatomical adaptation involves the strengthening of connective tissues such as tendon, ligament, fascia, and muscle that surround joints. Increasing the strength of such tissues equips the body to better withstand the stresses of power training that involves ballistic, high-velocity movements. Power training, normally included near the end of the off-season strength training program, incorporates more complex, multijoint, total body types of exercises. Athletes who fail to include an anatomical adaptation component in their off-season strength training programs have a much higher risk of sustaining training-related muscle-tendon injuries. Because of the more complex nature of the training program progression for the muscles of the lower extremities, a variety of specific exercises are described in this section.

* The movements at the hip, knee, and ankle during the downward portion of the pedal stroke (power phase) consist of simultaneous *extension* of the hip and knee along with some *plantar flexion* of the ankle. This is followed by the upstroke, commonly called the recovery phase, which involves simultaneous *flexion* of the hip and knee along

with continued *plantar flexion* of the ankle. These observations are strikingly similar to those reported by Cavanagh and Sanderson (1986) in their study of the cycling mechanics of 4,000-m pursuit track riders. While it is clear that the muscles responsible for hip and knee extension generate the majority of the force that drives the bicycle, the precise role of the plantar flexors of the ankle remains obscure. When interviewed, off-road cyclists reported that during the power phase they perceived active plantar flexion and that during the upstroke (recovery) their ankles were relaxed.

Muscles involved: gluteus maximus, adductor magnus, hamstrings, i.e., biceps femoris, semitendinosus and semimembranosus, gluteus medius, gluteus minimus, and piriformis. The knee extensors include the muscles of the quadriceps, i.e., rectus femoris, vastus medialis, vastus intermedius, and vastus lateralis (Barham & Wooten, 1973).

Recommended strength training exercises for the *anatomical adaptation phase*: Anatomical adaptation and basic strength can be achieved using basic, single-joint exercises such as the leg curl, leg extension, hip extension, and hip flexion. All of these exercises require weight machines in order to be executed. During the latter portion of the off-season strength training program, more complex, multijoint lifts for power development will be incorporated. Due to the nature of hip and knee actions during cycling, separate exercises are not required to develop power within the muscles involved.

Recommended strength training exercises for the *power phase*: Exercises in this portion of the program include the parallel squat (high or low, depending upon skill level), leg press, and high pull (from the floor). The actual exercises used in this portion of the program will be determined, in part, by the weight training skill and experience of the athlete. For example, the high parallel squat requires that the bar be resting high on the shoulders, at the base of the neck. This position is often used for athletes who are new to the exercise because less weight is used, reducing the risk of accidents. As an athlete becomes more proficient, the low squat can be executed; this involves placing the bar about 2 in. below shoulder level. This position decreases the length of the trunk lever arm, thereby allowing heavier loads to be lifted safely. An experienced athlete may be able to include a high pull or even a power clean as part of his or her leg power program; however, proper execution is essential for them to be effective and to avoid injury. Any cyclist wishing to use complex lifts such as a high pull or a power clean should first receive instruction from a qualified strength coach and then train to learn the correct mechanics of the lifts, as described by Radcliffe (1992).

Program Planning

To be competitive at the national and international levels, off-road cyclists must train on a year-round basis. The typical training year, known as a *macrocycle*, can be subdivided into smaller training periods, each having its own specific goals and objectives.

In general, these periods or phases are designed to provide for recovery from the competitive period, followed by progressive building for the next competitive season. Specific components within a macrocycle will have specific goals; for example, the early goal of a strength training program will be anatomical adaptation, as described earlier. Accordingly, this early strength training component, known as a *mesocycle*, will outline precise guidelines for the athlete relative to frequency, volume, intensity, and mode of training. Within a given mesocycle, each training session will have its own set of guidelines and goals, again designed on an individual basis. Individual training sessions can be grouped together to achieve a common goal, and are known as *microcycles*. The microcycle is the smallest unit within a training program.

A properly constructed year-round training program that incorporates appropriate mesocycles and microcycles follows the model of periodization as developed by Matveyev (1972). The process of periodization allows athletes to include progression in a training program while also providing them adequate recovery time to respond physiologically and psychologically to the training program and, equally important, to avoid injury. Training programs must be designed on an individual basis, but all should include the same basic components. The typical racing season for off-road cycling begins in late March within the United States and continues into late September. The NORBA National Championship Series (NCS), for example, begins in April and concludes in late August with the NCS Finals. This is followed by the UCI World Championships, which are held in September. Thus, the off-season begins in October and continues into the following year to early March, a period of approximately 6 months. During this time, depending upon geographic location, most riders will continue to train on their bicycles, at least a few days each week. For many riders, cross-training using road cycling, cyclo-cross, nordic skiing, roller blading, or other aerobic activities provides a way to escape from their off-road bike while maintaining aerobic fitness.

Any training program should be designed on an individual basis, and whenever possible, muscle strength and power status should be evaluated by way of objective measurements such as isokinetic testing. These data should be interpreted by an exercise physiologist in order to identify muscle weaknesses or imbalances. In addition, these initial data form an important reference point with which to gauge improvements later in the off-season training program.

Newton (1986) has developed guidelines for the off-season strength training program for road and track cyclists, and there is no reason these general guidelines cannot be incorporated into similar programs for the off-road competitor. Newton describes five specific phases of training for the off-season strength training program beginning in September at the end of the season. These are

1. **transitional**   October (2 to 4 weeks);
2. **hypertrophy**   November-December (4 to 6 weeks);
3. **basic strength**   December-January (4 to 6 weeks);
4. **power**   January-February (4 to 6 weeks); and
5. **maintenance**   March through season.

The transitional phase allows the rider to relax, take time away from the rigors of racing and training, and basically recover from the season. The hypertrophy phase, as described by Newton (1986), is essentially an anatomical adaptation phase, as described earlier. Using strength training to strengthen important connective tissues such as tendon, fascia, and ligaments is the goal of the hypertrophy phase. The basic strength phase is designed to develop the muscles for more ballistic work that will follow in both the power and in-season phases. The basic strength phase incorporates a training protocol that uses high intensity (amount of weight lifted) combined with fewer repetitions in each set of exercises. The power phase decreases the intensity but increases the speed of movement during each exercise so that the actual movement is rapid, even explosive. Once the racing season begins, the primary objective is to maintain the gains made during the off-season. Thus, the athlete returns to the weight room 1 or 2 days each week and continues to perform exercises, but on a reduced scale in relation to sets and repetitions. These phases are shown in greater detail in Table 10.1. Included are the recommended numbers of sets and repetitions per set as well as exercise intensity and suggested frequency for each of the phases.

With the exception of the power phase for the lower extremities, intensity in this program will be based upon the rider's 10 repetition maximum (10 RM), that is, the amount of weight that can be lifted correctly on a given lift 10 times, without stopping. This weight becomes the basis for planning the amount of weight for the next training session. For example, if 100 lb is the 10 RM for the biceps curl, then the weight to be used on each of five sets of biceps curls during the basic strength phase will be based on this weight. It is recommended that initial sets be done with a relatively lighter amount of weight, with the final sets using the maximum amount of weight. That means that the first set would contain lifts of 80% of 100 lb, or 80 lb; the next set would use slightly heavier lifts, say 85 lb, and the last set would use the full 10 RM, 100 lb.

Table 10.1 Strength Training Program Phases

Phase	Purpose	Sets/reps	Exercises	Intensity (10 RM)	Days/week (freq.)
Transitional	Adjust to strength training	1 to 3/15 to 20	General in nature: circuits, body weight resistance, etc.	Minimum	2 to 3
Hypertrophy	Build tissue	3 to 4/8 to 12	13, specific muscle groups: quadriceps, hamstrings, gluteals, lower leg, biceps, triceps, wrist, trunk.	Moderate (50 to 80% 10 RM)	3
Basic strength	Gain strength	5 to 7/1 to 6	13, specific muscle groups: quadriceps, hamstrings, gluteals, lower leg, biceps, triceps, wrist, trunk.	Heavy (80 to 100% 10 RM)	3
Power	Explosive power (lower extremities)	5 to 6/1 to 15	1 or 2, specific to the power zone.	Moderate (based on 3 RM)	2 to 3
Maintenance	Maintain strength	1 to 3/6 to 10	Work on weak areas, those not directly strengthened while cycling.	Light	1 to 2

Adapted from Newton (1986).

As the cyclist gets stronger, the 10-RM weight will necessarily be adjusted upward, depending upon the rate of improvement. As a general rule, when the 10-RM weight is easily accomplished for 10 repetitions, 5 to 10 lb of weight should be added and all subsequent sets should be adjusted to the new 10 RM. Development of power requires somewhat higher intensities (weight), and therefore weight calculations must be based upon a 3 RM rather than a 10 RM. Thus, to determine the appropriate amount of weight for exercises in the power phase, the maximum amount of weight that can be lifted for three repetitions should be used.

Given the requirements of off-road cycling described earlier, the off-season strength training program should focus on basic strength for the trunk and upper extremities and power for the lower extremities, particularly for the muscles of the power zone. During the initial phases, that is, the hypertrophy and basic strength phases, exercises will incorporate protocols that call for similar numbers of repetitions, sets, intensities, and frequencies for both the upper and lower extremities and the trunk. Eventually, the lower extremities will be progressed into a power phase, whereas the upper extremity and trunk programs will continue with the basic strength phase up to the beginning of the next competitive season.

Shown in Table 10.2 are the recommended exercises, in their suggested order, for each of the training phases, beginning with the hypertrophy phase.

Exercises that use body weight as the resistance, such as crunches, back hyperextensions, and bent-knee sit-ups, can be made progressive by manipulating variables such as numbers of repetitions per set and number of sets per workout, or even by adding some form of external resistance such as a weight held in the hands. The latter should be done with great caution, however, as such practices can result in training-related injuries.

To accurately record progress, a detailed training log should be developed. Such a log includes essential information from the strength training program, that is, weights, sets, and repetitions, as well as notes regarding subjective impressions on any or all aspects of a given workout. A training log sheet can be made to meet the individual needs of any athlete.

On days the cyclist is planning a training ride, it is advisable to conduct strength training in the morning hours and have the training ride in the afternoon or evening. During the power phase of the off-season strength training program, the cyclist should avoid doing sprint or interval work on the bike that same day.

This program combines free-weight and machine-weight exercises, providing both balance and convenience to the program. It is critical that

Table 10.2 Recommended Exercises for Each Training Phase

Phases	Exercises	
Hypertrophy	(1) Warmup and stretching	(8) Leg extensions/curls
	(2) Bench press	(9) Back hyperextensions
	(3) Shoulder shrugs	(10) Seated row
	(4) Standing barbell curl	(11) Hip extensions
	(5) Lat pulls	(12) Hip flexion
	(6) Wrist curls	(13) Seated overhead press
	(7) Crunches	
Basic strength	(1) Warmup and stretching	(7) Seated row
	(2) Seated overhead press	(8) Back hyperextensions
	(3) Bench press	(9) Seated leg press or parallel squat
	(4) Lat pulls	(10) Shoulder shrugs
	(5) Standing barbell curl	(11) Wrist curls
	(6) Crunches or bent-knee sit-up	(12) Front raise

(continued)

Table 10.2 (continued)

Phases	Exercises
Power—lower extremities only	(1) Warmup and stretching
	(2) Seated leg press or parallel squat
	(3) High pulls or power cleans (only for experienced lifters)
Basic strength—upper extremities and trunk only (continued during power training for lower extremities)	(1) Bench press or incline press
	(2) Seated overhead press or front raise
	(3) Standing barbell curl
	(4) Front raise
	(5) Crunches or bent-knee sit-up
	(6) Back hyperextensions
	(7) Lat pulls
	(8) Shoulder shrugs
	(9) Wrist curls
Maintenance	(1) Warmup and stretching
	(2) Crunches or bent-knee sit-up
	(3) Back hyperextensions
	(4) Bench press or incline press
	(5) Lat pulls
	(6) Shoulder shrugs
	(7) Parallel squat

all exercises be executed correctly in order to avoid training-related injuries. It is also important to remember that the goal is to improve off-road cycling performance, *not* to become a better weight lifter. Therefore there is no reason to attempt maximum lifts in this type of program. Athletes can assess their improvements by reviewing their training logs for a period of several weeks or more.

This program should not require more than 60 to 90 min per workout. Most cyclists do not want to spend any more time than necessary in the weight room. However, investing 3 to 4 hr each week during the off-season to develop strength and power will pay big dividends during the next racing season. Not only will performance improve, but early season muscle soreness as well as neck, shoulder, and back fatigue will be significantly decreased. In addition, the risk of training- and racing-related injuries will be reduced.

Directions for Future Research

While the training protocols described in this chapter are based upon the best information currently available, much has yet to be learned regarding the most effective protocols for improving performance in competitive off-road bicycling. Training programs must be tested as objectively as possible for their effects on athletes involved in this sport. For example, research is needed in order to verify that power training for the lower extremities does, in fact, result in improved ability to sprint and execute short, steep climbs on the bicycle. Although a virtual plethora of data exist to support the premise that specific types of resistive exercise improve one's ability to generate muscle power in a variety of sports, no studies have been published, to date, that used off-road cyclists as subjects. Until such endeavors are completed, and verified with reproducible results, athletes and coaches will continue to rely on data from other, related, sports in order to develop training programs for off-road cyclists.

Appendix

Strength Training Exercises

Back hyperextension

Adjust the apparatus so that the leg support is slightly below the level of the hip pad. With the hands and arms crossed on chest, lower the trunk to the point of a 90° angle at the hips.

Raise the trunk up, slowly, with the head/neck held upright, reaching the point of horizontal with the trunk. Repeat. Caution: The trunk should not be raised above the horizontal position.

Bench press

Lie on the bench with your eyes directly under the bar. Place hands evenly approximately shoulder width apart. Lift the bar off the rack in a controlled manner. Stabilize the bar over the upper part of the chest, elbows locked.

Lower the bar slowly, maintaining control, to the nipples of the chest and pause. Drive the bar up to the starting position. Keep the head and hips on the bench and feet flat on the floor at all times. Return the bar to the rack in a controlled manner.

Bent-knee sit-ups

With the knees flexed to 90° and arms crossed on the chest, raise up (trunk flexion), beginning with the chin to the chest; then raise the shoulders and midback.

Complete the sit-up by attaining the fully upright position; lower the trunk slowly, returning to the starting position.

Crunches

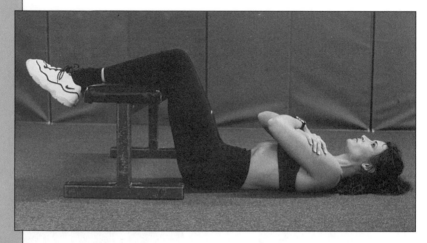

Lie on your back with knees bent and feet over a bench so that both the hips and knees are bent to approximately 90°, with your arms crossed on the chest.

Curl at the shoulders first, then curl at the upper back, and finally at the lower back. Pause, and then return to the starting position in a controlled manner.

Front raise

Select a weight light enough to allow execution of this lift. Using one arm at a time, grip the weight with the palm facing backward, keeping the elbow straight.

Raise the weight up (shoulder flexion) to the point of horizontal, as shown; then lower the weight slowly to return to the starting position.

High pull

Note. This exercise is to be performed by advanced lifters only.

Stand with the feet shoulder width apart. Point the toes out slightly. Grab the bar using an overhand grip, with the hands shoulder width apart. The bar should be touching the shins. Assume correct posture: arms locked, back straight, face forward, hips parallel to the floor, chest out.

Ease the bar off the floor by extending the legs. Do not pull with the arms. Bring the bar up straight, close to the body. The back and arms remain straight.

(continued) | **High pull**

Now pull the bar explosively by extending the legs and hips and shrugging with the shoulders, extending the body on the toes. Lower the bar under control back to the starting position.

Hip extension

Adjust the pad on the total hip machine so that it contacts the leg behind the knee, as shown. The starting position should place the exercising leg in 90° of hip flexion.

Extend the exercising leg backward (hip extension), keeping the knee flexed. Go as far as possible without stressing the lower back. Return slowly to the starting position and repeat.

Hip flexion

Adjust the pad of the total hip machine so that it contacts the leg just above the front of the knee, as shown. The starting position should be with the knee in slight flexion.

Flex the exercising leg (hip flexion), keeping the knee flexed. Go as high as possible without stressing the low back. Return slowly to the starting position and repeat.

Incline press

Sit comfortably with hips and back secure on the bench, legs to the side, shoulder width apart. Keep the feet flat on the floor and head on the bench.

Take the bar off the supports slowly, in a controlled manner. Lower the bar, under control, to the top of the chest above the nipple close to the chin. Pause, and keep body tight. Move the bar in a straight line. Return the bar to the rack carefully.

Lat pull

Place hands shoulder width apart while keeping back erect and head facing forward.

Pull bar in a controlled manner and touch the back of the shoulders while slightly bending the head forward. Make sure not to bring the bar down too quickly. Then return the bar to the starting position in a slow, controlled manner.

Leg curl

Lie face down on the machine, body straight, hands holding on to handles or edge of torso pad for stability. The head faces forward and the knees rest off the pad.

Curl the weight by flexing the knees, while keeping the pelvis flat on the machine. Once the knees are fully flexed, slowly bring the weight down to the starting position. It is important not to bounce the weight at the bottom. The torso should remain still throughout the movement.

Leg extension

Sit with the resistance pad on the lower part of the shin, close to the feet. In a controlled manner extend the leg (one leg at a time).

Once the leg is fully extended, gradually lower the weight into the starting position. Caution: Do not bounce the weight at the full extension position.

Leg press (seated)

Place the body in the seat so the knees are slightly bent. Begin to lower the weight in a controlled manner, so the thigh forms a 45° angle with the trunk.

Push with the legs to the starting position. It is important not to hyperextend at the knees when at the finished position, as this may cause a knee injury.

Parallel squat

Place hands evenly on the bar, shoulder width apart. Rest the bar across the upper back and shoulders. Keep the chest up and out, head up, and shoulder blades together, and torso straight and tight. Point the toes slightly out, keeping the feet flat on the floor.

(continued)

Parallel squat | *(continued)*

Bend at the hips first, then bend at the knees. In a controlled manner, squat to a position in which the thigh is parallel with the floor. It is important not to bounce in the parallel position. Drive up to the starting position, maintaining control.

Power clean

Note. This exercise should not be attempted without the guidance of a coach or exercise instructor who is knowledgeable on the proper coaching sequences involved in performing a "power clean" correctly.

Stand with the feet shoulder width apart. Point the toes out slightly. Grab the bar using an overhand grip, with the hands shoulder width apart. The bar should be touching the shins. Assume correct posture: arms locked, back straight, face forward, hips parallel to the floor, chest out.

By extending both the legs and hips, raise the bar to the level of the thighs. Bring the bar up straight, close to the body. The back and arms must remain straight. At this point, the bar should be contacting the front of the thighs, just below the groin level.

(continued)

Power clean (continued)

With a simultaneous extension at the knees and plantar flexion of the ankles (essentially a jumping movement), the bar will move upward quickly to rest on the shoulders.

Seated overhead press

Place the hands evenly on the bar with elbows under the bar. Sit with the back straight, head up, and feet to the sides, flat on the floor. Lower the bar slowly, under control, behind the head to ear level and pause. Keep the head facing forward and the back straight and tight.

Drive the bar upward and extend the arms to full length.

Seated row

Keep back erect with head forward. Grab grips tight and begin to pull the cable toward the chest while keeping the back erect and head facing forward.

Once the cable is pulled to the chest, control the weight when returning to the starting position.

Shoulder shrug

Stand erect with the feet shoulder width apart. Hold the bar close to the body with the arms straight, palms down, and hands shoulder width apart.

Raise the weight by shrugging the shoulders toward the ears; hold the weight for a pause; then slowly lower the bar back into the starting position.

Standing barbell curl

Stand with the feet shoulder width apart, body erect. Grab the bar with the hands about shoulder width apart, palms facing up. Hold your arms straight with the bar resting in front, close to the legs.

Curl the bar upward, keeping the elbows close to the body. Curl the bar all the way to the chin and pause. Slowly lower the bar back to the starting position.

Wrist curl

While sitting on the end of a bench, rest the forearms on the thighs while holding the barbell with the hands in the palms-up position.

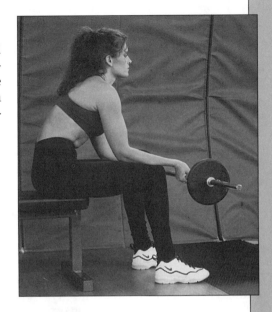

With the wrists in the "hanging" (extended) position, slowly flex the wrists to a full flexed position. Lower the weight slowly back to the starting position.

References

Barham, J.N., & Wooten, E.P. (1973). *Structural kinesiology*. New York: Macmillan.

Bompa, T.O. (1990). Periodization of strength: The most effective methodology of strength training. *National Strength and Conditioning Association Journal*, **12**(5), 49-52.

Burke, E.R. (1991-1992). Resistance training and improved cycling performance. *Conditioning for Cycling*, **1**(3), 3.

Cavanagh, P.R., & Sanderson, D.J. (1986). The biomechanics of cycling: Studies of the pedaling mechanics of elite pursuit riders. In E.R. Burke (Ed.), *Science of cycling* (pp. 91-122). Champaign, IL: Human Kinetics.

Guyton, A.C. (1986). *Textbook of medical physiology*. Philadelphia: Saunders.

Harman, E. (1994, April). Resistance training modes: A biomechanical perspective. *Strength and Conditioning*, 59-65.

Harman, E., Johnson, M., & Frykman, P. (1992). A movement-oriented approach to exercise prescription. *National Strength and Conditioning Association Journal*, **14**(1), 47-54.

Hedrick, A. (1993). Literature review: High speed resistance training. *National Strength and Conditioning Association Journal*, **15**(6), 22-30.

Marcinik, E.J., Potts, J., Schlabach, G., Will, S., Dawson, P., & Hurley, B.F. (1991). Effects of strength training on lactate threshold and endurance performance. *Medicine and Science in Sports and Exercise*, **23**(6), 739-743.

Matveyev, L.P. (1972). *Periodisienang Das Sportlichen Training* (P. Tschiene, Trans. into German with a chapter by A. Kruger). Berlin: Beles and Wernitz.

McArdle, W.D., Katch, F.I., & Katch, V.L. (1991). *Exercise physiology—energy, nutrition, and human performance*. Philadelphia: Lea & Febiger.

Newton, H. (1986). Strength training for cycling. In E.R. Burke (Ed.), *Science of cycling* (pp. 21-46). Champaign, IL: Human Kinetics.

O'Shea, P. (1985, February-March). The parallel squat. *National Strength and Conditioning Association Journal*, 74-79.

Pfeiffer, R.P. (1992, June). *Injury prevention strategies for the competitive "off-road" cyclist*. Paper presented at the annual meeting of the National Strength & Conditioning Association, Philadelphia, PA.

Pfeiffer, R.P. (1993). Movement oriented resistive exercise for the competitive off-road cyclist. *Conditioning for Cycling*, **2**(2), 11-18.

Pfeiffer, R.P. (1994). *1993 Injury survey of the norba pro/elite category*. Paper presented at the Role of Medicine and Science in Cycling conference, Crested Butte, CO.

Radcliffe, J.C. (1992). Training for power: Part I. *Conditioning for Cycling*, **2**(1), 6-13.

Young, W. (1993). Training for speed/strength: Heavy vs. light loads. *National Strength and Conditioning Association Journal*, **15**(5), 34-41.

11

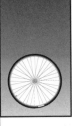

Preventing Overuse Knee Injuries

Maury L. Hull, PhD • Patricia Ruby, MS

Historically, knee pain has affected a large percentage of riders at all ability levels (Bond, 1976). However, only recently have statistics on this problem become available. Weiss (1985) evaluated injuries in a group of 132 cyclists who participated in an 8-day tour. Some degree of knee pain was reported in 35% of the riders, and 20% reported significant pain. In a longer-term study that covered a period of 7 years, Holmes, Pruitt, and Whalen (1991) treated more than 300 cyclists, and knee injuries headed the list as the most frequent problem. Knee injuries affected cyclists at all participation levels—from those who were national team members to those who were casual cyclists.

Because knee injuries are such a serious problem for cyclists, efforts have been made to understand causes of these injuries and to develop a technology for preventing them based on this understanding. With this in mind, the purpose of this chapter is twofold. One aim is to acquaint the reader with the types of overuse injuries and with current knowledge about their causes. The other is to survey scientific research that has been directed toward providing a foundation for preventative technology.

Injury Types

To appreciate the specific overuse knee injuries that occur, it is useful to have some understanding of the anatomy of the knee joint. As depicted in Figures 11.1 and 11.2, the knee joint is formed by the articulation (junction) of two bones, the femur and the tibia. Because the condyles (ends) of the femur are roughly spherical whereas the tibial plateau is nearly flat, the two bones have little conformity. The mating surface of each of the bones is covered with a thin layer of cartilage. To augment the conformity, sandwiched between the articulating surfaces are the menisci. Although the menisci augment the conformity to a degree, the joint would still be unstable (bones would slide freely relative to one another) if it were not for the ligaments. Internal to the knee are the anterior (front) and posterior (back) cruciate ligaments, which criss-cross. These ligaments mainly prevent anterior and posterior translation (sliding), respectively, of the tibia on the femur. They also prevent medial (inside) and lateral (outside) translation of the tibia. The remaining two principal ligaments are the medial collateral and lateral collateral, which run along the inside and outside of the joint, respectively. These ligaments prevent valgus (outward angulation of the tibia) and varus (inward angulation of the tibia) rotations, respectively.

Another joint of interest in an injury context is the patello-femoral joint. This joint is made up of the articulation between the patella

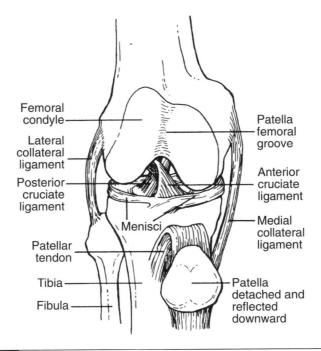

Figure 11.1 Anterior view of right knee showing the four primary ligaments.
Reprinted from Pruitt (1988).

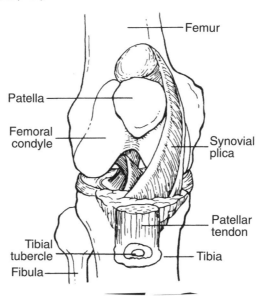

Figure 11.2 Anterior view of right knee illustrating the synovial plica.
Reprinted from Pruitt (1988).

(kneecap) and femur. As with the articulation between the tibia and femur, the articulating surfaces of the patello-femoral joint are covered with a thin layer of cartilage. The patella is an integral part of the tendon that attaches the powerful quadriceps muscles in the front of the thigh to the tibia at the tibial tubercle. The lower part of this tendon is called the patellar tendon and the upper part is termed the quadriceps tendon. As the knee is flexed and extended, the patella slides in the patello-femoral groove.

For each of the joints, the articulating surfaces (cartilage) are bathed in a lubricant called synovial fluid. This fluid is contained within the synovial membrane. On the medial side of the patella, this membrane has a fold that is termed the plica. The synovial membrane lines the inside of the joint capsule or retinaculum.

A large number of muscles cross the knee joint (see, e.g., Pruitt, 1988). Here the description will be limited to those in the front of the thigh. Four muscles form the quadriceps group, the group of muscles primarily responsible for extending the knee. As diagrammed in Figure 11.3, the

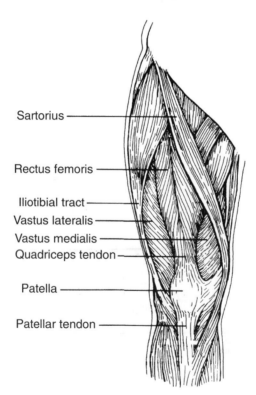

Sartorius

Rectus femoris

Iliotibial tract
Vastus lateralis
Vastus medialis
Quadriceps tendon

Patella

Patellar tendon

Figure 11.3 Anterior view of right leg illustrating the musculature of the thigh. Reprinted from Pruitt (1988).

quadriceps group includes the rectus femoris, vastus lateralis, and vastus medialis. Beneath the rectus femoris (and not apparent in Figure 11.3) is the fourth muscle of the group, the vastus intermedius. Spanning the lateral side of the joint is the iliotibial tract or band. This band is a thickening of the fascia lata, the tendinous tissue covering the musculature of the thigh.

Both because the knee joint is anatomically complex and because the structures of the joint are subjected to potentially large and repetitive stresses, the list of overuse knee injuries is a long one. Injuries most frequently occur to the anterior structures of the joint associated particularly with the patella (Bond, 1976; Dickson, 1985; Holmes, Pruitt, & Whalen, 1991; Weiss, 1985). Among these injuries are soreness on the underside of the patella, which can be due to chondromalacia (a degeneration of the patellar cartilage), patellar tendinitis, and quadriceps tendinitis. A less frequent ailment is Osgood-Schlatter's syndrome, an inflammation of the insertion site of the patellar tendon on the tibial tubercle. This ailment primarily affects adolescents rather than adults.

Structures on both the medial and lateral sides of the knee are also prone to injury, but the distribution depends on the levels of participation (Holmes, Pruitt, & Whalen, 1991; Weiss, 1985). For the noncompetitive cyclist, lateral structures are more commonly afflicted than medial structures with iliotibial band syndrome, a form of tendinitis, which is the most common ailment on the lateral side of the joint (Holmes, Pruitt, & Whalen, 1991; Weiss, 1985). For competitive cyclists, medial plica syndrome (a thickening and inflammation of the plica) and medial retinacular irritation occur about as frequently as patellar tendinitis and quadriceps tendinitis, respectively (Holmes, Pruitt, & Whalen, 1991), whereas these medial injuries are virtually nonexistent in noncompetitive cyclists.

Injuries Caused by Training Errors

Although the term "overuse" has been employed to describe all of the injuries just identified, there are actually two categories of overuse knee injuries that are distinguished by cause. One cause is training errors, and these are responsible primarily for anterior overuse injuries, the most common type. Among the common training errors are an inadequate training base, high-stress riding caused either by pushing high gears or by too much hill climbing, and failure to keep the knees warm enough when riding in cold weather (Dickson, 1985; Holmes, Pruitt, & Whalen, 1991; Powell, 1986; Wallach, 1989).

To appreciate the cause-and-effect relationship, some understanding of the loads developed on injury-prone tissues and their physiological response to these loads is necessary. As any cyclist appreciates, the muscles in the quadriceps group actively participate to develop the motive power in cycling. Because this group includes four muscles with a relatively large combined cross-sectional area, the force generation capability of the group can be substantial, reaching values as high as 7,000 N (Herzog, 1985). Because these forces must be transferred across the knee joint to the tibia through the patello-femoral joint, both the quadriceps and the patellar tendons must transmit these forces. In addition, a potentially large reaction force develops at the patello-femoral surface, particularly at larger values of knee flexion (Figure 11.4).

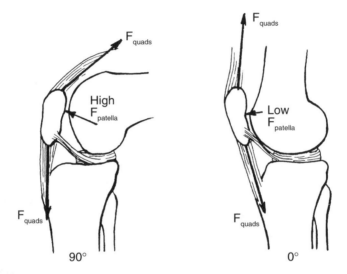

Figure 11.4 Equilibrium of patello-femoral joint with increasing knee flexion. At 0° flexion, the patello-femoral contact force ($F_{patella}$) is relatively low for a given value of quadriceps tension (F_{quads}). At 90° flexion, the contact force is high for the same quadriceps tension because of the increase in the component of tension directed toward the surface of contact. Adapted from Pruitt (1988).

The physiological response of connective tissues such as tendons and ligaments to repeated tension is determined by their morphology (form and structure). These tissues are composed of collagen fibers that generally run along the length. Although individual fibers follow a parallel course, they are interconnected to some degree (Woo & Young, 1991). When tension is initially applied, these fibers elongate, but they do not return to their original length immediately after tension is released. This phenomenon is known as preconditioning. Further cycles of tension will give rise to further elongation without full recovery up to some relatively low number (10-15) of cycles. So long as the tension is within limits, many cycles can be applied and the elongation will not increase further. However, repeated cycles of tension beyond these limits cause microstructural tearing of fibers and corresponding greater elongations. Consequently, the danger of high-stress training is that it causes repeated cycles of high tension that can lead to microstructural damage manifested as tendinitis. The mechanism of structural damage occurring as a result of repeated stress cycles is known as fatigue.

The ability of connective tissues to tolerate repeated tension without progressive damage depends on environmental factors. Both cross-sectional area and tensile strength of tendons have been demonstrated to increase over a period of time during which the tissues are subjected to tension through vigorous exercise (Woo & Young, 1991). This explains why cyclists who do not achieve a sufficient period of adaptation because of an insufficient training base are prone to overuse injury.

In the case of soreness on the underside of the patella, the tissue involved is cartilage rather than tendon. Degeneration of the cartilage in the form of wear is also a result of repeated high stresses, but here the mechanisms of damage include friction as well as fatigue. The articulating surfaces in human joints are separated by cartilage layers on each surface that act in conjunction with synovial fluid to lubricate the joint (Mow & Soslowsky, 1991). Analogous to a sponge, cartilage is composed of a porous-permeable solid matrix that holds an interstitial fluid. The thickness of the cartilage is not uniform; on the underside of the patella, for example, the thickness is greatest at the center—about 6 mm—but decreases to about 1 mm at the perimeter. In its normal state, the cartilage surface is relatively rough, approximately 20 to 50 times more rough than the rolling element in a ball bearing. A highly viscous liquid, the synovial fluid is the "oil" of the joint. Because of the geometric complexity of the articular surfaces, the spongelike action of the cartilage, and the lubricity of the synovial fluid, the lubrication of joints is complex; a number of different mechanisms have been identified. These mechanisms act to keep wear of cartilage to a minimum. And when wear does occur, there are cells that regenerate the tissue provided they are given sufficient time to perform this function. However, under conditions of repeated high loading, wear occurs. Once the wear process begins, it accelerates, with continued high loading leading to more severe degeneration and associated pain. When this degeneration reaches advanced stages on the underside of the patella, the condition is called chondromalacia. Obvious contributing factors to high cartilage compression are those that typify high-stress cycling, either riding in too high a gear or too much hill climbing.

A less obvious contributing factor to the high pressure that causes patellar soreness is seat height. As is evident from Figure 11.4, the reaction force on the patella increases in relation to the quadriceps force as the knee flexion angle increases. Inasmuch as increasing flexion angle accompanies a lower seat height, seat height bears a direct relation to patello-femoral pressure (Ericson & Nisell, 1987).

Injuries Caused by Anatomical Abnormalities

The second category of overuse knee injury is pathomechanical. As defined by Francis (1988), pathomechanical injuries are those that result from incompatibilities between the cyclist and the bicycle. The potential for incompatibility arises because the pedal platform surface fixes the orientation of the foot except in flexion-extension movements, whereas the complex linked system of joints in the lower extremity may prefer a different orientation, particularly when the joints are loaded. In this case, loads are developed at the foot-pedal interface because the foot is constrained from undergoing its natural movement. These loads will then be transmitted through all the joints in the chain. Since the chain includes the knee joint, these constraint loads may cause tissue structures to be unduly stressed, particularly if the constraint loads do not correspond to the natural motion axes of the joint.

To appreciate further the development of specific constraint loads as related to anatomical abnormalities, it is necessary to review each of the structures in the musculoskeletal chain starting at the hip and ending at the foot. Because each joint in the chain has the potential to undergo complex three-dimensional movement, a terminology is necessary to describe this. Typically, the motions are described in relation to the three cardinal body planes, the sagittal (side view), frontal (front view), and transverse (perpendicular to sagittal and frontal) planes (Figure 11.5).

The hip joint is a ball and socket joint that allows the femur (thigh bone) to freely undergo rotation in each of the principal planes. If a person is standing and the leg is straight (anatomical position), then the rotations are termed flexion-extension (sagittal plane), axial (transverse plane), and adduction-abduction (frontal plane) (Figure 11.6).

At the knee joint, the femur connects to the tibia (shin bone). Although at first glance the knee appears to behave as a simple hinge joint, in actuality its movement is more complicated owing to the complex geometry of the articulating surfaces in conjunction with the actions of the ligaments that bind the tibia and femur together. The motions of the knee can be described with the terminology indicated in Figure 11.6. As is evident in Figure 11.6, different terminology is used to describe the rotations of the knee and the hip. Again assuming a person in the anatomical position, rotations in the sagittal and transverse planes are flexion-extension and axial rotation, respectively, as before, but rotation in the frontal plane is varus-valgus. The movement of the knee can be conceived as occurring about two separate axes, one fixed to the femur

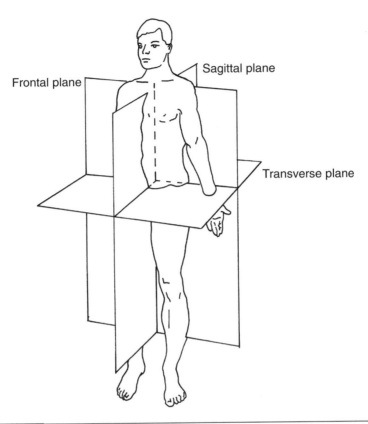

Frontal plane

Sagittal plane

Transverse plane

Figure 11.5 Definitions of the mutually orthogonal cardinal body planes.

and the other fixed to the tibia (Hollister, Jatana, Singh, Sullivan, & Lupichuck, 1993). Because the axis fixed to the femur is not perpendicular to the saggital plane but rather is oriented with a slight rearward and downward tilt toward the outside, movement about this axis produces primarily flexion-extension rotation accompanied by some amount of varus-valgus and axial rotations. As the joint is extended, valgus and external axial rotations occur with the directions of these rotations reversed as the joint is flexed. Movement in all three cardinal body planes is known as tri-plane movement (Figure 11.7). Rotation about the tibial fixed axis produces only axial rotation, which can occur independently of the axial rotation that accompanies flexion-extension.

To fully describe both the relative motions between the tibia and femur and the loads tending to cause these motions, it is necessary to introduce terminology for the translations (linear displacements) and corresponding force components. The complete terminology will be given later. For the time being, note that the terminology in Figure 11.6

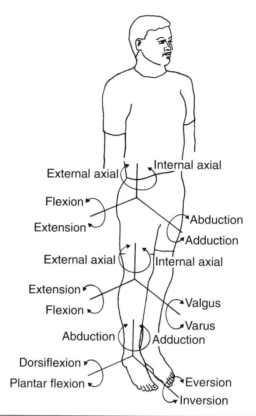

External axial

Internal axial

Flexion

Extension

Abduction

Adduction

External axial

Internal axial

Extension

Flexion

Valgus

Varus

Abduction

Adduction

Dorsiflexion

Plantar flexion

Eversion

Inversion

Figure 11.6 Terminology used to describe relative motions between the leg segments. Rotation directions are for the right leg and correspond to motion of the distal (lower) segment relative to the proximal (upper) segment.

is used not only for describing the rotational motions of the knee but also for describing the moment load components transmitted by the joint. For example, a moment tending to cause a varus-valgus rotation is called a varus-valgus moment.

Next in the chain is the ankle joint complex, which consists of two joints, the ankle joint and the subtalar joint. The ankle joint is formed by the articulating surfaces of the tibia at its distal end and the talus. In this case, the simple hinge concept is appropriate to characterize the movement, but, as depicted in Figure 11.8, the hinge axis is typically oriented with a slight rearward and downward tilt toward the outside (Inman, 1976). Accordingly, rotation about this axis produces primarily plantar flexion-dorsiflexion but also some degree of both inversion-eversion (rotation of the foot in the frontal plane) and adduction-abduction (rotation in the transverse plane). Again note that terminology different

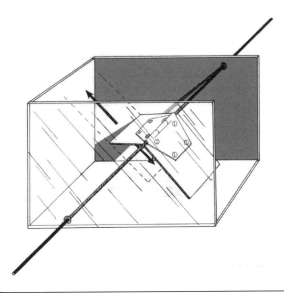

Figure 11.7 Phenomenon of tri-plane motion resulting from an axis of rotation that is not perpendicular to any of the three cardinal body planes. Rotation occurs in all three planes when the hinge arm is pivoted about the hinge axis. Adapted from Root, Orien, and Weed (1977).

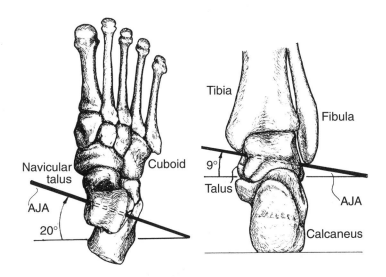

Figure 11.8 The orientation of the axis of motion for the ankle joint (AJA). On the left is a top view of the right foot showing the orientation with the axis projected onto the transverse plane. The right is a rear view of the right foot with the axis projected onto the frontal plane. The angles are averages. Reprinted from Root, Orien, and Weed (1977).

from both the hip and knee joint terminology is used to describe these rotations.

Beneath the ankle joint, the subtalar joint is formed by the articulation of the talus with the calcaneus (heel bone). As illustrated in Figure 11.9, motion between the two bones occurs about a single axis that forms average inclination angles of 42° with the transverse plane when viewed from the side and 16° with the sagittal plane when viewed from above (Root, Orien, & Weed, 1977). The axis tilt is upward toward the front and slightly inward. Thus, as with the ankle joint, the axis is not parallel to any of the three cardinal body planes, so complex tri-planar motions occur. However, the majority of motion is inversion-eversion and adduction-abduction rotation. With this axis orientation, inversion, adduction, and some plantar flexion occur together as do eversion, abduction, and dorsiflexion. The terms given to these combination rotations are supination and pronation, respectively (Figure 11.10).

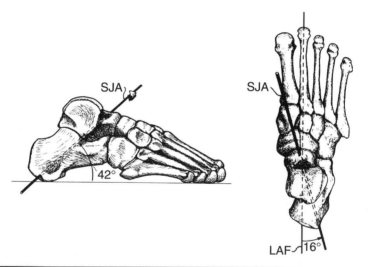

Figure 11.9   The orientation of the axis of motion of the subtalar joint (SJA). On the left is a lateral view of the right foot with the axis projected onto the sagittal plane. On the right is a top view of the right foot with the SJA shown in relation to the longitudinal foot axis (LAF). The angles are averages. Reprinted from Root, Orien, and Weed (1977).

Because of anatomical differences among individuals, a number of structural abnormalities can influence the loading that the knee joint ultimately transmits in cycling. These abnormalities can broadly be categorized as static and dynamic. Static abnormalities are evident from visual inspection under unloaded (i.e., non-weight bearing) conditions, whereas dynamic abnormalities become apparent when the leg is

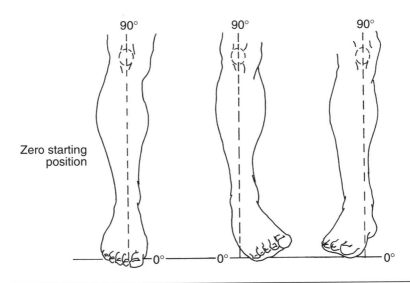

Figure 11.10 Complex tri-plane motions of the foot with respect to the shank as a result of axis orientations in the ankle and subtalar joints. Anterior view of right foot is shown. Supination (center) includes inversion, adduction, and plantar flexion. Pronation (right) includes eversion, abduction, and dorsiflexion.

loaded so that joint motions occur. Static abnormalities include malalignments of the forefoot and rear foot (Figure 11.11) and malalignment of the knees (i.e., bowleg, knock-knee) (Francis, 1986). Dynamic abnormalities include such actions as excessive pronation and abnormal angle of gait. The angle of gait is the degree of abduction-adduction that occurs when the foot is in full contact with the ground during level walking. The normal angle is 5° to 10° of abduction. Thus people who walk either pigeon-toed or excessively toed out have abnormal gait angles.

The consequence of either static or dynamic abnormalities is that the knee may be required to transmit potentially damaging loads. To illustrate how this is so qualitatively, two cases that are common clinically will be considered, forefoot varus and excessive pronation (Francis, 1986). In the case of forefoot varus, the forefoot is inverted while the rear foot is aligned neutrally. As explained by Francis (1986), when the foot is interfaced to a bicycle pedal that has no inclination to the transverse plane, the foot will be forced to evert. If the eversion rotation cannot be freely accommodated by the subtalar joint, then the knee will be forced inward, possibly creating a valgus moment at that joint (Figure 11.12). As a result, tissues on the medial side of the joint would be stressed and the patella might have a tendency toward lateral tracking.

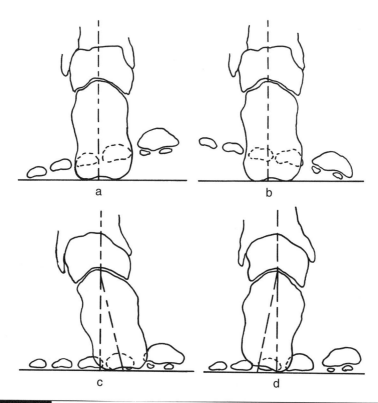

Figure 11.11 Malalignments of the forefoot and rearfoot as seen from a posterior view of the right foot. (a) Forefoot varus; (b) forefoot valgus; (c) rearfoot varus; (d) rearfoot valgus. In the neutral foot (no malalignments) the forefoot is horizontal and the rearfoot is vertical. Reprinted from Francis (1986).

When the foot pronates as a result of loads transmitted through the subtalar joint, the combination of eversion, abduction, and dorsiflexion of the forefoot relative to the rearfoot occurs. However, with the forefoot fixed to a bicycle pedal that can allow only dorsiflexion, the tibia will rotate internally as a result of the foot not being permitted to abduct. Assuming that the eversion is sufficiently small so that this motion can be accommodated by the subtalar joint, the internal tibial rotation will adduct the thigh when the knee is flexed, thus creating both an internal axial and valgus moment at the knee joint (Figure 11.12). Since the knee permits only limited axial rotation and essentially no valgus rotation, tissue on either side of the knee joint might be stressed.

In summary, the kinematics of the various joints of the leg are complicated by both the number of axes and their orientation relative to the three cardinal body planes. The knee has two independent axes of motion whereas both the ankle and subtalar joints have a single axis so

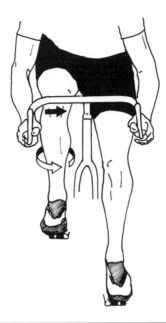

Figure 11.12 Movements of the leg as a result of forefoot varus and excessive pronation, examples of static and dynamic structural abnormalities, respectively. Forefoot varus leads to adduction of the thigh (black arrow), whereas both internal axial rotation (white arrow) and adduction of the thigh are consequences of excessive pronation. Reprinted from Francis (1986).

long as movements are confined within the natural limits of an individual (Root, Orien, & Weed, 1977). Both the location of the axes relative to bony landmarks and their orientation vary widely among individuals. Consequently, because of anatomical differences, both static and dynamic abnormalities occur. When cyclists with such abnormalities interface their feet to bicycle pedals with fixed orientations in both the frontal and transverse planes, constraint loads at the pedal may develop. Because these constraint loads must be transmitted through all of the joints in the chain, connective tissues (particularly at the knee joint) become subject to repeated stresses from each pedal cycle. Such stresses ultimately may lead to overuse injury.

Pedal Designs

Because pedals that fix the orientation of the foot in the frontal and transverse planes may give rise to damaging knee stresses, it is useful to consider the set of pedal design variables that might conceivably affect pedal constraint loads and hence knee loads. The two that come immediately to mind on the basis of the preceding are the adduction-abduction and the inversion-eversion orientations. Allowing some degree of abduction could reduce the internal axial knee moment created by the excessively pronating foot, whereas allowing some degree of inversion might reduce the valgus moment created by the forefoot varus.

In addition to the orientations themselves, there is also the manner in which these orientations are achieved. Orientations might be adjustable but be either fixed or free-floating. For the pronating foot, which is a dynamic abnormality, the amount of tibial rotation depends on the amount of force transmitted by the joint, so an abduction angle that varies continuously might be beneficial. In contrast, for a varus forefoot, which is a static abnormality, a fixed degree of inversion might be appropriate.

Because of the potential connection between foot orientation on the pedal and overuse knee injuries, a number of pedals that vary foot orientation have been designed. The first such design with which the authors are familiar is that by Davis and Hull (1981). These authors designed a pedal platform (i.e., device that interfaces the foot to the pedal) that allowed adjustability in three degrees of freedom: adduction-abduction, inversion-eversion, and anterior-posterior translation (Figure 11.13). This platform was mounted to a six-load-component pedal dynamometer that recorded the pedal forces and moments while subjects pedaled with cleated shoes and toe clips. The results of preliminary experiments with five subjects indicated that, of the six pedal load components, patterns of force development were relatively unaffected, whereas patterns of moment development were noticeably affected by fixed deviations in orientations from a reference orientation. However, there was no clear pattern of effects that emerged for all the subjects. One evident observation was an apparent interaction between the adduction-abduction and inversion-eversion pedal moments; changing one degree of freedom affected both loads.

A second device called the Biopedal also offered fixed adjustability in three degrees of freedom. The two rotational degrees of freedom were the same as those of Davis and Hull (1981), but the translational degree of freedom was one of height adjustment rather than longitudinal foot position (Hannaford, Morgan, & Hlavac, 1986). The height adjustment was included to address differences in leg length. The Biopedal was used in a clinical study involving eight subjects, five of whom had knee pain. The objective of the study was to establish a Biopedal orientation such that the tibial tubercle tracked a linear path as closely as possible. The motivation for establishing such a path was to minimize compensatory motions in the joints of the leg, and the investigators believed that such motions would manifest as deviations from the linear path. Of the five subjects who had knee pain, three reported improvements after use

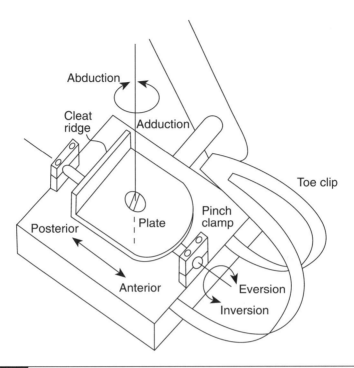

Figure 11.13 Diagram of pedal platform with adjustments in three degrees of freedom. Abduction-adduction adjustment is gained by rotating the plate with the cleat ridge. Inversion-eversion and anterior-posterior adjustments are made by loosening the pinch clamps and rotating or sliding the shaft, respectively.

of the Biopedal. Although this study did not attempt to relate pedal platform adjustment to pedal loads, it did address the need to customize any adjustments to the biomechanics of the individual.

More recently, pedal designs offering "free-floating" adjustability have been popularized by pedal manufacturers, most notably Look and Time. The Look products offer either a fixed or a free-floating adduction-abduction rotation adjustment, whereas the Time product allows both this rotation and medial-lateral translation.

The availability and widespread use of free-floating products have prompted scientific inquiry into their effect on pedal loads. Wheeler, Gregor, & Broker (1992) developed a five-load-component pedal dynamometer that could accommodate either the Look fixed or free-floating interface as well as the Time interface. This instrument has been used subsequently to record the pedal loads of 27 competitive cyclists free of knee pain (Gregor, Wheeler, Broker, & Ryan, 1993) as well as those of 7 cyclists with painful knees (Wheeler, Gregor, Broker, & Mandelbaum, 1993). For the asymptomatic cyclists, the free-float feature caused a reduction in the average extreme values of both the adduction moment (which occurred at maximum power in the downstroke region) and the abduction moment (which occurred throughout the upstroke region). For the symptomatic cyclists, the peak adduction-abduction moments were substantially greater than those of the average profiles of the asymptomatic group.

Biomechanical Model for Knee Loads

While these results suggest a potential benefit of the free-float feature in reducing knee loads, the true benefit can be appreciated only by analyzing loads at the site of injury. This is so because the knee loads are a complex superposition of all of the pedal loads (Ruby, Hull, & Hawkins, 1992). In addition, the knee loads are influenced by changes in segment kinematics. Because of these complexities, the effects of changes in pedal loads on knee loads cannot be inferred with any confidence.

To provide a computational tool for analyzing the effect of pedal design variables on knee loads, Ruby, Hull, & Hawkins (1992) developed a mathematical biomechanical model for computing all six of the load components transmitted by the knee. (Refer to Figure 11.14 for definition of the six load components at both the pedal and the knee.) The model actually consists of two components, one dynamic and one static. As illustrated in Figure 11.15, the dynamic component represents the leg system in the sagittal plane. Because the segments experience large movements in this plane, the inertial loads (loads resulting from acceleration) cannot be ignored, thus necessitating that the model dynamics be included in the analysis. The knee load components computed with this model component are the flexive-extensive knee moment $M_{y''}$ that must be developed by the muscles and both the anterior-posterior $F_{x''}$ and compressive-distractive $F_{z''}$ forces. To compute these load components it is necessary to solve the inverse dynamics problem. The solution to the problem requires writing equations that relate the joint loads to the pedal loads and segment kinematics (position, velocity, and acceleration). Once these equations are available, they can be solved for the unknown joint loads by measuring both the pedal loads and the segment kinematics.

The static component of the model (Figure 11.16) serves to compute the remaining knee load components, the varus-valgus $M_{x''}$ and axial $M_{z''}$ moments and the medial-lateral force $F_{y''}$. Because the movement of the segments in the frontal plane is small, the inertial loads can be ignored, simplifying the computation of the load components. As with the sagittal plane model, pedal loads are required as inputs to the

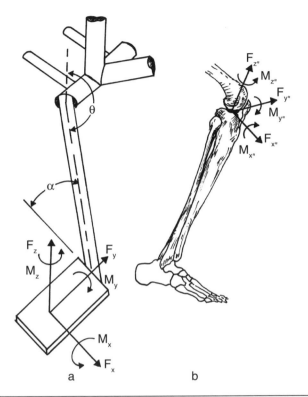

Figure 11.14 Axis systems for loads at the pedal and the knee. Loads in the pedal axis system (a) are those exerted by the foot on the pedal. The force components are the forward (+) and backward (–) tangential force F_x, the medial (+) and lateral (–) force F_y, and the upward (+) and downward – normal force F_z. The moment components are the inversion (+) and eversion (–) moment M_x and the adduction (+) and abduction (–) moment M_z. The moment M_y about the pedal spindle axis is zero. Loads in the knee axis system (b) are those exerted by the tibia on the femur. The force components are the anterior (+) and posterior (–) force $F_{x''}$, the medial (+) and lateral (–) force $F_{y''}$, and the compressive (+) and distractive (–) force $F_{z''}$. The moment components are the varus (+) and valgus (–) moment $M_{x''}$, the extensive (+) and flexive (–) moment $M_{y''}$, and the internal (+) and external (–) axial moment $M_{z''}$. The crank angle (θ) and the angle between the crank and pedal (α) are also indicated. Reprinted from Ruby, Hull, and Hawkins (1992).

static equations. Also required is the frontal plane position of the tibial tuberosity.

Measurement of the necessary inputs to the model components requires different techniques. Measuring the pedal loads requires a six-load-component pedal dynamometer such as that used by either Davis

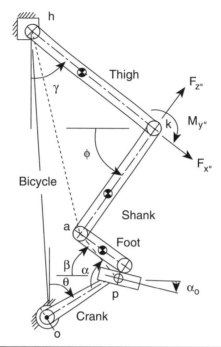

Figure 11.15 Sagittal plane model. h, k, a, p, and o denote the hip, knee, ankle, pedal, and crank spindle, respectively. γ, ϕ, β, and α_0 denote angles of the thigh, shank, foot link, and pedal, respectively from the references indicated. Reprinted from Ruby, Hull, and Hawkins (1992).

and Hull (1981) or Wheeler, Gregor, and Broker (1992). To determine the segment kinematics in the sagittal plane and the frontal plane position of the knee joint, video-based motion analysis techniques work well. These techniques attach markers to joint centers so that one can determine segment movements between frames.

In the development and application of the model by Ruby, Hull, and Hawkins (1992), one important result, relevant to studies seeking to relate pedal design variables to overuse knee injuries, was the complex relation between potentially damaging knee loads and the loads measured at the pedal. The equations for both the axial knee moment $M_{z''}$ and the varus-valgus knee moment $M_{x''}$ could be written in the general form

$$M_{x''} = M_{x''}(F_x) + M_{x''}(F_y) + M_{x''}(F_z) + M_{x''}(M_x) + M_{x''}(M_z) + \text{gravity term},$$
(11.1)

$$M_{z''} = M_{z''}(F_x) + M_{z''}(F_y) + M_{z''}(F_z) + M_{z''}(M_x) + M_{z''}(M_z) + \text{gravity term},$$
(11.2)

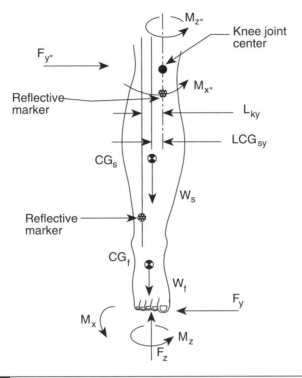

Figure 11.16 Frontal plane model. s and f denote the shank and foot, respectively, CG denotes the center of gravity, W denotes the weight, and L_{ky} and LCG_{sy} denote distances between the lines indicated. Reprinted from Ruby, Hull, and Hawkins (1992).

where the load components are as indicated in Figure 11.14. These equations indicate that all of the pedal load components (except M_y, which is close to zero) contribute to each of the knee moments. Thus, neither of the knee moments bears a simple relation to the corresponding pedal moment. This point is emphasized in Figure 11.17, which shows that the loads most profoundly affecting the axial knee moment are actually the tangential pedal force F_x and the transverse pedal force F_y. The pedal moment M_z bears essentially no relation to the knee moment $M_{z''}$. In fact, for this subject, eliminating M_z at the pedal would decrease the axial knee moment in the downstroke but increase it in the upstroke.

Knee Loads and Anatomy Variables

After developing the biomechanical model for computing knee loads, Ruby and colleagues used this model in two separate studies to investigate the effects of both anatomical variables (Ruby, Hull, Kirby, &

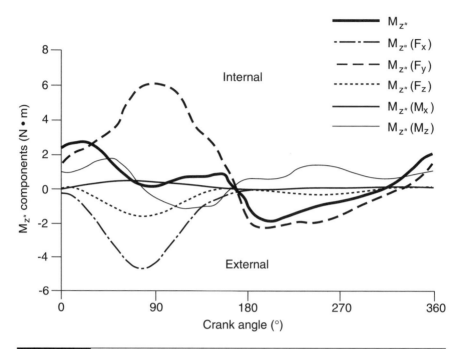

Figure 11.17 Sample plot showing contribution of pedal load components to the axial moment developed at the knee. The reference orientation for the crank is vertical and upward. A positive rotation is clockwise when viewed from the right side of the bicycle. Reprinted from Ruby, Hull, and Hawkins (1992).

Jenkins, 1992) and foot-pedal platform degrees of freedom (Ruby & Hull, 1993) on knee loads. The methods and results applicable to the anatomical variable study will be considered first. In order to describe both foot position and function, a total of 17 non-weight-bearing and weight-bearing measurements was made. The non-weight-bearing measurements focused on both the relative and absolute positions of the forefoot and heel while in a neutral position with no external forces being applied. The weight-bearing measurements focused on compensation of the foot and leg to an applied force. Measurements were made on a total of 23 subjects. The input data necessary to compute the six knee load components were measured while the cyclists pedaled at 90 rpm and 225 W.

The results indicated that the knee reached its most extreme medial position in the frontal plane in the region of maximum power. Simultaneously, for those subjects who had the greatest inverted forefoot position, both the posterior force and extensive moment were significantly higher in magnitude. Also there was a trend for both the varus moment and the internal axial moment (both developed throughout the downstroke region and peaking at maximum power) to be greater.

If one assesses the quantitative results in relation to those anticipated from both static and dynamic imbalances, the medial position of the knee and the corresponding internal axial moment are consistent for a pronating foot constrained by a fixed pedal. However, the development of the varus moment in the downstroke region is inconsistent with the load that would be expected to develop at the knee as a result of a forefoot varus condition. Recall that a valgus rather than a varus moment was expected as a consequence of the foot being forced to evert to match the orientation of the pedal surface in the transverse plane. However, as evident from Equation 11.1, the varus-valgus moment $M_{x''}$, like the knee axial moment $M_{z''}$, is a complex function of all of the pedal loads. The sample results in Ruby, Hull, and Hawkins (1992) demonstrate that the inversion-eversion moment at the pedal contributes almost negligibly to the varus-valgus moment at the knee. Rather, similar to the situation for the axial moment $M_{z''}$, it is the pedal forces and in particular F_y and F_z that are the major contributors to the varus-valgus knee moment. This emphasizes once again the danger in drawing conclusions about the knee loads based on a restricted view of pedal loads.

Not anticipated on the basis of any intuitive arguments surrounding joint function was the finding that both the posterior knee force and the extensive knee moment that developed during the downstroke were significantly larger (in a statistical sense) for the group of subjects who had the largest forefoot inversion. The importance of this finding is that it confirms the connection between high knee loads and anatomical malalignments. However, the inability to either predict or explain this finding points to the need for increased understanding regarding the relationship between anatomical variables and the lower extremity mechanics.

Knee Loads and Pedal Movements

Ruby and coworkers (1992) also used their biomechanical model to investigate the relationship between loads transmitted by the knee joint and the different degrees of freedom (described earlier) that the pedal might permit (Ruby & Hull, 1993). For this investigation, four interfaces were constructed, one fixed and the other three each permitting a different free-floating motion (Figure 11.18). The free-floating motions included not only adduction-abduction (± 15°) and inversion-eversion (± 10°) rotations, but also medial-lateral translation (± 7 mm). Each of the free-floating interfaces included a transducer for measuring the amount of displacement. Although the need for medial-lateral translation does not appear warranted on the basis of arguments concerning joint mechanics, this element was nevertheless included because the commercially available pedal by Time allows this motion. To provide the

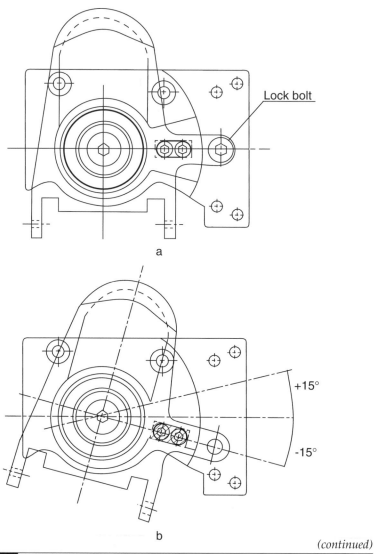

Lock bolt

a

+15°

-15°

b

(continued)

Figure 11.18 Motion platforms interfaced to six-load-component pedal dynamometer. Top views are shown for the fixed platform (a), the adduction-abduction platform (b), and the medial-lateral platform (d). The inversion-eversion platform (c) is shown in an anterior view. The numbers are the motion limits.

data for the comparative analysis of knee loads, 11 subjects pedaled with each of the four platforms at 90 rpm and 250 W.

Because the knee loads are cyclic and experience both positive and negative excursions (see Figure 11.17), a number of quantities were

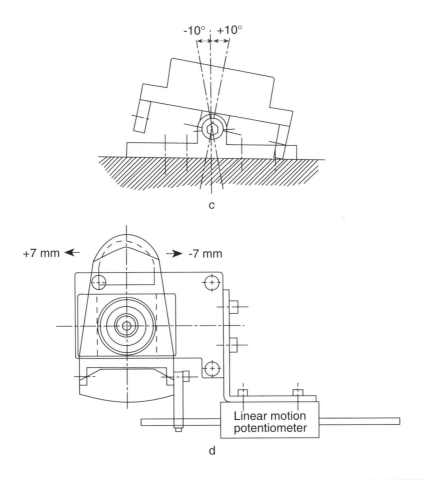

Figure 11.18 *(continued)*

computed to describe different attributes in both positive and negative regions as well as overall attributes. Region-specific quantities included the extreme, the area under the curve, and the average, while overall quantities included the total absolute area under the curve and the root mean square.

With use of the adduction-abduction platform, the foot remained abducted for the majority of subjects throughout the crank cycle. As a consequence of permitting this motion unrestrained, quantities of four of the six knee load components were reduced significantly when compared against the fixed. Both the peak anterior knee force developed during the upstroke region and the peak lateral knee force developed during the downstroke region were reduced significantly (Table 11.1). Because of the important role that the medial-lateral force plays in

Table 11.1 Multiple Comparison Tests of Knee Load Quantities for Cycling With Four Foot-Pedal Platforms

Load	Quantity	Ad-Ab vs. Fixed	Ad-Ab vs. In-Ev.	In-Ev vs. Fixed	Med-Lat vs. Fixed
$F_{x''}$	Minimum			<	
	Maximum	<			
	Total area	<		<	
	Avg |-value|	<		<	
	RMS			<	
$F_{y''}$	Minimum	<		<	
	|-area|	<		<	
	Total area	<			
	Avg |-value|	<		<	
$M_{x''}$	|-area|	<		<	
	Total area	<			
	Avg |-value|	<		<	
	RMS	<		<	
$M_{y''}$	Avg + value		<		
$M_{z''}$	+ area	<	<		
	Total area	<	<		
	RMS	<	<		

Note. The four platforms are the fixed, adduction-abduction (Ad-Ab), inversion-eversion (In-Ev), and medial-lateral (Med-Lat). A "<" sign indicated the quantity value for the first pedal platform in the comparison is significantly less than for the second platform. A blank space indicates no significant difference between the two platforms.

contributing to the knee moments, there was not only a reduction in the internal axial moment developed in the downstroke but also a significant reduction in the varus moment.

With the inversion-eversion platform, the foot remained inverted throughout the cycle for the majority of subjects. As with the adduction-abduction platform, quantities associated with four of the knee load components were reduced significantly when compared to the fixed case. The four load components were the same except that the inversion-eversion platform reduced no quantities associated with the axial knee moment but did reduce one quantity associated with the extensive knee moment.

Unlike the two rotational platforms, the medial-lateral platform did not significantly reduce any quantities for any load components when compared to the fixed case. The reason is probably that the platform always rested at the lateral motion limit for all subjects throughout the crank cycle.

Based on the above results, several important conclusions emerge. One is that there is no benefit to allowing medial-translation movement between the foot and pedal. Another is that allowing either inversion-eversion or adduction-abduction rotation is beneficial in reducing a large number of loads transmitted by the knee. Of the two rotations, adduction-abduction is more beneficial since it leads to reduction in both varus and internal axial knee moments, whereas inversion-eversion rotation leads to reductions only in the varus knee moment.

Directions for Future Research

While allowing free-floating adduction-abduction is clearly beneficial since this leads to reductions particularly in the two knee loads thought to be most damaging (i.e, axial and varus-valgus moments), there is one obvious question that merits further investigation. This is the issue of any added benefit that might be realized by permitting both adduction-abduction and inversion-eversion rotations simultaneously. Wootten and Hull (1992) described an interface specifically designed to address this issue, and the interface is presently being used for this purpose.

References

Bond, R.E. (1976). Almost everything you—and your non-cycling doctor—should know about knees. *L.A.W. Bulletin*, **12**(5), 14-15.

Davis, R.R, & Hull, M.L. (1981). Measurement of pedal loading in bicycling: II. Analysis and results. *Journal of Biomechanics*, **14**, 857-872.

Dickson, T.B. (1985). Preventing overuse cycling injuries. *Physician and Sports Medicine*, **13**, 116-123.

Ericson, M.O., & Nisell, R. (1987). Patello-femoral joint force during ergometer cycling. *Journal of the American Physical Therapy Association*, **67**, 1365-1369.

Francis, P.R. (1988). Pathomechanics of the lower extremity in cycling. In E.R. Burke & M.M. Newsom (Eds.), *Medical and scientific aspects of cycling* (pp. 3-16). Champaign, IL: Human Kinetics.

Francis, P.R. (1986). Injury prevention for cyclists: A biomechanical approach. In E.R. Burke (Ed.), *Science of cycling* (pp. 145-184). Champaign, IL: Human Kinetics.

Gregor, R.J., Wheeler, J.B., Broker, J.R., & Ryan, M.M. (1993). The effect of shoe pedal interface and load on pedalling kinetics in cycling. In *Book of Abstracts* (p. 508). Paris: 14th Congress of the International Society for Biomechanics.

Hannaford, D.R., Morgan, G.T., & Hlavac, H. (1986). Video analysis and treatment of overuse knee injury in cycling: A limited clinical study. *Clinics in Podiatric Medicine and Surgery*, **3**, 671-678.

Herzog, H. (1985). *Individual muscle force prediction in athletic movements*. Unpublished doctoral dissertation, University of Iowa, Department of Physical Education.

Hollister, A.M., Jatana, S., Singh, A.K., Sullivan, W.W., & Lupichuck, A.G. (1993). The axes of rotation of the knee. *Clinical Orthopedics and Related Research*, **290**, 259-268.

Holmes, J.C., Pruitt, A.L., & Whalen, N.J. (1991). Cycling knee injuries. *Cycling Science*, **3**, 11-14.

Inman, V.T. (1976). *The joints of the ankle*. Baltimore: Williams & Wilkins.

Mow, V.C., & Soslowsky, L.J. (1991). Friction, lubrication, and wear of diarthrodial joints. In V.C. Mow & W.C. Hayes (Eds.), *Basic orthopedic biomechanics* (pp. 245-292). New York: Raven Press.

Powell, B. (1986). Medical aspects of racing. In E.R. Burke (Ed.), *Science of cycling* (pp. 185-201). Champaign, IL: Human Kinetics.

Pruitt, A.L. (1988). The cyclists' knee anatomical and biomechanical considerations. In E.R. Burke & M.M. Newsom (Eds.), *Medical and scientific aspects of cycling* (pp. 16-24). Champaign, IL: Human Kinetics.

Root, M.L., Orien, W.P., & Weed, J.H. (1977). *Normal and abnormal function of the foot*. Los Angeles: Clinical Biomechanics Corporation.

Ruby, T., & Hull, M.L. (1993). The effect of foot pedal platform degrees of freedom on knee loads during seated cycling. *Journal of Biomechanics*, **26**, 1327-1340.

Ruby, T., Hull, M.L., & Hawkins, D. (1992). Three dimensional knee joint loading during seated cycling. *Journal of Biomechanics*, **25**, 41-53.

Ruby, T., Hull, M.L., Kirby, K.A., & Jenkins, D.W. (1992). The effect of lower limb anatomy on knee loads during seated cycling. *Journal of Biomechanics*, **25**, 1195-1207.

Wallach, R.M. (1989). Battle of wounded knees. *California Bicyclist*, **7**(1), 25-30.

Weiss, B.J. (1985). Nontraumatic injuries in amateur long distance bicyclists. *American Journal of Sports Medicine*, **13**, 187-192.

Wheeler, J.B., Gregor, R.J., & Broker, J.P. (1992). A dual piezoelectric bicycle pedal with multiple shoe pedal interface capability. *International Journal of Sport Biomechanics*, **8**, 251-258.

Wheeler, J.B., Gregor, R.J., Broker, J.P., & Mandelbaum, B.R. (1993). Cycling knee pain and shoe pedal interface kinetics. In *Book of Abstracts* (p. 1458). Paris: 14th Congress of the International Society for Biomechanics.

Woo, S L-Y., & Young, E.P. (1991). Structure and function of tendons and ligaments. In V.C. Mow & W.C. Hayes (Eds.), *Basic orthopedic biomechanics* (pp. 199-243). New York: Raven Press.

Wootten, D., & Hull, M.L. (1992). Design and evaluation of a multi-degree of freedom foot/pedal interface for cycling. *International Journal of Sports Biomechanics*, **3**, 152-164.

Index

A

Adenosine triphosphate (ATP), 74
Aerodynamic drag, 7-10
Aerodynamic equipment and energy expenditure, 178-181
Aerodynamics
  and body type of cyclist, 27, 30
  and rider position, 26-27
  of wheels, 20-24
Air resistance, 68, 169-170
Allsop suspension system, 57
All-terrain bicycles, 40-41. *See also* Off-road cycling
Alternative drive mechanisms, 37-39
Anatomy
  abnormalities of, and knee injuries, 258-265
  and knee loads, 271-273
Ankle joint, 260-262
Arms and clip-on handlebars, 94-95

B

Back
  and clip-on handlebars, 94-95
  hyperextension exercise, 227
Basic strength phase of training, 220-224
Bearing friction, 18-19
Bench press exercise, 228
Bent-knee sit-ups, 229
Bicycle drag, 28, 31
Bicycles, weight of, 11-12
Biomechanics, 146-165

and cycling optimization, 162
and injury prevention, 163
joint power of hip, knee, ankle, 159-161
and knee loads model, 268-277
and muscle activation patterns, 157-159
and optimization estimates of pedaling cadence, 106-107
and pedals, 146-157
Biopace noncircular chainring, 38, 133, 139
Biopedal, 266-267
Bioperformance, 147
Blood glucose, 186
Boardman, Chris, 27, 30, 75-76, 161-162
Bodily carbohydrate stores, 186-187
Body positioning, 80-99
  and aerodynamics, 26-27
  alternative, 161-162
  and crank arm length, 92
  and energy expenditure, 174-175
  and foot position, 92-93
  and handlebars, 90, 91, 92, 93-97
  and leg length, 86-88
  on mountain bicycles, 81-82
  on road racing bicycles, 80-81
  and saddle, 83-86, 88-89
  and stem length, 90
  on time trial bicycles, 82
  upper, 89-91
Body size, 66-77
  effects during downhill cycling, 73-74

Body size *(continued)*
    effects during level cycling, 69-71
    effects during sprint cycling, 74
    effects during uphill cycling, 71-73
    optimum, 75-76
Body type of cyclist, 27, 30
Body weight versus human power, 3, 4
Breathing and clip-on handlebars, 96-97
Bump-pedal feedback, 62

C

Cadence. *See* Pedaling cadence
Carbohydrate consumption
    after exercise, 196-200
    daily, 188-189
    during exercise, 191-196
Carbohydrate stores, body, 186-187
Cartilage and knee injuries, 257
Cartridge wheel bearings, 18-19
Casing construction of tires, 13
Cavanagh, Peter, 36
Chains, 19
Chain-suspension interaction, 59-62
Chin and clip-on handlebars, 94-95
Cleat position, 93
Clipless pedals, 146-147
Clothing, 33-37
Compression damping, 53-54
Computers, bicycle, 39-40
Conventional motion cycle, 127-130
    cadence optimization, 127
    multivariate optimization studies, 127-130
Cosmopion, 34-35
Cost functions
    and muscular stress, 125
    for noncircular chainrings, 133
    in optimization analysis, 123-126
    torque-based, 125-126
Crank length, 92, 129
Crunches exercise, 230
Cup and cone wheel bearings, 18-19
Cycling equipment, 1-43
    bicycle frames, 25-30
    clothing, 33-37
    drinking systems, 33
    and resistance forces, 5-19
    shifting systems, 30, 33
    wheels, 20-25
Cyclists
    body type of, 27, 30
    disabled, 156-158

D

Damping, suspension, 51-54, 56
Disabled cyclists, 156-158
Downhill cycling, 73-74
Drafting and energy expenditure, 175-178
Drag
    aerodynamic, 7-10
    bicycle, 28, 31
Drinking systems, 33
Drive mechanisms, alternative, 37-39
Drive torque, 17
Dupont bicycles, 30
Dynamic abnormalities, 262-263
Dynamic optimization, 136-140

E

Effective force, in pedal loading, 149-152
Elbow joint, 215
Endurance and human power, 3
Energy expenditure, 67-69, 168-184
    and aerodynamic equipment, 178-181

and body position, 174-175
and drafting, 175-178
and outdoor measurements,
    170-172
and riding speed, 172-174
and wheels, 178-181
and wind tunnel studies, 170
Energy loss in springs, 53
Energy production and efficiency
    in pedaling cadence, 103-104
Enveloping of tires, 46
Evaporative cooling, 35
Excessive pronation, 263-265
Exercises
    resistive, for off-road cycling,
        208-225
    strength training, 227-250

F

Feet abnormalities, 263-265
Fingers, 216
Flat back and clip-on handlebars,
    94-95
Foot position, 92-93
Fore and aft saddle position, 88-89
Forefoot varus, 263-265
Forward dynamics-based optimi-
    zation analysis, 119-120, 121,
    123, 124
Frames, 25-30, 82
Free-floating pedals, 267-268
Frequency response in suspension,
    54-57
Frictional resistance, 168-169
Frontal area of bicycles, 9
Front raise exercise, 231

G

Glenohumeral joint in movement
    analysis of off-road cycling,
    214-215
Glycemic foods, 198-199
Gravity forces, 68

and speed, 10-12
Gross efficiency, 108-109
Ground reaction line, 60-61
Guichard, Don, 30
Guimard, Cyrille, 85

H

Handlebars
    clip-on, 93-97
    height of, 90
    position of, 92
    width of, 91
Head tube angle, 81
Helmets, 35-36
High pull exercise, 232-233
Hip extension exercise, 234
Hip flexion exercise, 235
Hip joint, 258
Hooker bicycle, 30
Horsepower records, 2
Human power, 2-5
    versus body weight, 3, 4
    and endurance, 3
Hydraulic damping, 53-54
Hypertrophy phase of training,
    220-224

I

Inchworming, 60
Incline press exercise, 236
Indurain, Miguel, 75-76
Inertial forces and speed, 12
Inseam length to measure saddle
    height, 84-85
Instrumented pedals, 148-149
Instruments, 39-40
Inverse dynamics-based optimiza-
    tion analysis, 119-121, 122

J

Joint power of hip, knee, ankle,
    159-161

K

Knee injuries, 252-279
  and anatomical abnormalities, 258-265
  and biomechanical model for knee loads, 268-277
  cartilage in, 257
  and knee joints, 252, 258-259
  and knee ligaments, 253
  and pedal designs, 265-268
  and pedal loading, 154-156
  and training errors, 255-258
  types of, 252-265
Knee loads
  and anatomy variables, 271-273
  biomechanical model for, 268-277
  and pedal movements, 273-277
Knees and clip-on handlebars, 96
Kyle, Chester, 30

L

Lat pull exercise, 237
Leg curl exercise, 238
Leg extension exercise, 239
Leg length discrepancies, 86-88
Leg press (seated) exercise, 240
LeMond, Greg, 35, 75, 85, 90
Level cycling, 69-71
Light-reflective clothing, 35
Liver glycogen, 187
Load on wheels, 16-17
Look products, 267
Lower extremities
  movement analysis of, 217-218
  resistive exercises for, 217-218
Lubricants and wheel bearings, 18-19

M

Macrocycle, 219
Maintenance phase of training, 220-224
Mathematical model of cycling, 119

Maximum power, noncircular chainring, 133-135
Merckx, Eddy, 2, 75
Mesocycle, 219
Microcycle, 219
Minimum mechanical work, optimization analysis, 135-136
Monocoque bicycles, 30
Mountain bicycles. *See also* Off-road cycling
  body positioning for, 81-82
  versus road bicycles, 40-41
  seat tube angle of, 82
  and suspension, 47
Movement analysis of off-road cycling, 212-218
  of elbow joint, 215
  of shoulder (glenohumeral) joint, 214-215
  of trunk (low back and abdomen), 216-217
  of wrist joint and fingers, 216
Movement-oriented resistive exercises, 208-209
Multilink suspension systems, 61
Multivariate optimization studies, 127-130
  of crank length-cadence, 129
  of pedal height, 129
Muscle glycogen, 186-189
Muscles
  activation patterns of, 157-159
  contractions, 208-209
  endurance of, 211
  of lower extremities, 210-211
  strength, power, and endurance, 210-212
  of upper extremities and trunk, 211-212
Muscular stress, 125

N

National Off-Road Bicycle Association (NORBA), 209, 210

Natural frequency, 54
Net joint torques, 120
  cost functions of, 125
Noncircular chainrings, 38
  cost functions for, 133
  dynamic optimization, 136-140
  and maximum power, 133-135
Nutrition, 186-206
  and blood glucose, 186
  and bodily carbohydrate stores, 186-187
  and carbohydrate consumption after exercise, 196-200
  and carbohydrate consumption during exercise, 191-196
  and daily carbohydrate consumption, 188-189
  and glycemic foods, 198-199
  and liver glycogen, 187
  and muscle glycogen, 186-189
  and performance, 188-189
  and preexercise carbohydrate consumption, 189-191

O

Obree, Graeme, 27, 36, 161-162, 182
Off-road cycling. *See also* Mountain bicycles
  movement analysis of, 212-218
  and muscles of upper extremities and trunk, 211-212
  muscle strength, power, and endurance demands of, 210-212
  and pedaling cadence, 114
  physiologic demands of, 209-210
  resistive exercises for, 208-225
  strength training exercises for, 227-249
  training program planning for, 219-225
Optimization analysis, 118-143
  and biomechanics, 162
  and cadence, 127

and conventional motion cycle, 127-130
cost function in, 123-126
dynamic, 136-140
forward dynamics-based techniques of, 119-120, 121, 123,124
inverse dynamics-based techniques of, 119-121, 122
and minimum mechanical work, 135-136
multivariate, 127-130
and unconventional motion cycle, 130-140
Outdoor measurements and energy expenditure, 170-172
Overuse knee injuries, 252-279
Oxygen consumption of cyclists, 71

P

Parallel squat exercise, 241-242
Patella injuries, 255
Patello-femoral joint, 252-254
Pathomechanical knee injuries, 258-265
Pavement roughness and tires, 13
Pedaling cadence, 102-116
  biomechanical optimization estimates of, 106-107
  and cycle touring, 114
  and energy production and efficiency, 103-104
  multivariate optimization studies of, 129
  and off-road riding, 114
  optimization analysis of, 127
  optimizing, 108-113
  perceived exertion of, 107-108
  rate of, 107
  and skill level of cyclists, 105
Pedal loading, 149-157
  and disabled cyclists, 156-158

Pedal loading *(continued)*
  effective force of, 149-152
  ineffective force of, 152-154
  and pressure distribution on foot, 156
  and torsion and knee injuries, 154-156
Pedals, 36-37
  clipless, 146-147
  design of, 265-268
  height of, 129
  instrumented, 148-149
  and knee loads, 273-277
  piezoelectric, 148-149
Pedal torsion and knee injuries, 154-156
Perceived exertion and pedaling cadence, 107-108
Performance
  and body size, 66-77
  and nutrition, 188-189
Physics of cycling, 168-170
  air resistance, 169-170
  frictional resistance, 168-169
  rolling resistance, 169
Physiologic demands of off-road cycling, 209-210
Piezoelectric pedals, 148-149
Positioning. *See* Body positioning
Power clean exercise, 243-244
Power meters, 40
Power phase of training, 220-224
Power zone of muscles, 210
Preexercise carbohydrate consumption, 189-191
Preload suspension, 50-51
Pressure distribution on foot, 156
Pressure drag, 9
Pruitt, Andy, 80

R

Rear suspension systems, 58-62
  bump-pedal feedback, 62
  multilink, 61
Resistant forces, 5-19
  aerodynamic drag, 7-10
  bearing friction, 18-19
  gravity forces and weight, 10-12
  inertial forces, 12
  rolling resistance, 12-17
Resistive exercises, 208-225
  and aerobic power, 209
  and anaerobic power, 209
  for lower extremities, 210, 217-218
  and motor skill, 210
  movement-oriented approach to, 208-209
  and muscle contractions, 208-209
  and muscle strength and endurance, 209-210
  for upper extremities and trunk, 213-217
Resonance of suspension systems, 55-56
Restoring force of springs, 49
Road bicycles versus all-terrain bicycles, 40-41
Road racing bicycles, 80-81
Rolling resistance, 12-17, 169
Rotational Adjustment Device (RAD), 93

S

Saddle
  height of, 83-86
  position, 88-89
  tilt, 89
Seated overhead press exercise, 245
Seated row exercise, 246
Seat tube angle
  on mountain bicycles, 82
  on road racing bicycles, 80
Shifting systems, 30, 33

Shimano Biopace noncircular chainring, 38, 133, 139
Shoes, 36-37
Shoulder in movement analysis of off-road cycling, 213-215
Shoulder shrug exercise, 247
Skill level of cyclists, 105
Skin suits, 34-35
Speed
 an energy expenditure, 172-174
 resistance forces affecting, 5-19
Springs
 energy loss in, 53
 and suspension, 48-50
Sprint cycling, 74
Sprockets, 19
Standing barbell curl exercise, 248
Static abnormalities, 262-263
Steering angle and rolling resistance, 17
Stem length, 90
Subtalar joint, 262
Surface friction drag, 9
Suspension systems, 46-64
 and damping, 56
 and frequency response, 54-57
 ideal, 48
 lockout of, 53
 in mountain bicycles, 47
 preload, 50-51
 rear, 58-62
 resonance of, 55-56
 and springs, 48-50
 and travel, 48-49, 50
 and unsprung weight, 57-58
 without suspension, 46-47
Synovial fluid, 254
Synovial plica, 253

T

Time products, 267
Time trial bicycles, 82

Tires
 and casing and tread construction, 13
 cross-sectional diameter of, 17
 and drive torque, 17
 enveloping of, 46
 and load on wheel, 16-17
 and pavement roughness, 13
 pressure of, 16
 rolling resistance of, 12-17
 speed of, 17
 and steering angle, 17
 temperature of, 17
 tube construction of, 13, 16
 types of, 14-15
 and wheel diameter, 17
 width of, 25
Torque-based cost functions, 126
Tour de France, 1994, 75-76
Touring and pedaling cadence, 114
Training errors, knee injuries due to, 255-258
Training program planning for off-road cycling, 219-225
 phases of, 220-225
Transitional phase of training, 220-224
Travel, in suspension, 48-49, 50
Tread construction, 13
Trunk in movement analysis of off-road cycling, 216-217
Tube construction of tires, 13, 16
Tubes of bicycles, 9

U

Unconventional motion cycle, in optimization analysis, 130-140
Union Cycliste Internationale (UCI), 30
Unsprung weight, 57-58
Uphill cycling, 71-73
Upper body position, 89-91

Upper extremities and trunk
  in movement analysis of off-road cycling, 213-217
  resistive exercises for, 213-217

W

Weight of bicycles, 11-12
Weight reduction and cycling, 5
Wheel bearing friction, 18-19
Wheels, 20-25
  aerodynamics of, 20-21, 24
  diameter of, 17
  and energy expenditure, 178-181
  size of, 20-24
  and tire width, 25
  type of, 24-25
Wind tunnel studies and energy expenditure, 170
Work efficiency, 109
Wrist curl exercise, 249
Wrist joint, 216

About the
Contributors

Jeffrey P. Broker, sport biomechanist for the U.S. Olympic Committee, has been involved in cycling research since 1986. While earning his doctorate at UCLA, he studied the detailed musculoskeletal mechanics of cycling, helped develop a pedal instrumentation system, and coordinated cycling clinics that focused on pedaling technique. Dr. Broker now works as a sport biomechanist with the U.S. Cycling Federation in Colorado, where he helps to prepare U.S. cycling teams for international competition. He enjoys cycling himself, particularly mountain biking in the Rockies.

J. Richard Coast is a professor in the Department of Health, Physical Education, Exercise Science, and Nutrition at Northern Arizona University in Flagstaff. Specializing in the study of respiratory and exercise physiology, particularly cycling physiology, Dr. Coast is currently the director of the S.A. Rasmussen Exercise Physiology Laboratory. He has over 20 publications or presentations in the cycling field, many of them focusing on the metabolic cost of cycling. He teaches exercise physiology, respiratory physiology, and exercise testing at Northern Arizona.

Robert J. Gregor is a professor of Health and Performance Sciences at The Georgia Institute of Technology in Atlanta. He has been involved in cycling research since 1974 and has published 17 scientific papers and given over 20 presentations, concentrating on lower extremity mechanics related to musculoskeletal performance, performance efficiency, and injury prevention.

James Hagberg is a professor of Medicine at the Applied Exercise Physiology Laboratory at the University of Pittsburgh. He has a longstanding interest in cycling research, beginning with his graduate training at the University of Wisconsin. Along with Steve McCole, Dr. Hagberg has been funded by the U.S. Cycling Committee for the last 3 years to study cycling at the University of Florida and University of Maryland.

Maury L. Hull is currently a professor in the Department of Mechanical Engineering and chair of the Biomedical Engineering Graduate Program at the University of California—Davis. He directs research programs in several areas, including knee biomechanics, muscle mechanics and neuromuscular control, cycling biomechanics, and off-road cycle structural components and suspensions. An avid cyclist, Dr. Hull has more than 20 years of recreational and competitive cycling experience.

Shane R. Johnson, an exercise physiologist in the Department of Pulmonary Research at the VA Medical Center in Boise, Idaho, was a competitive powerlifter and Olympic weightlifter at Oregon State University from 1987 to 1990. His current research involves physiological adaptations and demands on pulmonary and cardiovascular dynamics in response to resistive strength training in power athletes. He studied at Oregon State under John Patrick O'Shea, one of the world's best-known research authorities on weight training and weightlifting.

Steve A. Kautz is a biomedical engineer at the Rehabilitation Research and Development Center at the VA Medical Center in Palo Alto, California. Dr. Kautz's most recent interests are in cycling biomechanics and the neural control of pedaling—including work with cyclists with neurological deficits. In his current studies, he is using optimization analysis and computer simulations to interpret experimental data.

Chester R. Kyle earned his PhD in engineering from UCLA and is now Adjunct Professor of Mechanical Engineering at California State University in Long Beach. He has consulted for years in bicycle design and performance and currently works as a Bicycle Design Coordinator for the U.S. Cycling Team. Dr. Kyle has over 100 publications in the mechanics and biomechanics of sports, particularly cycling. His current research work involves the aerodynamics of racing cycles and cycling equipment and the dynamics of racing cycle motion.

Steve McCole earned his MS at the University of Pittsburgh and is now a doctoral student in exercise physiology at the University of Maryland. His recent work involves the interaction of physiology and biomechanics in the performance of competitive cyclists. He is currently working with Dr. Hagberg on research funded by the U.S. Cycling Committee.

John Olsen is a senior test engineer at PACCAR Technical Center and a technical editor for *Bicycling* magazine. During his 12 years of writing bicycle journalism, he has had the opportunity to test virtually every type of cycle suspension. He has designed equipment for Honda and Boeing.

Ronald P. Pfeiffer received his EdD and ATC from Boise State University, where he worked in the Human Performance Laboratory. He has since lectured extensively on conditioning for mountain bike racing. From 1987 to 1990, Dr. Pfeiffer raced competitively and won several major events in the western region. He has recently published a text on sport injury.

Andrew L. Pruitt is Director of Sports Medicine at Western Orthopaedic Sports Medicine and Rehabilitation Clinic in Denver, Colorado. His cycling research includes work with clinical pathomechanics, 3-D gait analysis, and the use of force pedals in cycling. Dr. Pruitt is also Medical Coordinator for the U.S. Cycling Team.

Patricia Ruby is the Director of Biomedical Engineering at Hayes Medical, Inc., in Sacramento, California. She is currently involved in medical device research and development. Her research work has been primarily in sports biomechanics, with an emphasis on cycling. She is a U.S. Cycling Federation Category 2 competitor.

W. Michael Sherman is Co-Editor-in-Chief for the *International Journal of Sports Medicine*. He has published extensively in the area of carbohydrate metabolism, emphasizing its implications for optimal athletic performance and its influence on diabetes. Dr. Sherman is an exercise physiology professor in the School of Health, Physical Education, and Recreation at The Ohio State University.

David P. Swain, Director of the Wellness Institute and Research Center at Old Dominion Universtiy in Norfolk, Virginia, has published many studies on the energy cost of cycling. He also conducts research on the role of exercise in promoting health. Dr. Swain is a Fellow of the American College of Sports Medicine.

About the Editor

Ed Burke, who has written or edited ten books on cycling, is renowned for translating the latest scientific research into practical applications for cyclists. In addition to being the executive editor of *Cycling Science* and managing editor of *Performance Conditioning for Cycling*, he has written extensively on cycling physiology, training, and nutrition for *Winning Magazine*, *NORBA News*, and *Bicycling*.

Ed received a doctorate in exercise physiology from The Ohio State University in 1979. A staff member of the 1980 and 1984 U.S. Olympic cycling teams, he is now coordinator of sports science technology for the national cycling team. He is a member of the American College of Sports Medicine, the U.S. Cycling Federation, and he is Vice President of Research for the National Strength and Conditioning Association. An associate professor in the Department of Biology at the University of Colorado, Ed lives in Colorado Springs with his wife, Kathleen.

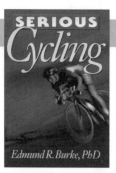